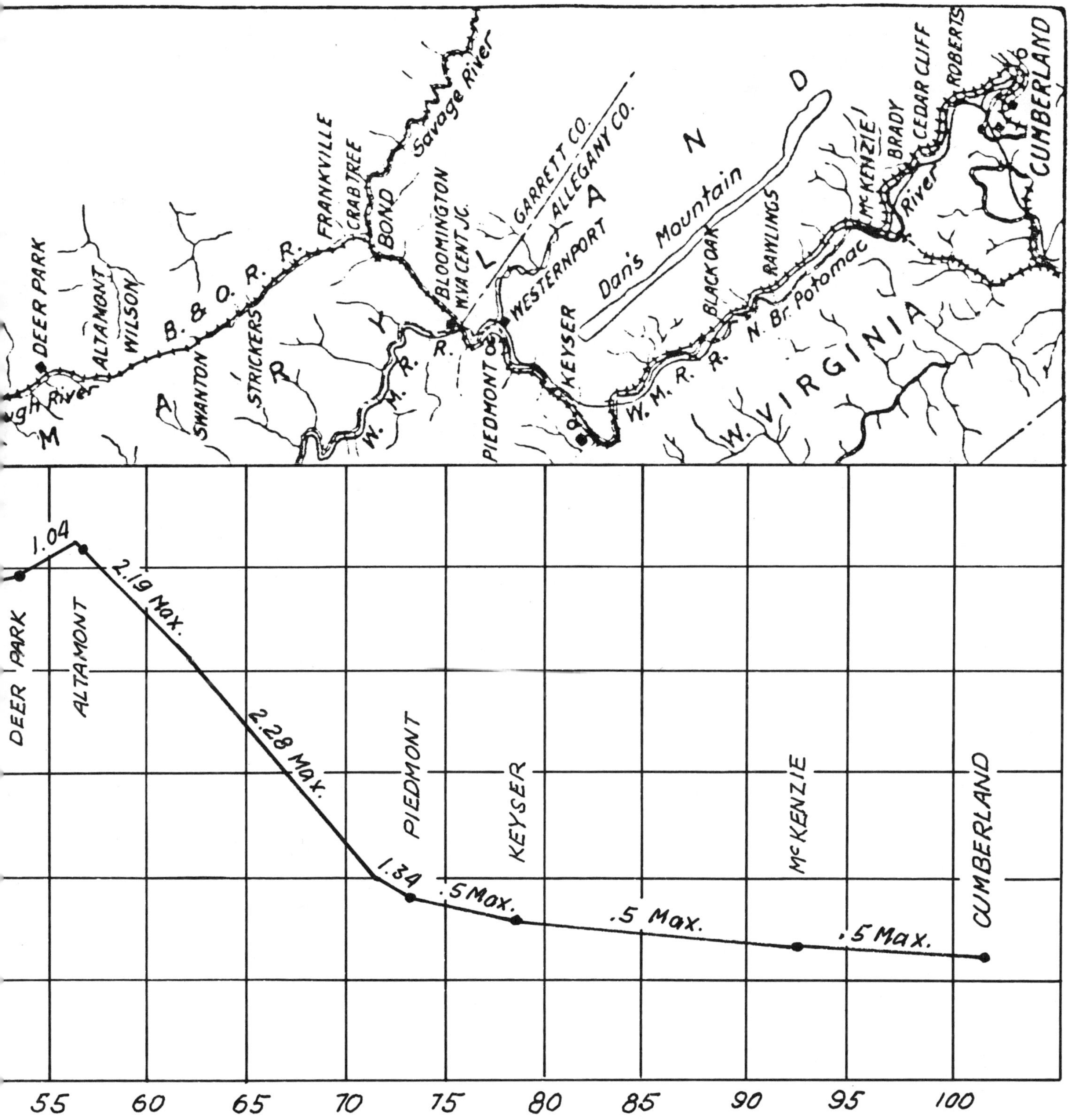
DEER PARK
ALTAMONT
WILSON
B. & O. R. R.
SWANTON
STRICKERS
FRANKVILLE
CRABTREE
BOND
Savage River
BLOOMINGTON
W.VA CENT JC.
GARRETT CO.
ALLEGANY CO.
WESTERNPORT
PIEDMONT
KEYSER
Dan's Mountain
BLACK OAK
RAWLINGS
McKENZIE
BRADY
CEDAR CLIFF
ROBERTS
CUMBERLAND
N. Br. Potomac
River
W. M. R. R.
M A R Y L A N D
W. VIRGINIA
1.04
2.19 Max.
2.28 Max.
1.34
.5 Max.
.5 Max.
.5 Max.
55
60
65
70
75
80
85
90
95
100

WEST END

Cumberland to Grafton 1848-1991

by Charles S. Roberts

COPYRIGHT © 1991 BARNARD, ROBERTS AND CO., INC.
Manufactured in the United States of America

FIRST EDITION October 1991

All Worldwide rights reserved. No part of this book may be reproduced in any manner without permission in writing, except in the case of critical reviews.

Published by
BARNARD, ROBERTS AND CO., INC.
P.O. Box 7344
305 Gun Road
Baltimore MD 21227
(410) 247-2242

Library of Congress Catalog Card No. 91-74019
ISBN 0-934118-18-3

FRONTISPIECE: EL5 7163 and EL2 7211, both compound as built, shove a drag through Salt Lick Curve on 13 March 1949. Photo by Howard N. Barr, Sr.

COVER: Photograph by the author. Details on page 193.

CREDITS: "B&OHS" acknowledges material from the archives and collections of The Baltimore and Ohio Railroad Historical Society, P.O. Box 13578, Baltimore MD 21203. Memberships in the Society are available at modest cost.

DEDICATION

To the late Everett L. "Tommy" Thompson, 1911-1989

From boyhood to the dawn of a new life, the West End's premier chronicler, photographer and devotee. We hope there is a reading room in his present abode.

QUOTES OF MOMENT

"There is but one railroad and it is the Baltimore and Ohio. There is but one division and it is the Cumberland. There is but one subdivision and it is the West End."

attributed to Carl W. Stillwell

"The Baltimore and Ohio is not a railroad . . . it's a religion."

Elizabeth C. Barringer

"The true railfan has two favorite railroads . . . the Baltimore and Ohio and another one."

Barnard, Roberts and Co., Inc.

A JEALOUS MISTRESS

Almost a third of a century ago, we took upon ourselves a mistress. This affair of the heart did not begin with a glance across a crowded room. The hormones began to flow when we read an article about M&K Junction by the late Frank E. Shaffer in the March, 1962, issue of *Model Railroader*. It was love at first sight.

We could not get enough of her. The pursuit ultimately encompassed the entire West End (if you will pardon the pun) of the Cumberland Division. It was obvious early on that we would have to share her, but we would take her on any terms . . . as the late Maurice Chevalier put it, one percent of something is better than one hundred percent of nothing.

We have modeled her, praised her, worshipped her, photographed her and now we're going to write about her.

She is 143 years old and, to be sure, she has faded a bit. She is still alluring and, candidly, she is still a vicious bitch. She has tried to kill us three times, maim us once and ambush us twice, with guns. The lady claims two fathers, one of them being Thomas Swann. Since Mr. Swann was our great-grandmother's brother, a touch of incest lurks in the heat of the dalliance.

There is none other like her.

Oh, certainly there are other mountain railroads. And there are those with sharper curves, steeper grades and heavier tonnage. *None in the world combine grades, curves and tonnage like the West End.*

By the latter part of the last century, railroading in the U.S.A. had evolved into three major trunk lines . . . . in order of size and power, the Pennsylvania Railroad, the New York Central System and the Baltimore and Ohio.

These three railroads were almost one-quarter of American railroading during most of rail history, and their descendants are still major players.

But only the Baltimore and Ohio had the West End.

Charles Swann Roberts
21 May 1991

TABLE OF CONTENTS

1	Breaching the Great Barrier	9
2	Approach March	17
3	Seventeen Mile Grade	35
4	The Glades	58
5	Cranberry Grade	77
6	M&K Junction	93
7	Cheat River Grade	113
8	Newburg Grade	140
9	Power	158
10	Trains and Cars	180
11	Glimpses (Color Plates)	193
12	Operations	209
	Miscellany	217
	Bibliography	221
	Index	222

DEFINITIONS

WEST END

Our jealous mistress has been known by at least seven names that we know about and it is not improbable that there might have been more as the lady got around a bit. When built from Cumberland through Grafton, she was the *Third Division* from Piedmont ... east of Piedmont was made part of the Second Division which began at Martinsburg. By 1886, she was the *Western Division* from and including Keyser ... by 1889 she was back to Third Division Keyser to Grafton and stayed such until 1900. In c. 1901 the B&O dropped "Main Stem" to describe Baltimore to Wheeling in favor of "Main Line System" and then she was the *Second Division* Keyser to Grafton. In 1902 the Cumberland Division was created to Keyser but she remained Second Division until c. 1903 when she was included as part of the *Cumberland Division* with no specific West End reference we have found. In the U.S.R.A. era 1918-20 she was the *Keyser Division* from Viaduct Junction to East Grafton. By 1920 she was Cumberland Division *West End* subdivision and held that name until she was renamed *Mountain Subdivision* in the early 1970s ... the name she retains today (1991). To students of the B&O in most of this century, she was simply the West End and we have chosen to call her by that name throughout. Tommy would have wanted it that way.

THE HILL

While hyperbole is not unknown to English-speaking people, understatement is employed when the subject is grim. Most railroaders refer to the looming hulk in front of them as the Hill ... on the West End it was The Hill out of respect and with full knowledge that there were more than one. The Hill was the one you were on.

CSX

A conglomerate composed of many fine railroads, the management of which decided to meld them all into one entity and The Baltimore and Ohio Railroad died at age 160 in 1987. Since that was only four years ago, we have opted to use "B&O" exclusively. The thought has crossed our minds that such usage may convey our disdain for those who ignore the importance of heritage and tradition; the glue that holds all of us together.

DRAG

B&O parlance describing a heavy train carrying low time-priority contents, usually coal, coke, ore, stone and grain. Always run as extras, the goal is to tie onto the train the absolute maximum amount of tonnage to keep cost down. The great majority of trains run eastbound on the West End have always been Drags hauling coal. In the early years such trains were simply called Coal Trains. Slow Freight and Tonnage are synonymous with Drag.

COAL CARS

The B&O term describing empty open-top cars going back to the mines for more. The predominant westbound movement on the West End, these trains are usually run in solid blocks. As with Drags the maximum tonnage is tacked on.

QD

For Quick Dispatch. QD trains carry higher value, time-sensitive ladings. Sometimes scheduled and sometimes extras, these trains also have been known as Time, Export, Symbol, Named, Timetable, Piggyback, Ordinary, Other, Timesaver and, in the early days, Burden freights. Livestock trains were QD. In the *very* early days, such trains were called Tonnage, but that term ultimately came to mean Drag. QD was actually the highest speed priority, but we are using the term to describe all non-Drag loaded freight trains. For all QD trains, the aim was speed ... weight of the train and the power deployed was adjusted to maintain schedule.

SHOVE

B&O slang describing helper-on-rear configuration. Just about all trains on the West End throughout history had helpers somewhere in the train ... front, middle or rear. Cutting off rear helpers "on the fly" was classic B&O procedure on the West End until the recent advent of End of Train Devices. A dramatic sight ... slow to five-or-so miles per hour, pull the pin on the caboose, let the air hose pop and the helper goes into emergency. The train keeps going. We miss it.

Chapter 1

Breaching the Great Barrier

The name of the nation's first true railroad was The Baltimore *And Ohio* Rail Road Company. In a struggle that can only be called Herculean, the B&O had reached Cumberland in Maryland on 5 November 1842, 178 miles west from Baltimore and fifteen years from conception. And in Cumberland they sat for seven more years, still over two hundred miles from the Ohio River and, in the event, ten years from fulfilling the promise of their name.

These years were not wasted. The B&O had to invent or evolve every item and aspect of the construction and operation of a railroad, from the mundane to the sublime, and that they succeeded is one of the great adventure stories of all time.
C. S. Roberts

During the years 1842-1848 it can be said that the B&O perfected the whole concept of railroading and were rewarded with steadily growing revenues and earnings.

There are only three basic industries ... growing things, making things and carrying things. The railroad revolutionized them all and was the catalyst that transformed human society from a waterbound, beastbound affair into a vast and interdependent industrialized era known as the Industrial Revolution. And the B&O showed the way.

The Golden Fleece was the great Midwest. Exploding population and growth in the early nineteenth century made apparent that the middle

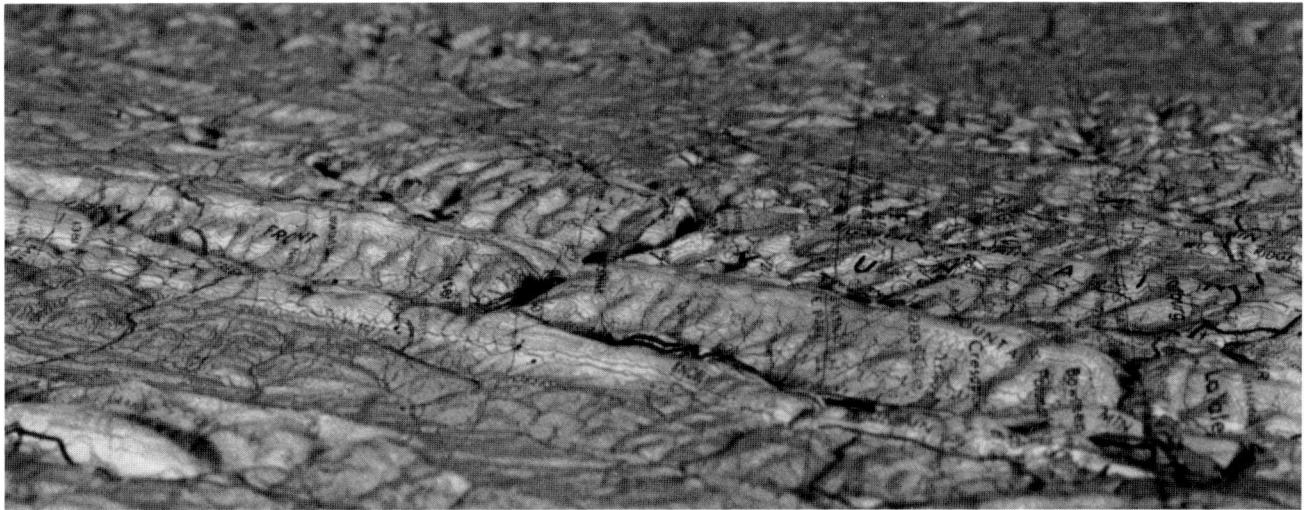

IT IS JUST AS WELL that man had not taken wing when Messrs. Swann and Latrobe were planning the breach of the Great Barrier. This photo of a relief map of the terrain they had to cross gives the impression of an angry North Atlantic winter storm, enough to give pause to the bravest of men. Cumberland is the complex on the right; the straight slash in the center shows the path of the Potomac and Savage Rivers. The Glades bump along from the top of the slash toward a jumble of mountains at the upper left. There was no other way to get there from here, as the saying goes, but we are glad these two heroes did not have to look at this perspective ... even they may have wavered.

WEST END

of the United States would be the nucleus of a great nation. Until the coming of the railroad, waterborne transport was the only transport and the Midwest was blessed with an abundance of rivers and lakes ... almost all flowing south.

The cities of the east coast regarded this trend of events with understandable alarm. The original cities and States were in danger of being bypassed and isolated, to "wither on the vine," as expressed at the time.

The danger to the eastern seaboard was even greater than they thought because the vast natural resources in the Midwest and environs were then undiscovered. When tapped, they would feed an unprecedented industrial expansion.

How to grasp a share of this prize was the question of the day. Nature had placed a Great Barrier between the East and Midwest ... a thick chain of mountains running from Georgia to Maine, pierced only by a few rivers.

New York was the first to respond with the Erie Canal, taking advantage of the Hudson River and the relatively flat profile of upstate New York. Most historians agree that this canal established New York City as the commercial capital of the nation ... later, railroads like the Erie and those lines which ended up as the New York Central System confirmed the leadership. New York City's canal and railroads went around the mountains, a solution not available to Philadelphia and Baltimore ... they must go over.

Both cities toyed with the canal approach and Philadelphia even built a few, but one wonders what was in their minds when they contemplated the mountains ... we will later allude to the aspirations of the Chesapeake and Ohio Canal in this regard.

Baltimore decided to build a rail road, thus the B&O was born. This Band of Brothers knew nothing and were guessing at everything. It has been said that Great Britain acquired and then dissolved her Empire in fits of absentmindedness and one cannot recall this conclusion without thinking of the founders of the B&O. Long on vision and courage, short on everything else, they decided to have a go. And what a go it was.

By 1848, the "New York" railroads had reached the Great Lakes and what was to become the mighty Pennsylvania Railroad had reached Pittsburg (the "h" would come later), although not with a continuous railroad. The B&O was still stuck at Cumberland and mired in a debate. The rational choice would be to reach the Ohio at Pittsburg, already a large city and with an easy single crossing of the mountains. The machinations of the Pennsylvania Railroad put paid to that plan ... with more political than railroading skill at that time, the PRR so rigged certain laws that the B&O could not even touch Pennsylvania, let alone Pittsburg, in their quest for the Ohio.

And Virginia was little better. They would grant B&O a charter, but only if they reached the Ohio at Wheeling.

And railroads were abuilding in the Midwest, reaching for the Ohio and the East.

What to do? Simply stop at Cumberland? Build to Wheeling, but only a piece at a time? Build to what would become Grafton and hope to persuade Virginia to relent and allow B&O to reach the Ohio at Parkersburg, with higher water and a more direct approach to Cincinnati and St. Louis? Or swallow the pill and build to Wheeling in one bound?

The original Band of Brothers were gone or worn out. A new hero was needed and one appeared ... on 11 October 1848, Baltimore businessman Thomas Swann was unanimously elected President of the B&O and the decision was made. Go to Wheeling in one bound and fulfill the promise of our name ... the Baltimore *and* Ohio.

Great Generals need great lieutenants and Thomas Swann had one in Chief Engineer Benjamin H. Latrobe. An engineer with the railroad from the beginning, save for a brief period with another road, Latrobe *knew*. A modest man, and with skills complementary to Thomas Swann, the two were a great team. "Conquer and overcome" was the battle cry and, to jump ahead, on New Year's Day in 1853, the line was operating as promised to Wheeling and victory was proclaimed. The B&O was now 379 miles long and about to pluck the Golden Fleece. The reality however, wasn't that simple.

Man, in his rise to become the predominant species on Spaceship Earth, developed of necessity an urge to make war ... sometimes with glee and greed, at other times with reluctance, and always with ferocity. Thus military analogies abound when man sets forth upon a mission and when he

Thos. Swann

Benjm H Latrobe

completes it. The Tocsin call of War draws man like a magnet draws metal and the assault upon the "great Allegheny barrier," as Mr. Latrobe called it, was war in every sense of the word. And it would prove to be a very long war, indeed.

Mr. Latrobe had surveyors in the field during 1848 and the reports were clear. There was only one practical way to get to the Ohio from Cumberland. First, a simple river line railroad from Cumberland along the North Branch of the Potomac River to the mouth of the Savage River, exploiting the gap conveniently carved by the river between Allegheny Front and Dan's Mountains ... a mere skirmish to this point. Then the main assault, up the Savage River canyon on the side of Backbone Mountain, thence up Crabtree Creek on the back of Backbone Mountain to a summit at Altamont ... seventeen miles, hence Seventeen Mile Grade. An easy trip then across the Glades, a lovely, rolling plateau, to Cranberry Summit. A plunge down the side of Briery Mountain for about eleven miles to the Cheat River ... cross the river and then another assault up the side of Laurel Mountain for about five miles ... the Cheat River Grade ... and then punch through Laurel Mountain with a tunnel and begin the descent along Raccoon Creek and Three Forks Creek to the Tygart River, soon to be called Grafton. From there to Wheeling across broken, rolling country.

The main battlefield would be from the Savage River canyon entrance to the foot of the west side of Laurel Mountain, the famed West End.

Swann and Latrobe decided to let all the contracts for construction from Cumberland to Wheeling at one time, dividing the path into sections of approximately one mile in length. Many place names along the route were taken from this decision and remain to this day ... hence "21st Section Bridge" south of Cumberland and "76 Fill" west of Rowlesburg.

Almost all contracts were let by June 1850. Rail would be of iron 58 lbs to the yard with ties two feet on centers, ballasted to a depth of two feet and of proven T design. Bridges would be of masonry or iron.

William Prescott Smith, B&O official and its first historian, published a book in 1853 and made suitable military allusions to "General-in-Chief" Latrobe "leading his army of sappers and miners to conquer and overcome the immense barriers of nature that stood frowning in his path, with their peaks penetrating the clouds."

WEST END

War would not be war without fear, however. Mr. Latrobe caused a horsepath to be constructed along the general trace of the road and invited Mr. Swann and a small party to travel it. Mr. Swann recalled later, "It would be impossible for me to describe to you now the effect which this first impression left upon me. I was almost brought to the conviction that our assailants were not without some ground of complaint ... my anxiety was such that I deemed it important that they not be permitted to transpire ... if the people of Baltimore could have witnessed what we were about to attempt the road would have been abandoned ... I might have been a shining mark in some lunatic asylum." Mr. Swann swallowed his fears and covered up ... if the call of the trumpet is uncertain, who shall follow and, besides, he was in too deep to turn back.

We have traversed and explored every inch of the West End with awe, finding it hard to believe that a railroad could be built, let alone operated, through such terrain. Whistle *Scotland the Brave*, lads, it's going to be a jolly war.

Swann and Latrobe were not fools. Swann knew the line had to be built ... Labrobe knew that it was possible.

Problems surfaced early on as contractors defaulted on their contracts ... Latrobe took over all such and had company forces do the jobs.

And labor turned out to be a problem. Strong Irish backs were imported in large numbers and Latrobe soon learned that, indeed, it was true that an Irishman's two avocations are drinking and brawling. He also learned that, though sparsely populated, the locals knew how to make whiskey. "Harbors for those who rend the poison are so readily found in that wild country," he lamented.

"The numerous body of foreigners, with their old country feuds and intemperate habits, made necessary the early establishment of an armed police." Desertions were high and replacements violently resisted by earlier factions. "A large majority upon this line are from one section of Ireland and have done much to deter countrymen from other provinces from coming to the work," reported Mr. Latrobe. He did what he had to do and, from the tone of his reports, the "armed police" shot first and asked questions later. A veteran engineer on the Piedmont helper some years ago told us of his father and grandfather relating that Seventeen Mile Grade was in fact a vast graveyard, all unmarked.

Apparently, upwards of 5,000 men and 1,000 horses were employed on the line from Cumberland to Wheeling, although we see no evidence that accurate records were kept ... of workers or casualties. No jury trials are mentioned.

For all his skill, knowledge, zeal and experience, Mr. Latrobe had some unpleasant surprises coming—another aspect of war. And these could not be dealt with as handily as replacing recalcitrant contractors or applying summary discipline.

The first unpleasant surprise had to do with, of all things, geology.

Mr. Latrobe and his fellow engineers were thoroughly familiar with the geology east of Cumberland and saw no reason to think there would be any difference west of that place. On the surface there is no difference ... below is another matter.

No one in that era had any inkling of how mountains were formed. It would be late in this century before the truth was discovered ... that whole continents were moving, sliding, crumpling, heaving, sinking, shaking and generally doing what they damn well pleased.

Mountains both east and west of Cumberland began at the bottom of a vast inland sea and were composed of sandstone, limestone, coal and shale ... sedimentary materials that accumulated on the bottom and were compressed by the weight of the successive layers.

The immense powers of Continental drift pushed the seabed up into mountains and the sea waters flushed out.

Mountains are noble, elitist and reach for the stars. Water is egalitarian, determined to level out everything and the lower the better. Mountains and water are implacable foes.

East of Cumberland, water had eroded almost all components except sandstone, the hardest of the lot and, hence, the most stable.

For various reasons, the process west of Cumberland had been much slower ... the mountains there were unwashed and the sedimentary layers were intact.

Sadly, most of the elements composing West End mountains decompose rapidly as soon as they are exposed to air and water. Worse, water lubricates the layers of sediment and, if the angle is right, they begin to slide.

Ambush is another element in war, and Mr. Latrobe walked right into one. At first his reports referred to firm slate rock and how it would be unnecessary to line tunnels and how fortunate it was to have such nice rock in cuttings.

He was not looking at slate ... it was shale. Heave a piece of slate against a wall and it will fragment. Heave shale and it will turn to grit.

All tunnels on the West End were bored for double track, generally 22 feet wide. They began to collapse. Mr. Latrobe counterattacked with timber linings and was repulsed. The tunnels continued to collapse and the timber linings were another trap ... unable to carry the weight, they had to be removed, and, in the process, dumped tons of rock upon the workmen, closing the line. Only brick, stone, and, in some cases, cast iron linings would do the job. And whatever lining was used, it took up space and left little or no room for two tracks.

The cuttings presented even more of a problem. Water would get into crevices, freeze, expand, and spit rocks down upon the railroad. Incoming.

As we relate the history of each part of the West End, we will expand upon these tribulations ... suffice it to say for the moment that it was not until 1858 that Mr. Latrobe announced "the most important event of the history of the company since the opening of the road to the Ohio River ... the arching of every tunnel on the Main Stem has been completed."

Are mountains alive? To be classified as "alive," students of such issues aver, the subject must consume matter and convert it into energy, throw off waste, reproduce, and adapt to or change its environment. Mountains appear to do all these things.

Historians are required to come to conclusions, but on this one we will pass. Nevertheless, we will state with certainty that every B&O man who fought on the West End *thought* that the mountains were alive.

And then there is the weather. Messrs. Swann and Latrobe did not have the benefit of years of meticulously compiled weather reports to contemplate before they decided to build a railroad through these mountains. This subject is of such moment that we discuss it separately ... it is enough for now to say that Mr. Latrobe's reports, year after year, alluded to "severe winters" that "almost closed down the railroad" until it finally dawned on him that *all* winters in that lovely plateau called The Glades were severe ... that it was the Land of Three Seasons: July, August and Winter.

Alive or not, the mountains had allies in the war with the B&O ... weather was one and water another. We recall the opening statement in our introduction to field engineering: "The greatest enemy to man's works is water, in each of its three forms." As a liquid moving down sharp grades, it assumes the character of concrete and takes all with it ... after all, water carved those mountains. As a solid—snow and ice—we will see some of its effects. Even as a gas, it plagued the West End. Mr. Smith was all too correct when he mentioned "peaks penetrating the clouds." There is little fog, *per se*, in The Glades and its approaches. It is low cloud, and we can testify that, of the two, we'll take the fog.

July, August and Winter

A few miles north of the B&O main line through the Glades, straddling the Maryland-West Virginia border, is the Cranesville Swamp. Called the Great Pine Swamp by pioneers, it is a protected sanctuary. Why?

It has existed since the last Ice Age and is a subarctic environment awash with arctic flora and fauna. Some trees found here are at their southernmost location in North America. The swamp thrives.

Most of the B&O rails through the Glades traverse Maryland's Garrett County, named for B&O president John Work Garrett. Average yearly snowfall in the county is 82 inches. It regularly snows for three or four days. Deep Creek Lake, an enchanting resort lake near the B&O, has an average winter ice thickness of 18". Average winter temperature is 28 degrees F ... summer 66 degrees.

In every single month of the year, including July and August, it snows somewhere in Garrett County. One year it snowed on July 4th and the locals were puzzled ... was this a late storm or an early one?

It was a typical December in 1951. At 2:00 a.m. on the sixteenth, the following tower temperature reports were made: Hardman 14°, Blaser 8°, Terra Alta 4°, Altamont 2°, Cumberland 16°.

Cumberland Division West End Adjusted Tonnage Ratings (printed in full later in this book) dated 15 August 1949 mandate the following "Adjustment

WEST END

> in Tons *Per Car*:" 35°+, 4 tons; 20-35°, 6 tons; 0-20°, 8 tons; below 0°, 10 tons.
>
> Every few years a cold snap hits the Glades. Temperatures then drop into the 30-35 degree range *below zero*. Wind chill is beyond comprehension.
>
> For many years we visited the Glades area in October and December, and for four years owned a cottage near Altamont, spending many summer and winter weekends. All of the following accounts reflect actual, personal experience.
>
> The wind always blows in Garrett County. By the end of winter, the snow on the lee side of buildings is as high as the building. You use windward doors.
>
> The wind currents are such that, frequently, huge amounts of snow are suspended in the air and then suddenly dumped in one place. On a day of mere snow flurries with bare fields everywhere, we drove into a six-foot drift that hadn't been there an hour before.
>
> Returning to our cottage one evening in the lightest of snow flurries on a winding country road at about 35 m.p.h. and on a curve, a complete whiteout occurred. A yellowish glow illuminated the interior of the auto. The windows were opaque white. The auto was moving. Suddenly the glow dissipated. We were still on the road and twenty years older. A mile later it happened again.
>
> We entered the cottage one winter evening and someone commented, "I think it's warming up... it's up to zero." We learned that the snow particles are so cold that they are mildly abrasive and give good traction. During a cold snap, we met a lad who needed a lift... his tires had frozen to the ground and his battery and transmission had frozen solid. During another cold snap, we returned a daughter to college and heard a campus policeman shout, "Don't turn off your engine... it will freeze solid in two minutes." During the entire day, we noted that the temperature gauge needle never left the peg.
>
> We recall a veteran engineer with steam experience relating how they would regularly build a coal fire on the deck plate to get some heat... in the cab of a steam locomotive, mind you... and laughing because one time the bonfire had buckled the steel plate and they were still freezing. Then we watched his face turn red with anger as he remembered the daily war with the Altamont operator... the helper engine crew wanted to turn on the wye and go down head first to keep the wind on the nose and out of the cab. Some warmth was gained from the heat of the profanity when the operator shook his head.
>
> We rode the Piedmont helper to Altamont three times one April day and saw three seasons... summer at Piedmont, spring at Swanton and winter at Altamont.
>
> Another veteran engineer pointed out that in the winter you had to keep the train moving on the grades... if you stopped all the journals would freeze in a matter of seconds and then "you were really hung up." And they worried about air leakage from contracting air hose joints and hoped the compressors could keep up.
>
> We must also say that the Glades are very dangerous in another way... a siren, if you will... a captivating place with natural beauty and vistas in all seasons that leaves one breathless with delight. Shangri La must be like this, you think... here is where we want to stay forever. A daughter did so... she took a few college courses and stayed.
>
> And the Glades are the home of a hardy, handsome, independent, friendly, proud and feisty people... admirable in every way.
>
> One wonders if Messrs. Swann and Latrobe would have had second thoughts if they could have read this account.
>
> Perhaps, perhaps not.

That gravity was another ally of the mountains is obvious, but its impact was insidious. The first lesson taught to neophyte field artillerymen is that the problem is *not* going uphill. With enough power and traction, you will get up. The problem is going *downhill*. Artillery and trains are quite heavy and made to move. The severe grades on the West End went down as well as up, and a good case could be made that the downgrade legs haunted B&O more than the upgrade. The latter is a matter of economics... the former is one of survival.

So the West End was astride The Hill and its allies. At the famous Wheeling celebration, one of the interminable toasts proclaimed "a fair fight and an honorable peace." We recall that incomparable man, W. C. Fields, when pestered by a young interloper, growling "Go away, boy, you bother me." Did The Hill hear the call for peace? If so, it replied, "You wanted war and now you will get all the war you wanted."

Mr. Latrobe preferred to use the word "breach" in reference to The Hill. He avoided "conquer." He was a realist as well as an engineer and knew well the military axiom "you may order attacks by regiments and divisions and corps, but you come in contact with the enemy by squads and platoons

BREACHING THE GREAT BARRIER

Another Ally, Another Enemy

In 1861 The Hill picked up another ally—the Confederate States of America. The B&O could have learned to do without another enemy.

History is replete with accounts of the devastation wreaked upon the B&O in the Civil War, particularly east of Cumberland. The West End was not spared.

The Rebels started having fun immediately, burning cars at Piedmont and destroying 21st Bridge early in 1861. For the B&O, it was all downhill from there.

One particularly unpleasant episode occurred in the spring of 1863. General Robert E. Lee ordered what would become known as the "Great Raid" and gave Generals John D. Imboden and William E. Jones orders to take out the B&O from New Creek to Wheeling. Of course, the B&O was defended by Federal troops and the Rebels did not win everywhere... for example, they were repulsed at Rowlesburg and Tray Run. They did not lose everywhere, either.

Track was destroyed in numerous locations. What is now known as Bridge 88 west of Oakland was destroyed, and raiders at Altamont set loose a westbound train that got that far. Actually, they meant to send the train the other way, but fouled up... west it went, and ended with its pilot wheels hanging over the bridge abutment. The Newburg engine house, machine shop and sandhouse were destroyed. Water stations were burned with abandon.

In his After Action report, General Jones claimed to have burned 16 railroad bridges and one tunnel in addition to other structures. General Lee was pleased and his endorsement stated, "the expedition was conducted with commendable skill and vigor and was productive of bountiful results... the enemy will be induced to keep troops to guard the railroad who might otherwise be employed against us." The B&O groaned.

And in 1864 and 1865 more raids occurred... structures and trains burned, telegraph cut, track torn up and general hell raised.

Even war can produce amusement. In Oakland, Rebel troops rode across the lawn of one Alexander MacInnes, a recent Scottish immigrant. "Get off my property, sir!" proclaimed the Scot. "I am a British subject and I will appeal to Her Majesty, the Queen!" Since the officer commanding was in rebellion against a government far closer than London, he was not impressed. He was, however, tired, and said so. The Scot invited him in to tea. Perhaps Sir Winston Churchill was correct when he said that the American Civil War was the last one between gentlemen.

The Civil War, at long last, ended.

The war against The Hill did not.

---

and that is where the issue is decided." He was a wise man and he knew the war would go on for a very long time.

B&O would have victories... literally millions of them to date. They would come one train at a time, one movement at a time, one day at a time. And there would be many, many defeats, with attendant casualties.

The war has gone on for almost a century-and-a-half and is going on at this very moment. And The Hill is winning.

The history of the war can be divided into eras, in terms of construction and power.

The West End started as single track and was open only a few months in 1853 when Mr. Latrobe reported that the traffic was heavier than expected and that single track was already inadequate, with "stoppages and interferences fatal to the success of Burden trains." A drive to double track started at once, but it would be 1888 before the entire West End was double tracked.

The double track era lasted only about twenty years... constantly growing traffic pressed the B&O into a vast improvement operation which resulted in extensive triple tracking by c. 1910-12. In 1973, most of the line reverted to double track. A flood in 1985 and an accident in 1989 resulted in the Cheat River Grade, and the bridge over the river, being single tracked.

Powerwise, three eras ensued... single engine, mallet and diesel.

Trafficwise, the history is one of almost continuous growth interrupted only by assorted panics and recessions, almost always occurring after some large improvements were made. Until the mid-1980s, that is, when the B&O began surrendering to The Hill.

And, as was suspected from the very beginning, the tonnage was and is overwhelmingly eastbound, as indeed it was and is for the entire B&O system. Loads east and empties west was the pattern. For example, in 1851 revenue tonnage east 79%, west 21%... and this before the line was open to Wheeling. Even in 1857, of the 83% ton-

WEST END

nage east, over three-quarters was coal. In 1911, equipment mileage was 95% loads east, empties west 72%. And, of course, most of the tonnage east was coal. Today, it is almost all coal.

Single/double/triple. Single/mallet/diesel. Tons east, empties west. The West End, with a profile like the back of a dinosaur. The West End, the majestic mountain railroad.

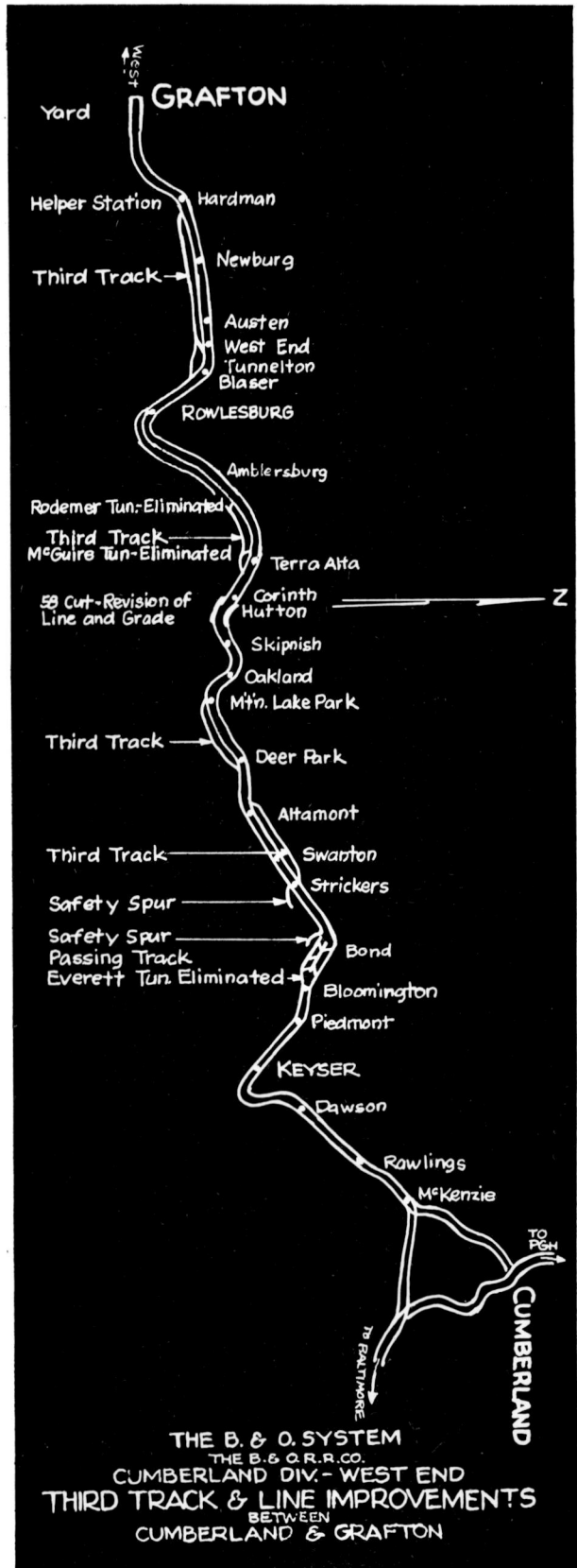

THE B. & O. SYSTEM
THE B. & O. R.R. CO.
CUMBERLAND DIV.- WEST END
THIRD TRACK & LINE IMPROVEMENTS
BETWEEN
CUMBERLAND & GRAFTON

Mr. Latrobe says it all....

Following are mildly edited excerpts from Mr. Latrobe's report to the President dated 1 October 1853 in which he establishes himself as a writer as well as an engineer, and summarizes the essence of the West End with clarity:

"Location ... of the line is of primary concern in every railway. There are difficulties connected with it upon almost every line, either in the face of the country or in the interests which ... divert it from its true course. Both of these classes of obstacles have embarrassed this Road, and the former in an eminent degree."

"The necessity of adhering to Virginia in seeking a route to Wheeling forced the B&O over a country of much harder features than that upon which it was originally planned through Pennsylvania in 1839. The mountain summits were higher and more numerous and the approaches to them on both sides more rugged and abrupt."

"The passage of the Alleghenies involves a higher grade than had been previously employed upon lines of general traffic ... that they require some increase of motive power was known and admitted beforehand ... its supposed dangers have been found to be entirely groundless ... owing clearly to the greater caution observed upon them."

"Winter was unusually severe 1851-52 and the success with which the grades were passed through the snow and ice of that winter must be conclusive upon this ground of apprehension."

"The grades of the B&O present one feature somewhat more marked than those of its competitors for the Western trade but that is confined to the central 60 of its 380 miles. This subject appears to be still an occasion of reproach to this great work and of invidious comparison with other lines which boast that they possess the best pass over the great Allegheny barrier. None of them compare with the B&O in directness of connection with the commercial centers of the Mississippi Valley."

Mr. Latrobe also mentioned that the "breadth of roadbed is for two tracks ... except at a few points."

As one reads this account with the advantage of almost a century-and-a-half of knowledge and observed experience, it is easy to conclude that Mr. Latrobe missed his calling. He was a great engineer ... he would have been an even better public relations man.

Chapter 2

Approach March

Cumberland and Patterson Creek to Piedmont

In military terms, an Approach March is a forward movement toward the enemy, preliminary to battle. The building of the B&O toward the mountains met this definition and, while not without problems, the construction was easy and proceeded swiftly. By July of 1851, the single track line was completed to Piedmont (literally "foot of the mountain") and traffic was beginning to flow, particularly from mines being opened between Keyser and Piedmont.

Much of the line was graded for two tracks, but it was 1872 before the entire line from Cumberland to Piedmont was double tracked. Many side tracks were constructed, however, and water tanks were generously deployed, so traffic was moved satisfactorily.

Beginning at Viaduct Juction in Cumberland, the line crossed Wills Creek on the Cumberland Viaduct and immediately entered a fairly deep cut on the edge of Haystack Mountain. Using modern names and spelling, the following towns were then passed ... Roberts, Amcelle (for the large factory of American Cellulose and Chemical Company erected in the mid-1920s), Brady, McKenzie, Potomac, Lowndes, Rawlings, Black Oak, Dawson, 21st Bridge, Keyser and Piedmont. In the early 1920s, the Kelly Springfield Tire Company built a large factory between Viaduct Junction and Roberts ... between it and "Amcelle" B&O received a lot of traffic until both plants closed in the 1980s.

Grades were dreamlike. Officially, maximum grades were .5% Cumberland to Piedmont ... actually most were less. In fact, in the twenty-and-a-half miles between Viaduct Junction and 21st Bridge, about seven miles were perfectly flat. And even these slight grades were ascending westward ... they were favorable to the heavy eastbound tonnage.

The last half of the last century was marked by constantly increasing tonnage on both the West End and the "Chicago" line from Pittsburgh (modern spelling) and Cumberland was becoming a bottleneck. The B&O decided to build the Patterson Creek Cutoff to relieve the pressure and it was opened in 1904.

Double tracked from inception, the Cutoff left the main line at Patterson Creek and followed the creek through rolling country to Knobly Mountain, which was pierced with a 4,160' tunnel. Grades ranged from .65% to .93% to just east of the tunnel ... from there to McKenzie, where the main line was rejoined, grades against eastbound traffic were from .28% to .35% with only .26% through the tunnel. The Potomac River was crossed, of course, between the tunnel and McKenzie.

At the time of opening, the Cutoff was touted as saving 10½ miles of road and 808' of curvature ... all true, but the main reason for the Cutoff was to bypass Cumberland congestion and this role was accomplished nicely.

For over half-a-century, from 1904 to c. 1960, the 6.9 mile line remained double tracked except for closure of #4 track during the Great Depression, 1933-39. The Cutoff was reduced to #3 track c. 1960, but the single track was signalled in both directions. The line was closed permanently c. 1974, but was almost reborn during the 1980-81 Great Coal Boom. That boom dissipated and so

17

WEST END

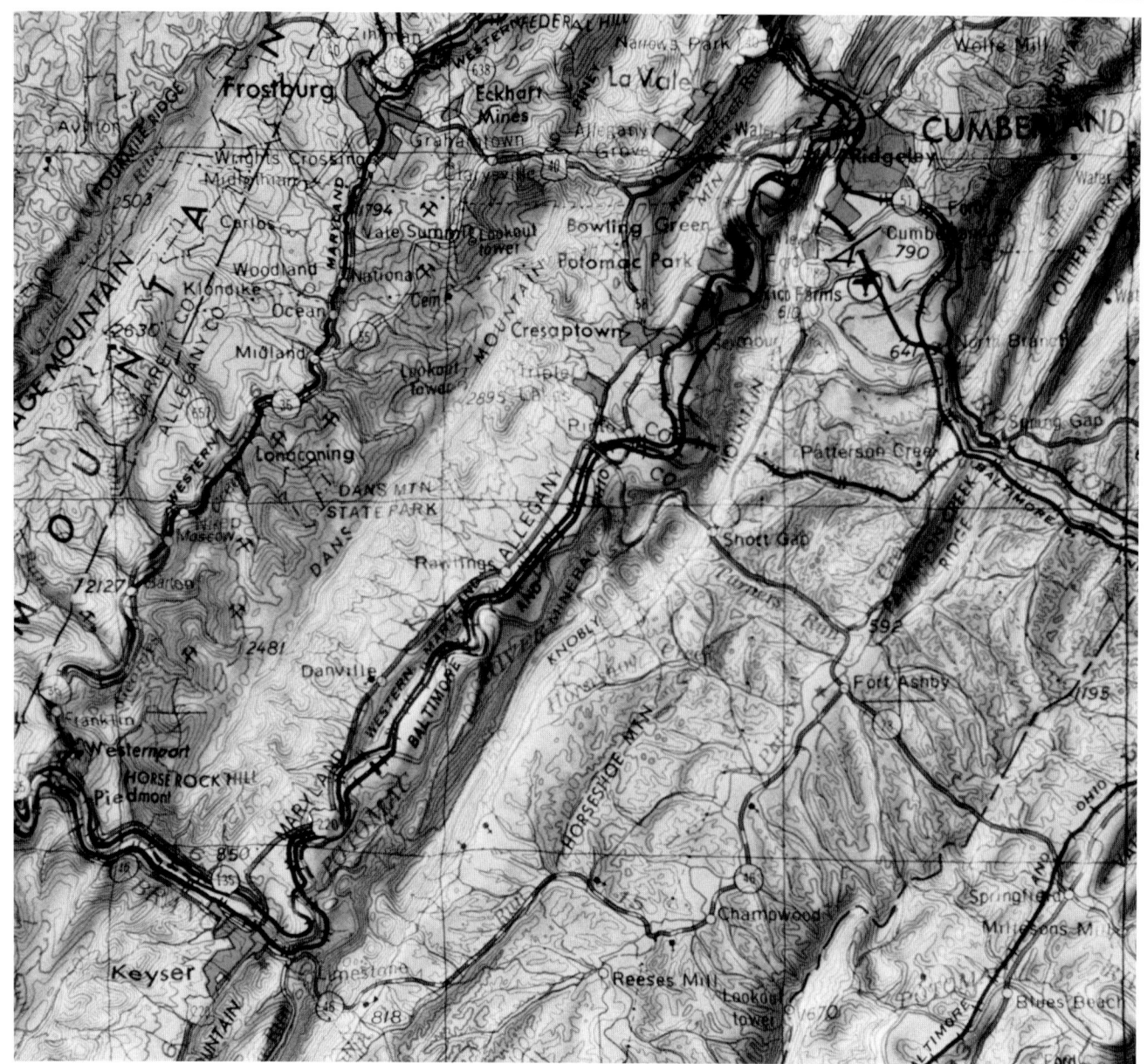

C. S. Roberts

THE WEST END begins at Cumberland at upper right and at Patterson Creek where it enters the Potomac River a bit above right center. The double (//) slashed black line is the B&O; the single (/) slashed is the Western Maryland, formerly West Virginia Central and now part of CSX. The line from Cumberland begins at Viaduct Junction (call letters ND), crosses Wills Creek on a viaduct and wanders up the Potomac River on the north shore until 21st Bridge, where it crosses the Potomac and enters West Virginia. On the way, at McKenzie (CO) the line meets the Patterson Creek Cutoff which has left the Potomac at Patterson Creek, follows the creek to Knobly Tunnel through the mountain of the same name and crosses the Potomac to join. The B&O crosses Limestone Run and New Creek to enter Keyser (originally New Creek), a major yard and shop point for many years. The B&O then follows the river line to Piedmont (P) opposite Westernport in Maryland. The Georges Creek Valley, a major source of coal from day one until today, traces northeast from Westernport to Frostburg. Gentle country, gentle weather, gentle grades, gentle curves ... a land of milk and honey compared to what is to come.

did the plans to reopen the line. McKenzie (CO) tower was closed in January 1958 and operated remotely from Patterson Creek (FN).

The crush of traffic in the 1850s and 1860s resulted in another decision by B&O long before the Cutoff was built and that decision created a new yard and gave a town a new name ... New Creek became Keyser c. 1872, probably named for a B&O officer of that era.

Tonnage was pouring off the mountains but, of necessity, in short trains because of the grades and, in addition, the Georges Creek Valley was becoming a major source of tonnage. There was too little flat land at Piedmont to accommodate the crush, so the great yard at Keyser was created. By 1875 a 44-stall roundhouse with 60′ turntable was completed, along with a machine shop, coal chutes, stock yards and, of course, a multitude of yard tracks. Four tracks were installed between Piedmont and Keyser by 1875, and from then on until the next century the story of Keyser was one of constant expansion. In 1897, a new car repair shop 80′ × 500′ was completed and another was built in 1907. In 1902 and 1919 large expansions in yard capacity were completed.

Keyser's fundamental mission was to "double up" tonnage streaming east from the West End; *e.g.*, in the heavy steam era 50-55 car drags were received and dispatched to Brunswick and east via the Cutoff as 100 car drags. The mountain passage was hard on cars, so repairs in progress were also a major activity at Keyser.

Westbound, the opposite was the case ... coal cars were received in long trains and "singled," so to speak, into trains of about 60-80 cars for the climb west.

Power and cabooses piled up in Keyser, an inevitable result of doubling up, so there was never any shortage of westbound power. In the steam era, power often was sent west light, and cabooses were tacked onto any convenient westbound train *including* passenger trains. In the diesel era, six or more unit lashups of power were, and are, commonplace.

Keyser also became a major car building facility and many famous cars were constructed there, including 125 I12 wagontop cabooses in 1941 and 1945, 100 N34 wagontop covered hoppers, and probably thousands of the B&O's unique M15 and M53 wagontop box cars. As late as 1964, cars were being converted at Keyser, but by that date the facility was in decline.

The westbound yard was flat, but the eastbound yard had a hump. Apparently the hump was rather low because several trimmers were usually employed to close up cars and, in cold weather, an engine had to be assigned to move receiving yard cars to and fro to warm up journals so they would roll down the hump. A B&O yardmaster's lot was not a happy one, at least not at Keyser.

B&O Museum

A VERY EARLY PHOTO of the Cumberland Viaduct over Wills Creek just west of Viaduct Junction, complete with a westbound passenger train pulled by a diamond stack 4-4-0. Completed in 1851, the viaduct consisted of fourteen 50′ brick arches laid on stone piers and abutments. About 850′ long, the viaduct rose about 28′ above Wills Creek and was built as a double track structure. It was rebuilt and strengthened c. 1909 with poured concrete.

WEST END

THE TOWER AT VIADUCT JUNCTION in the late 1920s, shot from an eastbound passenger train coming off the West End. Tommy Thompson loved to take photos from moving trains and, considering film speeds in those days, this is one of his best and earliest. ND Tower was built new in 1901.

E. L. Thompson/B&OHS

For many decades, a typical day at Keyser involved well over a thousand cars, weighed, humped, and dispatched east, and an equal number west. The yard was active until the early 1980s and then the crash of the Great Coal Boom spelled its demise. By c. 1982, road crews were handling switching and there were no yard turns. Another factor in the decrease of activity at Keyser was the advent of unit drags in the early 1960s, which in effect meant that many trains were pre-blocked and did not require classification.

Two other points are worth mentioning in regard to Keyser. The Northwestern Turnpike, generally following the path of present day Route 50, preceded the B&O into this country and a connecting road ran from the pike to New Creek. In fact, the pike roughly paralleled the West End on the south until a crossing at Thornton, near Grafton, with feeders touching the West End at various places, providing B&O with access during construction.

Keyser was an interchange point with the Twin Mountain and Potomac Railroad, a 36" gauge line that ran south from Keyser to, believe it or not, Twin Mountain. Reportedly financed by millionaires from Fairmont W.V. to tap lush orchards south of Keyser, the 26-mile line lasted from 1913 to 1918. B&O got the job of scrapping it—down to the last spike—which probably resulted in more revenue to B&O than the interchange traffic. The TM&P met B&O just east of New Creek bridge. The fate of the millionaires is unreported.

A happier interchange point was Piedmont. Selected by Mr. Latrobe as a major location for shops, and a jump-off point for the main assault on The Hill, Piedmont evolved into a legendary spot on the B&O. Across the Potomac River from Westernport, an ancient river town, Piedmont was also opposite the entrance of Georges Creek to the Potomac, and to this day benefits from the vast coal fields that underly the entire area.

Two engine houses and a workshop were constructed at Piedmont ... all were completed c. 1854. Mr. Latrobe described the engine houses as "sixteen sided polygons (for the same number of engines), 150 feet interior diameter; walls of brick on stone foundations; roof of iron supported from the ground within the walls of the building by leaning columns resting on stone pedestals and running up to the lantern. The peculiarity of the structure is the independence of the roof upon the walls, which are therefore made much lighter." We will not pretend to be architectural engineers, but to us it sounds like Mr. Latrobe might have been a skyscraper pioneer in a later age.

APPROACH MARCH

C. S. Roberts

VIADUCT JUNCTION is the geographic and traffic focal point of the entire B&O system. The B&O describes a giant Y, from St. Louis and Chicago at the two extremities to Baltimore and east at the bottom ... they meet at ND. The St. Louis line enters the interlocker over the viaduct from the West End on the left and the Chicago line from the right. The other view shows the viaduct today. Both photos were taken 3 May 1991.

WEST END

B&OHS

PATTERSON CREEK'S FN Tower, built in 1893, marks the beginning of the Patterson Creek Cutoff. The cutoff passed through the truss bridge at left background, later replaced with a deck plate girder bridge and strengthened for EM1s in 1945. The line to Cumberland diverges to the right of the righthand semaphore signal. The white line and arrow on the tower marks the high water mark for a mid-1920s flood. This tower was destroyed by a derailment c. 1957 and was replaced by a new brick tower against the hill out of sight to the left. The new FN tower was scheduled for closure in the summer of 1991 as this was written.

APPROACH MARCH

The workshop was not a small affair, measuring 320 by 100 feet. It was of more conventional construction.

As Keyser gained in importance, Piedmont declined, and by early in this century the shops were gone.

The Georges Creek Railroad bridged the Potomac between Westernport and Piedmont by the spring of 1853 and the coal began to flow. The GCRR was taken over by the C&P in 1863 after it, in turn, was bought by Consolidation Coal, which, in turn, was controlled by the B&O for many years, all of which means the B&O had a lock on the tonnage.

It should be noted that coal was to be found in abundance from Keyser west, and mine after mine opened along B&O rails deep into West End territory.

A lot of tonnage moved from these mines, but as time went on they were depleted and West End coal tonnage evolved into through rather than originated revenue.

Piedmont. The end of the beginning. Now the beginning of the real West End.

Gary Schlerf

THE NEW FN taken from the rear of an Amtrak train in Feb. 1973 and proving that Tommy was not alone in taking photos from moving trains. The train is on the line to Cumberland ... the Cutoff is the line to the right.

WEST END

B&OHS

McKENZIE TOWER (CO), the western end of the Patterson Creek Cutoff. The cutoff runs straight through … the diverging line to the left runs to Cumberland. On the cutoff about three-quarters of a mile east, the line crosses the Potomac and plunges into Knobly Tunnel. This point was originally named Potomac Station, but was McKenzie by 1889. An amusing incident occurred here in 1951 … the operator erroneously diverted an eastbound drag toward Cumberland. The engineer realized the error but could not stop until the headend was well past the tower. The train was in a sag and could not be backed clear, so a locomotive had to be sent from Keyser to help out. There was no way the poor operator could cover up that one.

APPROACH MARCH

TYPICAL SCENERY along the Cumberland-Keyser railroad looking south from west of McKenzie on a delightful May 3 of 1991. Note how green the valley ... later this same day, we were in the Glades and not one leaf was out.

C. S. Roberts

B&O Museum

TWENTY-FIRST BRIDGE c. 1872, located in the 21st section from Cumberland. This crossing was a headache for Mr. Latrobe as two successive contractors failed to perform so the B&O had to do the job. The very first single track structure, finished in 1851 and named Potomac Bridge, was of wood and consisted of two 156' spans ... it must have been quite a sight as Mr. Latrobe described it in the 1853 Annual Report as "trusses supported by a wrought iron, parabolic, suspension chain, stiffened by diagonal rods." Hard to visualize but easy to destroy ... the Rebels burned it early in 1861 during one of their early forays. The structures pictured, which appear to be Bollman designs, were built at separate times ... one of the two was completed in 1868 in connection with double tracking to Piedmont. The road leading to the site is "21st Lane," a name we hope endures.

25

WEST END

C. S. Roberts Collection — TWO LATER INCARNATIONS of 21st Bridge ... the postcard, postmarked 1912, shows a double track through-truss bridge with the Western Maryland bridge in the background, while the photo taken 3 May 1991 depicts a curved deck plate girder bridge. The WM bridge remains. — *C. S. Roberts*

KEYSER YARD LOOKING EAST on 18 May 1921, a panoramic view of the West End's largest and, in fact, only major yard. Roundhouse, powerhouse, engine servicing facilities, huge car repair facilities and eastbound classification tracks fill a smoky, busy scene. — *B&O Museum*

APPROACH MARCH

C. S. Roberts Collection

THREE VIEWS OF KEYSER STATION (KY), built in 1875. The two postcard views are undated but are probably turn-of-the-century era. The other print was taken in June of 1983. The station still existed in May 1991, but to call it in disrepair would be complimentary. KY was a busy place for decades ... westbound passenger trains picked up helpers here during station stops, front or rear at different times in history. Major feature trains such as the National Limited, Diplomat and Cincinnatian used the Patterson Creek Cutoff and bypassed Cumberland, much to the annoyance of the citizens of that fair town who had to come to Keyser to board.

C. S. Roberts

WEST END

C. S. Roberts Collection

KEYSER YARD LOOKING NORTH in the days of glory, the roundhouse on the left, car repair building on the right and classification tracks in the background ... circa turn-of-the-century.

LOOKING WESTWARD ON 3 MAY 1991, it is hard to believe that Keyser Yard was ever alive. Except for the station, which is just out of sight to the lower left, the only hints that this might have been a place of importance are the flat cinder beds on both sides of the main line and the remnant of the ladder track on the right leading to nowhere.

C. S. Roberts

APPROACH MARCH

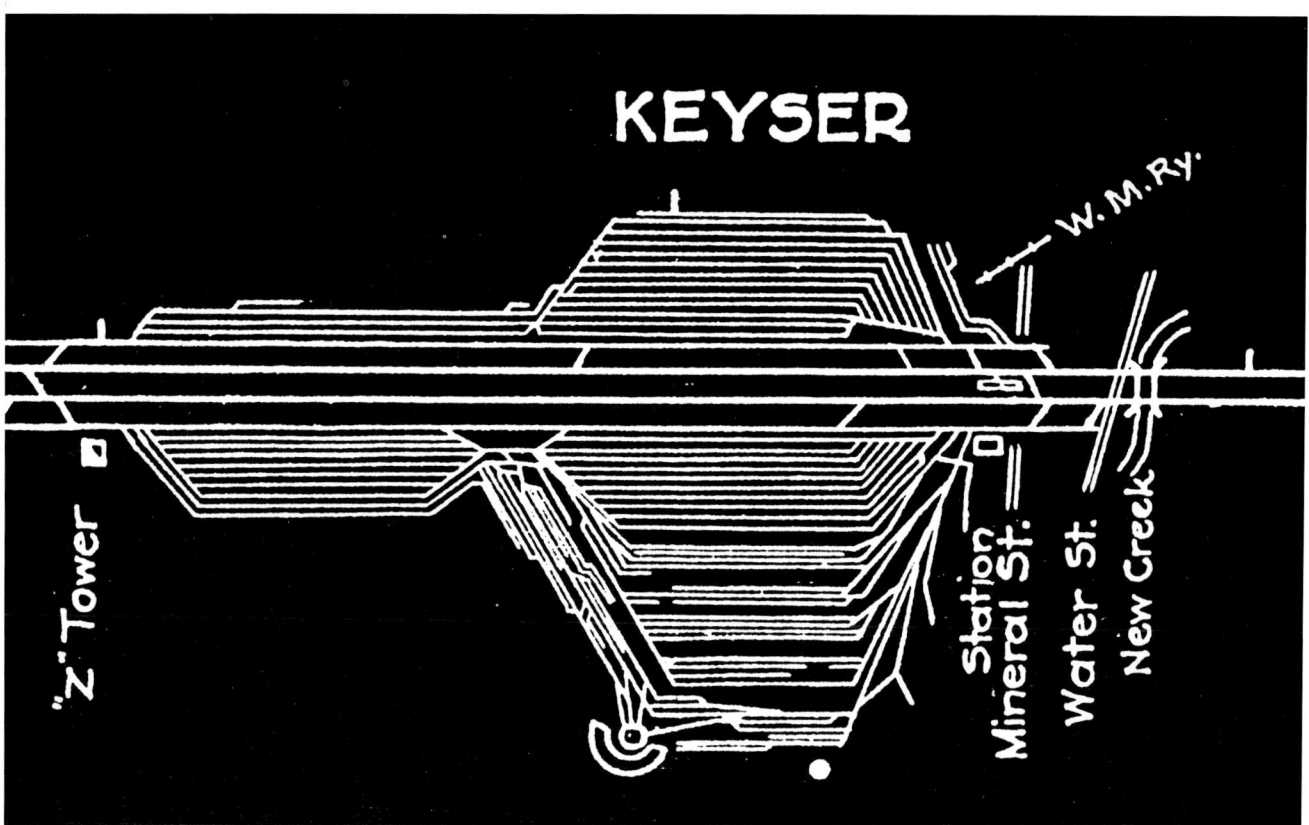

KEYSER YARD TRACK CHART in 1931 dramatically shows the extent of the facilities at this important location, a panoply that was extant until deep into this century. Eastbound drags off the grades would enter the eight receiving yard tracks just east of Z tower. (A large numeral designating which track a given train was to enter was displayed in a tower window for the information of the crew ... those placards were still there in 1984, awaiting calls that would never come again.) The drags would then be weighed, humped, classed and doubled up for eastbound movement, usually over the Patterson Creek cutoff. Note that the class tracks were not long enough to hold a doubled train ... sawing was necessary. Westbound the drill was the same, except that longer trains were the rule because the traffic was overwhelmingly coal cars (empties). QD trains passed through Keyser for Cumberland or Brunswick for classification, so KY was always a vast sea of coal. The whole yard is slightly less than two miles long, which points up the problem implicit in improvement of power and train length. The yard was constantly being enlarged from opening c. 1872 until finally the limit was reached ... there was no room short of removing a mountain or paving over the river. And, of course, each day had its charming highlights to brighten the mood of dispatchers, yardmasters and other assorted officials. In 1951 the EM1 on an eastbound drag ran out of coal and steam with the headend just on a receiving track, thus blocking up everything west as tight as the proverbial drum. This occurred in the same month, but not on the same day, of the sag affair at McKenzie and definitely establishes that Murphy was active that long ago. The engineer had cut it a little thin and it is easy to guess that the road foreman of engines cut it thinner still.

WEST END

WEST KEYSER (Z), in service in 1906 and still active in May 1991. In 1956 the next tower west (Piedmont-P) was closed and Z has handled that interlocker remotely ever since. Helpers to assist westbound coal car and QD trains were usually tied on the rear at P, although in recent years they are sometimes put on at Z depending upon train length. The yellow SD on the right is the Piedmont Helper, awaiting a call and a crew. The CSX SD beyond the signal bridge works local coal traffic on the Georges Creek line, hauling it west up the Potomac on the ex-WM line to a power plant at Mt. Storm and Westvaco at Luke. Most eastbound coal on that line also ends up at Mt. Storm, so very little traffic moves east from here. There is little here to remind one that this was once one of the hottest points on the West End, with traffic teeming in both directions.

C. S. Roberts

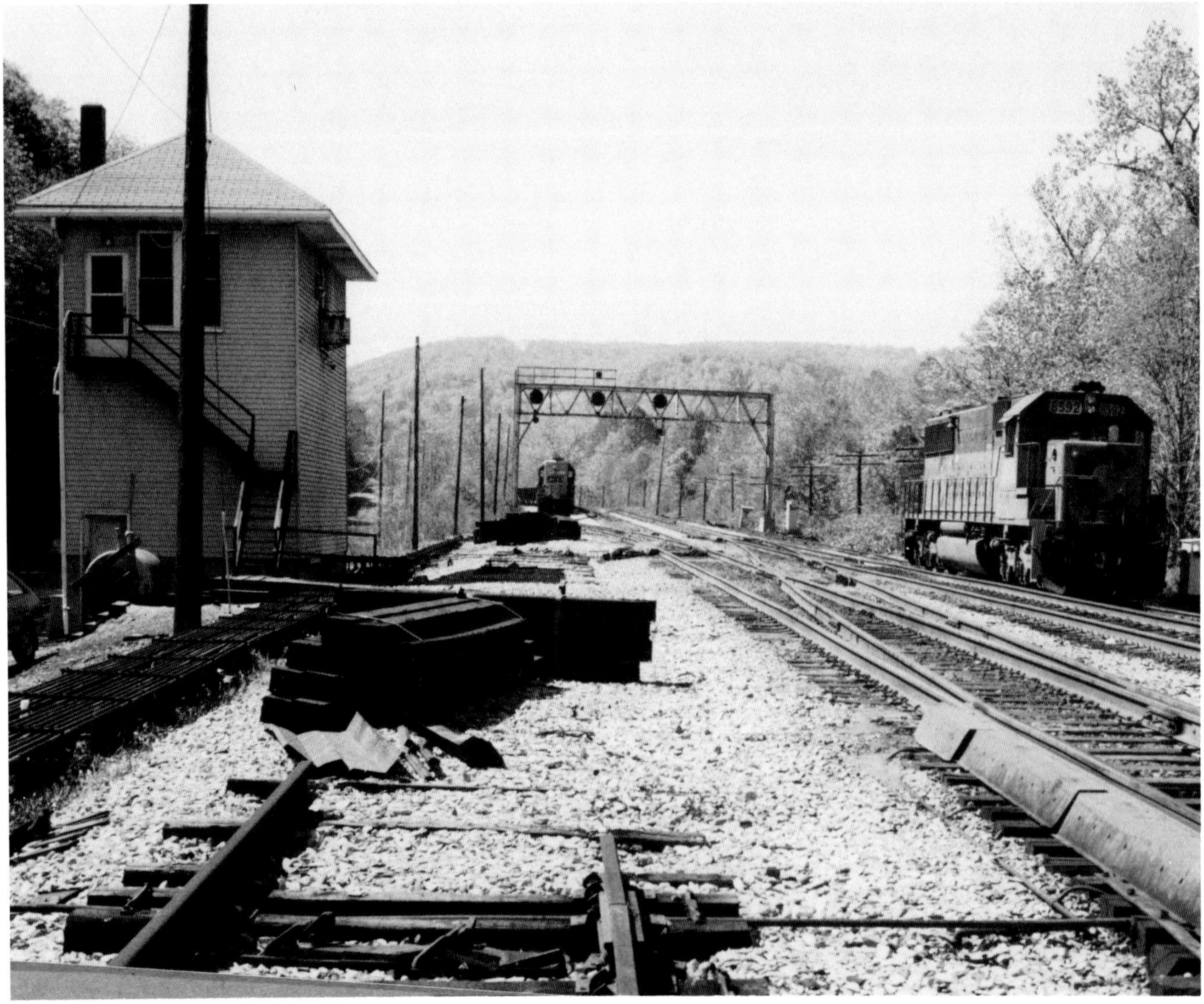

B&O Magazine

Left ... Piedmont at its height in the last century, looking east with the shop complex at lower left and combination station with freight house upper right. The C&P station is across the tracks to the left of the B&O Station and the B&O main line sweeps around to the lower right.

B&O Museum

Above ... Piedmont in 1872 with the B&O station and freight house under construction just left of center and the C&P station similarly under way to right of center. Note the long string of "pot" hoppers loaded with coal coming off the C&P and Georges Creek Valley just to the right of the C&P station. To far upper left you can see the edge of the easternmost B&O polygon engine house. *Right* ... the same general scene c. 1857 from the book "The Great Railway Celebrations of 1857."

C. S. Roberts Collection

WEST END

B&OHS

PIEDMONT (P) TOWER, located just east of the B&O Station on the south side of the main line and a busy place as helpers for trains bound up Seventeen Mile Grade were tied on here ... in fact, many still couple up at this spot. In 1956 this tower was closed and the action handled remotely from West Keyser (Z), next tower to the east. The tower is still painted red in this photo and a Color Position Light signal is off the photo to the right, so the era is probably c. 1940.

Gary Schlerf Collection

THE PIEDMONT SHOPS looking west c. 1872. Note the balloon-stack power at the extreme right. This photograph clearly shows that the engine houses were "many-sided" rather than round as depicted in contemporary drawings. The design for these engine houses was suggested by Mr. Latrobe and executed by assistant Albert Fink, who was also well known for iron bridge designs. Four such engine houses were planned for Piedmont, but only two were built ... Keyser would be the location for further expansion because there was more room.

PIEDMONT COALING DOCK just east of P tower in the 1920s, primarily used to coal helpers for Seventeen Mile Grade. The two wooden hoppers are interesting as they appear to be N16 composite cars built in 1918 to save steel, a retrogression that also occurred in World War II. In company coal service in this photo, they weighed 21 tons and carried 55 tons ... inside length was 31'. Similar, but somewhat shorter, designs were used in the last century before the steel hopper era dawned.

B&OHS

C. S. Roberts

C. S. Roberts

FOUR PIEDMONT SCENES ... the B&O Station and Freight House a little forlorn in June 1983 and reborn as a warehouse in May 1991. The postcard scene looks west circa turn-of-century with the B&O Station on the left and the C&P Station on the right. And another shot, in May 1991, shows the remnants of the C&P Station without its second story but not in apparent use. There is nothing left of the tracks to the right of the station and someone had the temerity to put a building right in the middle of the "tracks."

C. S. Roberts Collection

C. S. Roberts

Chapter 3

Seventeen Mile Grade

Piedmont To Altamont

One of the nine principles of war is "maneuver," by which it is meant that an attacking army should so approach the enemy that a flanking attack can be delivered. Frontal assault against an enemy's main defenses should be avoided if at all possible. One facetious ditty directed at donkey generals goes like this:

> Hey, diddle diddle
> The Cat and the Fiddle
> Let's go
> Right up the Middle

And take ninety percent casualties. Unfortunately, if the enemy has done his job correctly, the attacker is forced to assault frontally. Sadly, Backbone Mountain had so arranged itself that Mr. Latrobe had no choice but to go "right up the middle."

Less than a mile west of Piedmont, at what became West Virginia Central Junction, the assault had to begin even before crossing the Potomac . . . the grade stiffened to 1.57% to the river. (The WVC, incidentally, became the Western Maryland Railway and was ultimately absorbed into CSX . . . across the river from the junction at Luke is located the Westvaco paper mill, an important shipper and receiver from the late 1800s to this day.)

Once across the Potomac and back into Maryland, the line immediately hit a 2.20% grade for about a half-mile until Empire where it soared to 2.29% for a mile-and-a-half to Everett Tunnel. The grade through the tunnel was "eased," if one can use that word to describe such an incline, to 2.07%. From there to Swanton, grades ranged from a low of 2.08% to a high of 2.23%.

The grades were bad enough . . . the curvature almost beyond belief. In the eleven miles from the viaduct to Swanton, only about 1.6 miles was tangent (straight) track and almost all of that was transitioning from one curve into another.

For a few hundred feet at Swanton the grade flattened to .45%, but then resumed in a range from 1.36% to 2.1% to Altamont. Nearing Wilson and Altamont there was actually some tangent, each a mere half-mile long.

And the visage was something less than comforting . . . here are extracts from an 1855 journal: "The gorges are very deep, really frightful to contemplate . . . monstrous artificial embankments . . . frightful black, yawning precipices." B&O passenger traffic men must have winced at such descriptions and we suspect they decided that it might be better to have passenger trains traverse the West End at night . . . certainly a lot of them ended up that way.

And there were bridges . . . once the road turned up Crabtree Creek it was necessary to cross that stream six times to reach Altamont.

With transportation available, coal mining and lumbering became economically feasible and various settlements were created along the line of road.

Just across the Potomac into Maryland, the town of Bloomington blossomed with several mines . . . so did Empire a half-mile west.

Empire (MX) became an important tower on the railroad from the early years until triple tracking in 1910 . . . in fact, a new tower was constructed in 1907. MX was closed when Big Curve (BC)

35

WEST END

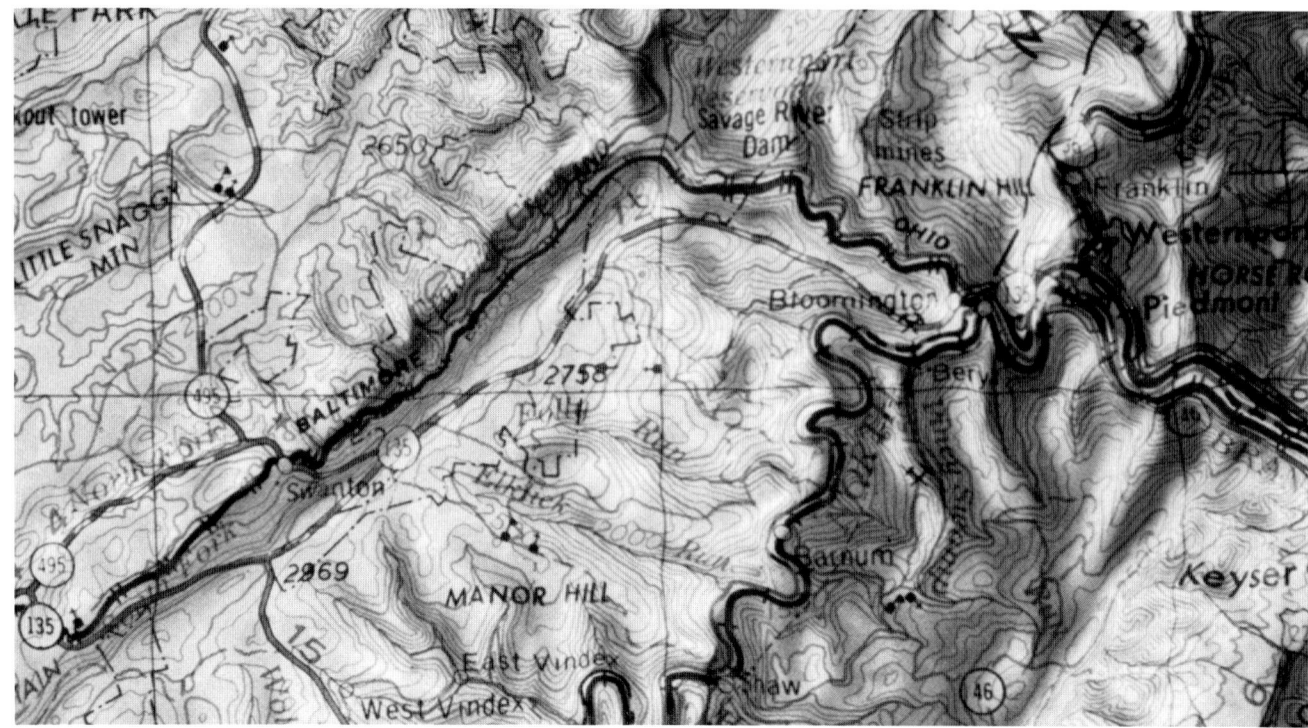

C. S. Roberts

THE HEART OF THE WEST END, and the actual boundary of the old Third Division, begins at Piedmont, right center. The line negotiates a loop in the Potomac River and crosses at Bloomington ... then it claws its way up the Savage River Canyon along the side of Backbone Mountain, turning up Crabtree Creek just west of the present-day Savage River Dam (finished in 1951) and clings to the back of Backbone Mountain to Altamont, at lower left, by Road 135. Note the church marker just to the right of 135 ... this is a tiny Episcopal Church "Our Father's House–The Log Church" and is opened for services only a few times a year. It has no windows, only shutters, and has to be one of the few if not the only house of worship right on the Eastern Continental Divide. A raindrop east of Altamont ends in the Atlantic Ocean ... to the west, in the Gulf of Mexico. Note the edge of the lake, left center. It is hard to believe, but true, that the Chesapeake and Ohio Canal intended to follow this same route to the west and to create a lake at the site of present day Deep Creek Lake to feed water to the locks. Assuming 24 foot locks, they would have needed about seventy of them to get to the top and a comparable number to get to the Ohio on the other side! A case could be made that the B&O saved the canal company from itself. If it had been built, it would have been a great tourist attraction and monument to engineering insanity. The lake itself was created for hydroelectric purposes in 1925 and has been a world-class resort area ever since.

What's in a name?

We have ventured forth up the Savage River canyon, both on the railroad and by road along the river. More than once we thought the river aptly named. Flanked on the northeast by Big Savage Mountain and Backbone Mountain on the southwest, the gorge is best described as malevolent. Curiously, the names of the river and of the mountain are not related, either to each other, or to the savagery of the terrain. In the winter of 1736, a foolhardy band of surveyors found themselves out of food in the area and decided to resort to cannibalism. The nominee for entré was one John Savage, selected because he was the "most worthless, with poor eyesight." A relief expedition arrived just in time, and the river was named for him in appreciation for a service he did not perform ... the first geographic feature in Western Maryland to receive a European name. One assumes that Mr. Latrobe's surveyors took along ample rations, and secreted their spectacles.

As to the mountain, a frontiersman named Colonel Cresap killed a very large Indian on its flanks and named the mountain accordingly. The Colonel apparently enjoyed firefights, for he tangled with some Indians on another mountain nearby and his black slave, loyal to the end, died defending his master. Hence, Negro Mountain, one of the few B&O did not annoy.

Mercifully, B&O did not have to touch Big Savage Mountain in this campaign, although it would cross it farther north on an easier grade when the Pittsburgh line was built.

Today, the Savage River is renowned for white river rafting, which hints of its ferocity.

SEVENTEEN MILE GRADE

C. S. Roberts Collection

BLOOMINGTON VIADUCT from the West Virginia shore of the Potomac looking westward late in the last century. The viaduct was designed to be built of brick, but the contractor failed and B&O took over the work. Brick quality was inferior, so B&O built the stately structure of white sandstone with three 56 foot spans with the roadway about 50 feet above the river. The original name was Savage Viaduct even though it did not cross that river ... all evidence indicates that the name was changed rather early. Completion was in 1851.

C. S. Roberts Collection

THE VIADUCT LOOKING DOWNSTREAM circa turn-of-century with a classic passenger train with double-headed Ten-Wheelers on the point and working hard ... they are now on Seventeen Mile Grade. The town of Bloomington shows at upper left.

37

WEST END

opened in 1911. A crossover remained until 1955 when it was removed.

The closing of MX and opening of BC was related to the deroofing of infamous Everett Tunnel (a story we will tell separately) and triple tracking from Bond east to BC in 1910. In the event, Big Curve was not open very long ... it was closed by 1916 and its interlocker handled remotely from Bond.

In the early years, Crabtree was the next point on the railroad where it turned up the creek. A road crossing still exists at Crabtree to serve a few homes.

About a mile-and-a-half west of Crabtree was the small town and tower at Frankville (FK), named for Francis Thomas. Mr. Thomas was an ex-governor of Maryland and presidential aspirant who became involved in a sticky divorce which ended his political career. He retired to his estate at Frankville and was killed by a helper engine in 1876. FK was closed in 1911 in conjunction with the opening of Strecker (HX) in 1912.

We will tell the stories of Bond, Strecker and Swanton in more detail in captions ... the next point of note on the railroad was Wilson (originally Wilson's Store) about a mile east of Altamont.

By 1853 there were ten sidings between Bloomington and Altamont, many for traffic purposes. Double tracking proceeded for a few miles every year and we believe it was completed by c. 1874, but this date is not confirmed.

There were a number of water stations on the grade in the early years but it has been difficult to find evidence as to exact locations. We believe there was one just west of Everett Tunnel and another near Crabtree.

We do know that there was a water station at Bond ... it was closed in the late 1930s.

The most famous water station on the grade was No. 37. Located a little over a mile east of Swanton, it was definitely in place by 1889 and we suspect it was built in 1855. By the triple track era, it consisted of two tubs, two penstocks and a setoff track.

B&OHS

B&O WIDENED the viaduct c. 1916 by adding to the upstream side with poured concrete ... the downstream side was unchanged. Note how extensive the addition ... provision was made for three tracks although there is no evidence three tracks were ever laid. Ample width was allowed for mallet locomotives coming into service and we assume B&O wanted to be generous in providing for possible future needs.

SEVENTEEN MILE GRADE

NEMESIS EVERETT TUNNEL early in the war circa 1855, taken from a contemporary woodcut and looking east. Mr. Latrobe was only a little over two miles into the grade when The Hill started a sixty-year long riposte, proving the military adage that the most perfect plan of attack lasts as long as it takes to come into contact with the enemy. Called a "short tunnel" by Mr. Latrobe in 1850, it was finished in July 1851 with a length of 300 feet, deep approach cuts, 22 foot width for double track and no lining. The Hill slashed back and timber lining was installed. By 1855 the timber was removed and a brick arch fitted. In 1873, with B&O desperate for two tracks, the brick arch was removed, the tunnel widened, cut stone put in and the tunnel lengthened to 500 feet because the cuts were an open sore. In 1893 it was widened and re-arched again with new side walls. And all this action was just the *first* battlefield on the West End. Incidentally, this illustration accurately depicts how B&O was clinging to the side of Backbone Mountain and how vulnerable the railroad was to decomposing rock.

Warren Somerville

SIXTY YEARS INTO THE BATTLE and with mallets coming into service, B&O finally had enough and tore the roof off the damn thing, finishing in April 1911. This photo shows the removal operation at the eastern portal looking west. And this time the resulting cut was widened for three tracks, although the third track ended at Big Curve *west* of the tunnel cut. We suspect that The Hill responded with incoming and B&O decided to stick with two tracks to leave room for the dead rounds.

B&OHS

WEST END

C. S. Roberts

CURVES AND CUTS with the only tangent track in sight transitioning into another curve, these five photos say it all about Seventeen Mile Grade below Swanton. The rear-end photos were taken 20 October 1978 from the deck of the Piedmont helper ... the QD train is Gateway 97. Tommy took the photo of No. 75 *Cincinnatian* Engine 5302 22 January 1947 near Big Curve from, of course, the vestibule.

E. L. Thompson/B&OHS

SEVENTEEN MILE GRADE

Early locomotives had small tenders and did not use water efficiently, so a number of water stations were needed to surmount the grade. Steam locomotive superheaters reduced water consumption and c. 1920 B&O began to use larger tenders to cut down on water stops. Ultimately there was only one water station on the grade and it was No. 37. Almost all freights and many passenger trains took water at 37 ... Tommy was on board No. 75 *Cincinnatian* when even that lordly train had to stop. Even helpers took water at 37 when returning because the tub at Piedmont was privately supplied and expensive. When the EM1 7600s came on the railroad in 1944-45 with their 22,000 gallon tanks, 37 could be passed by them if everything went just right. Unfortunately, we have not found any photos of this strategic facility. When diesels finally took over all movements in the mid-1950s, you can be sure B&O closed 37 and all the others with joy ... supplying water was an expensive and frustrating activity.

In fact, everything about Seventeen Mile Grade was frustrating. It was steep, unstable, serpentine and, above all, *long*. When Congress was granting charters to the transcontinental railroads, the members looked at Seventeen Mile and wrote into the law that no railroad could build a main line with more than a 2.2% grade.

Thus the first seventeen of Mr. Latrobe's "central sixty miles." Only 43 miles to go.

E. L. Thompson/B&OHS

BOND (BD) on a rainy day in March of 1945 from the safety spur looking west presents a rather grim scene befitting its primary function of bagging runaway trains. Initially Bond was merely a junction with the railroad of the DuBois and Bond Brothers Lumber Company which was built in the early 1900s to harvest timber from the Savage River area and the switch was installed c. 1903. The company was active, under various ownerships, until c. 1916 when the area was "logged out." B&O triple-tracked the line for 1.5 miles east from Bond to Big Curve, completing the expansion in October 1910. The tower and safety spur were opened in May 1912 along with a similar station at Strecker to the west. The spur was on a 12% grade and extended up the side of the mountain for about 62 car lengths. The switch was always set for the spur ... a downhill train had to consume a fixed amount of time after triggering a circuit at the distant signal before the operator could align the switch for the main. As we shall see, the spur was visited on occasion. Another major function for the tower was inspection. *All* eastbound drags and QD trains had to stop at Bond for inspection by carmen and to cool wheels and brakeshoes before resuming the descent. Usually this inspection was on No. 2 track nearest the mountain and took about fifteen minutes. This procedure continued until deep into the 1950s when all freight trains had diesels with dynamic brakes and flat maintaining brake systems. Bond was closed and third track removed February 1980 and burned down by vandals shortly thereafter ... the safety spur was removed c. 1958. Shifts of carmen were brought to and from Keyser on regular passenger trains which made unscheduled stops at the tower. The story of Bond is proof of our contention that the downhill leg, particularly on Seventeen Mile Grade, was a constant source of trouble and expense for B&O.

A Personnel Problem ...

Apparently the Bond Brothers, who operated the lumber company, were rather liberal employers and worked closely with their people during their tenure. It is also recorded that they went to the trouble of leaving stands of new growth for the benefit of future generations ... certainly the area is now a lush parkland. Solving domestic disputes was one of management's duties in the isolated mill town and one of the Bonds was faced with the following problem one day. A man and his wife were at odds ... his wife complained that they lived in one room with eleven children and her husband insisted on keeping their piglets in that room. The husband replied that the piglets were worth more than the children and he fully intended to keep them indoors. History does not record how Solomon Bond resolved that little gem.

WEST END

Howard N. Barr, Sr.

ACTION AT BOND on 9 June 1949 ... No. 75 Engine 5301 pounds upgrade and passes eastbound drag with EL2a 7209 on the point entering No. 2 track for inspection.

Howard N. Barr, Sr.

SEVENTEEN MILE GRADE

B&OHS

Safety Above Everything

CUMBERLAND DIVISION

YES, VIRGINIA, THERE IS A SANTA CLAUS and, yes, Virginia, trains did go up the safety spurs. Even if Virginia remained skeptical, you can be sure that the Bond operator thought old St. Nick was real as this runaway of 67 cars spared the tower on Christmas Day in 1913. Note that the relief crane requires two locomotives to negotiate the 12% grade and get at the mess. Nor was this the only incident ... B&O was and remains reticent about acknowledging unpleasantness, but Tommy whispered to us that the prestigious National Limited went up the spur one night and had to be brought down one car at a time. And others have been reported to us ... always mumbled and off the record. The joys of bringing a 5,000 ton train down a 2.2 plus percent grade for seventeen miles would appeal only to a masochist.

WEST END

Gary Schler

THIS MOST DRAMATIC AND ILLUSTRATIVE photograph was taken in September 1968 of a drag descending Seventeen Mile Grade near Bond. In spite of the dynamic brakes on the headend diesels, the train brakes are causing a smoke storm that makes one wonder if the wheels and shoes will melt. "Its supposed dangers have been found to be entirely groundless ... owing clearly to the greater caution observed upon them." Tell us about the rabbits again, Mr. Latrobe.

SEVENTEEN MILE GRADE

B&OHS

HITCHCOCK–THE CUT that became a tunnel. Mr. Latrobe originally planned to bore a tunnel at this location in 1850 but was taken in by all that nice rock and instead chopped through with a 108 foot deep cut. In short order he learned that this was a mistake and began to arch the cut ... in effect, building a shed over the tracks. The arching project was about a third finished by June 1861 when Civil War destruction forced a halt and work was not completed until 1865. In 1901 it was necessary to enlarge the tunnel, a project that must have caused some heartburn as The Hill was using the shed as a dumping ground for tons of rotten rock in a determined effort to take back its ridge. The overburden is getting deeper and deeper. It is easy to speculate that, sooner or later, The Hill will prevail. In this c. 1875 photograph, the process was already well advanced.

WEST END

LOOKING EASTWARD from the top of Hitchcock Tunnel c. 1875, the viewer beholds a scene that says it all for Seventeen Mile Grade from Bloomington to Swanton... curves, crumbling cuts and steep, crumbling embankments. Look just to the east of the second pole from the shack and notice the vertical dropoff. B&O kept extending the eastern portal until just short of this precipice and could go no farther. On our first trip on the Piedmont helper we were on that side of the locomotive and glanced down into a bottomless pit... with the overhang of the locomotive well past the cribbing that supports the track, the view was alarming. On succeeding shoves we refused to look.

SEVENTEEN MILE GRADE

Howard N. Barr, Sr.

THE SAME VIEW as the preceding photo about seventy-five years later on 23 July 1950 and not very much has changed. F7 DH1 181 with the inevitable coal cars threads its way west with its train wrapped around curve after curve. Note the detritus along the eastbound track, particularly by the fifth car from the engine ... the line had obviously been blocked shortly before. Mr. Barr climbed down from his perch on the portal and entered the tunnel to walk west. He was in the tunnel only a short distance when The Hill spit another load of rock down on the railroad.

WEST END

C. S. Roberts

THE PIEDMONT HELPER dropping east on 20 October 1978 on No. 1 track, with train orders, about to enter the west portal of Hitchcock Tunnel. Poor Mr. Latrobe ... he built a tunnel at Everett when he should have built a cut and the opposite at Hitchcock.

STRECKER (HX) on 23 April 1945 looking west from the safety spur appears to be a duplicate of Bond and, in fact, the two interlockers were near-twins even so far as birthdates ... both opened in May 1912. The spur at HX was also on a 12% grade and would hold slightly more cars. A third track had opened from HX to Swanton (SN) in January 1911. HX worked in coordination with Bond to facilitate traffic flow on the two tracks between them ... even B&O couldn't figure out a way to triple track that tortuous stretch. We know the spur was removed in October 1958 and believe the tower was closed c. 1961 and burned down by B&O. Curiously, a temporary train order station was opened at HX during the coal boom c. 1980 ... it went with the boom. Bond was always Bond, but Strecker's name changed over the years ... it evolved from Stricker's to Stricker to Strecker's to Strecker. To the locals, it was and always will be Stricker's.

E. L. Thompson/B&OHS

SEVENTEEN MILE GRADE

Howard N. Barr, Sr.

LOOKING EAST from the spur, Mr. Barr caught EL2a 7213 grinding downhill with a drag and EM1 7620 pounding west with coal cars in a classic West End scene. It was not easy to get to HX ... one had to follow a 150' trail down to Crabtree Creek, cross on a rickety company-maintained bridge, climb a stairway to the tracks and walk a half-mile to the tower.

SWANTON (SN) c. 1908 looking westward ... right in front of the tower you can see the beginning of the third track to Altamont, opened in 1902, and the extant combination station built in 1905. Prior to the opening of the third track to Strecker in January 1911, SN was a very active tower on Seventeen Mile Grade but lost its role to HX and was closed by late 1911.

C. S. Roberts Collection

49

WEST END

C. S. Roberts Collection

SWANTON looking eastward c. 1908 ... obviously the third track improvement in 1911 took the tower. In c. 1973 the third track was removed to Strecker. In the 1870s a private narrow gauge lumbering line reached Swanton, although we have found no evidence of just where the lumber was loaded into B&O cars.

C. S. Roberts

LONELY SURVIVOR ... the Swanton station from the front in October 1977 and the rear on 3 May 1991. There is no other evidence that Swanton was once a hot spot on the West End.

C. S. Roberts

SEVENTEEN MILE GRADE

SWANNTON

All local residents and historians are convinced that Swanton was named for Thomas Swann when the railroad was first built through the area and, if they are correct, this is the way the station sign should have read. The sign pictured was made for us as a Christmas present when we owned a lake cottage served by the Swanton post office ... a daughter lives just west of Swanton, providing a tiny bit of legitimacy to the local lore. With all deference, we believe the location was named for a John Swan, Sr., and/or one of his two sons, John, Jr. or Robert. The Swan family was active in extensive land speculation in the early 1800s in what became Garrett County and we have noted that a John Swan owned land next to the station in the 1870s. The road crossing at Swanton was originally the old Cumberland and Clarksburg road, reputedly the first wagon road built in this country. Early historians traveling the West End in 1853-55 noted that Swanton was an abandoned clearing with remains of an old mill, lending some credence to our version. We hope the locals are correct, if for no other reason because nothing on the West End was named for either of the two heroes of the saga, Messrs. Swann and Latrobe. But please spell his name right.

C. S. Roberts

Warren Somerville

ALTAMONT–"HIGH MOUNTAIN"–at 2,628 feet, the summit of the Alleghenies on the B&O and the highest point on the railroad, the top of Seventeen Mile Grade and the Eastern Continental Divide. This drawing, taken from a contemporary woodcut made in the early 1850s, graphically shows the line beginning its plunge to the Potomac and the 30-foot deep cut at the very top. The second track is a siding. There was a small settlement here when B&O arrived named Summitville and the Post Office, with its usual celerity, took until 1869 to rename the town Altamont. It was always Altamont (AM) on the B&O and that was that.

ALTAMONT in the mid-1870s showing the line west of the summit cut, with the original wye at the left. The County Road across the top of the map was ultimately extended to the right and crossed the cut on a road bridge apparent in later photos and still extant.

B&OHS

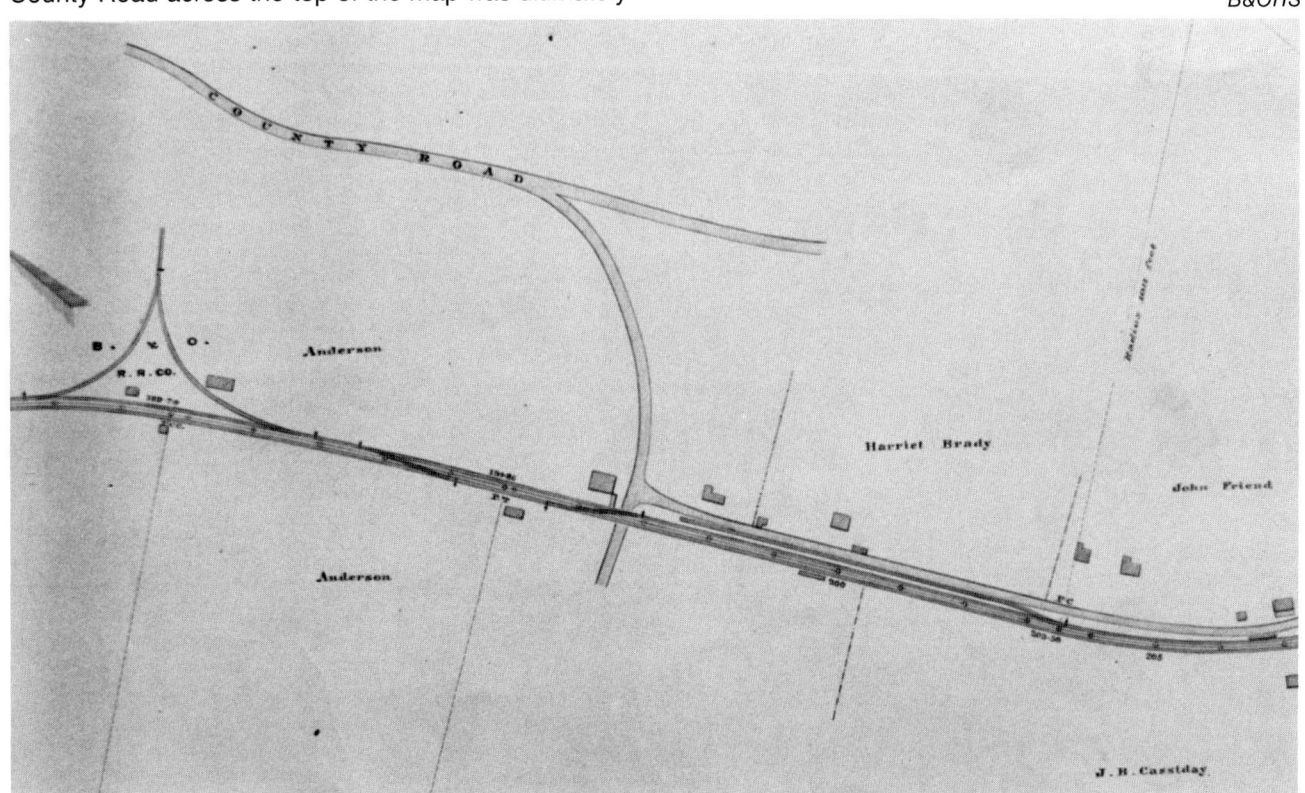

WEST END

THE BALTIMORE BEEF, one of several eastbound livestock trains run through the West End every day from the opening of the line until the late 1950s, has just topped the grade and is beginning the descent c. 1952. The wye to the left of the train is the "new" one built, we believe, in the early 1900s. The track on the right runs about a mile downgrade to Wilson ... the other three tracks are mainline in this photo. Westbound helpers on the rear of freight trains cut-off on the fly just to the left of the caboose and then followed the train to the tower for return orders.

C. S. Roberts Collection / Pontin

LOOKING EAST in May 1991, the scene is substantially the same. The wye was closed c. 1973 by removal of the eastern leg ... the remaining leg in this photo is a storage track. A fourth track was also removed in this era, but the right track still rejoins at Wilson.

C. S. Roberts

SEVENTEEN MILE GRADE

E. L. Thompson/B&OHS

NINETY-FIVE COAL CARS west, with EL5a 7168 on the point and S1 6123 shoving, pass the wye on 28 September 1948.

ALTAMONT was the top of *two* grades ... the lesser known Deer Park Grade also ended at AM and in the steam era drags required help from Mountain Lake Park. On 28 September 1948 we see Extra East 7610 with 51 cars about to top the summit. If you look just over the roof of the house right-center you will see the smoke of Engine 4423 shoving. AM tower appears just over the cab of the EM1 and the Altamont waiting shelter is seen at far left. The helper will cut-off near the tower and the train will stop with its caboose just east of the tower for retainers to be turned up. The most famous historical marker on the B&O can be seen at lower left.

E. L. Thompson/B&OHS

WEST END

E. L. Thompson/B&OHS

TRAIN 11 *Metropolitan Special* Engine 5087 is about to top the grade and come to a stop to allow the 4426 to cut-off from the rear ... passenger train helpers did not cut on the fly. This action took place on 26 May 1946 and is significant for a reason that is not apparent. During the steel passenger car era, passenger helpers were attached on the rear at Keyser and shoved to AM. A few months later, B&O operating executive A. K. Galloway was in his office car on the rear of No. 1 *National Limited* and was irritated by the jostling of his car by the helper. He had the train stopped at AM, went into the tower and issued orders then and there that no more passenger trains would be helped from the rear. He rejected admonitions of coupler strain on the severe grade and from then on passenger trains were helped from the front ... "because I said so." Note the road bridge in the background and the smoke of the helper just east of the bridge.

HELPERS AT AM in the mid-1940s awaiting return orders ... Big Six 6107 has shoved up Seventeen Mile Grade and the Mikado up the Deer Park Grade. It is always windy and cold at AM, so the trip to the outhouse was always an experience for the operator.

Bob Lorenz Collection

SEVENTEEN MILE GRADE

C. S. Roberts

COAL CARS WEST at AM in October 1977 ... GP9 6495 leads a gaggle of odd units typical of operations in that era and a pair of helpers led by B&O's first SD40 7591 trail behind. Note that the tower has been repainted and the outhouse moved next to the tower. Not quite all the comforts of home, but a marginal improvement.

C. S. Roberts

C. S. Roberts

AM IN THE SPRING of 1991, still active and materially improved. The outhouse is now in the tower, but the steps have been moved to the other side so the operator has an even longer walk than he had in steam days.

WEST END

FIFTY-TWO more loads go over the top on 19 October 1947 with Deer Park helper 4406 on the verge of cutting off and letting the 7209 on the front handle the long slide down. The old wye was located just to the west of the embankment at far left center.

E. L. Thompson/B&OHS

TRAIN NO. 11 on 21 March 1948 just west of the interlocker with an I12 caboose on the rear. Sometimes as many as four cabooses were tacked-on westbound passenger and express trains, but this is the only photo we have ever seen that confirms the procedure on film.

Bob's Photo

SEVENTEEN MILE GRADE

WATER WAS AVAILABLE at AM from the opening of the road until c. 1927. The reservoir and two penstocks were opposite the new wye as you can see from this track chart. Considering all the moisture that falls on the West End, you would think that water would be readily available. The problem is that most of it runs off, which left B&O with the constant problem of finding and holding enough to feed thirsty steam locomotives. With the closure of the water station at AM, westward trains had to water at No. 37 east of Swanton or hold out until Mountain Lake Park. Of course, it was downhill to the latter and little steam would be used en route.

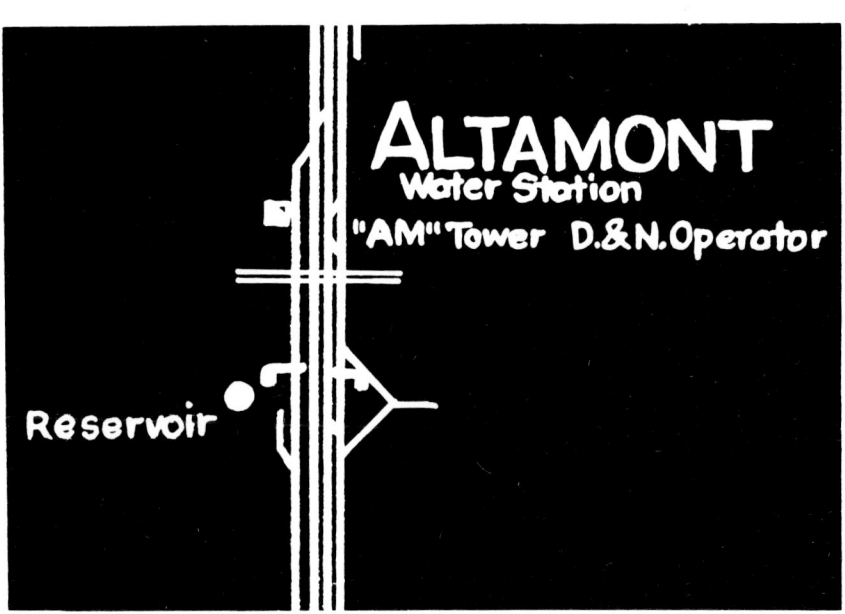

THE COVERED RESERVOIR at Altamont, built c. 1874, had a 50-foot diameter and was 14 feet deep. The valuation photographer who took this photo had an apparent shutter flaw in his camera.

B&O Museum

Chapter 4

The Glades

Altamont to Terra Alta

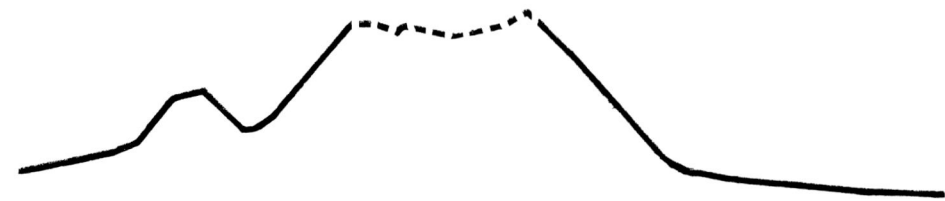

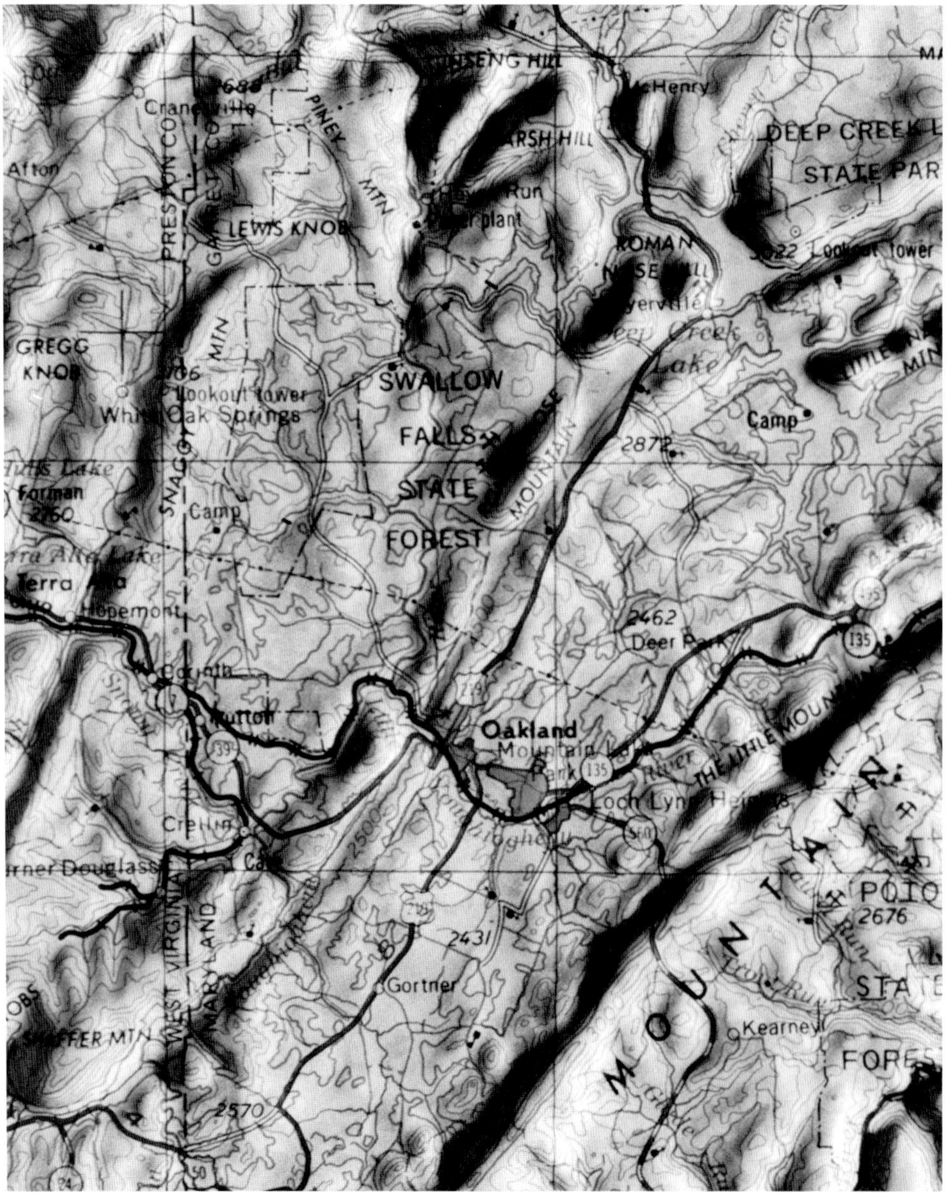

WEST FROM ALTAMONT, the next eighteen or so miles was positively arcadian for B&O. From Altamont (135 on the map), the line dropped down a slight (by West End standards) grade to Deer Park, then passed Mountain Lake Park/Loch Lynn to Oakland, crossed the Little Youghiogheny River (the "Yock") which had cut a convenient opening in the hills, rolled through Hutton, Corinth, Hopemont and Terra Alta (originally Cranberry Summit on the railroad) to the end of paradise. Even this Garden of Eden had a few snakes in it, however, as we shall see.

C. S. Roberts

THE GLADES

For those who survived the main assault up Seventeen Mile Grade, entry into the Glades must have appeared as a vision from Heaven. Certainly it seemed that way to early railroad travelers through this idyllic terrain.

"Beautiful, natural meadows ... charming valleys ... lovely vistas ... verdure bright and fresh ... streams of singular clearness and purity abound in trout ... hemlocks and laurel thickets," waxed William Prescott Smith in 1853.

And in 1856 ... "forest groves in all their native wildness ... pure air highly rarefied, cool and bracing throughout the sultry summer months ... streamlets flowing at every side leaping in innumerable sparkling cascades." Deer, bear, panthers, wildcats and wild turkey roamed the Glades and meadows were lush for grazing. Mr. Smith did strike one slightly sour note when he noted a snowstorm on the first of June, but it was a pretty scene so he let it pass.

It was all true. Construction of the B&O through the Glades was a piece of cake. Long stretches of tangent, a few gentle curves, no tunnels, no incoming and only one major water crossing over the Youghiogheny just west of Oakland, easily accomplished with a timber and iron single span of 180 feet in length that would later become known as Bridge 88. To be sure, there were two grades of consequence ... one at Hutton and the other approaching Altamont. They were irritating because they faced eastbound tonnage, but in comparison to the rest of the West End they were minor.

The loveliness of the Glades spawned a resort industry, with numerous hotels at Deer Park, Mountain Lake Park, Loch Lynn and Oakland. The virgin forests also attracted loggers and heavy lumber traffic blessed the B&O at Deer Park, Oakland, Skipnish, Hutton and Rinard.

The first logging operation touched B&O at Deer Park, which we will discuss. The last one, from 1915-25, was operated by one George D. Browning and met the B&O just west of Oakland ... its rails ran to the Deep Creek area and, in fact, it was taken over by the builders of the Deep Creek Dam in the 1920s to haul construction materials.

Another interesting logging narrow gauge line touched B&O at Skipnish, about a mile east of Hutton, and lasted until the late 1890s. This line reached property owned by the Garrett family and, while separate, was in reality operated by the B&O.

Hutton proved to be a major source of traffic for B&O from 1891 to as late as 1960 ... when the forests were cut over, the Preston Railroad found coal which kept the rails shiny for some years. Oak

Warren Somerville

THE GLADES turned out to be the land of the sparkling waters ... Deer Park spring water was used in B&O dining cars and is marketed to this day throughout the east. The privately-owned facility depicted above was in operation from 1908-1916 and shipped bottled water by the carload ... it was located about two miles west of Altamont on a curve still known on the railroad as "Bottling House Curve." The B&O bottling plant was at or near this location ... secondary passenger trains made unscheduled stops at the plant and loaded cartons of water in the baggage car for distribution to B&O commissaries.

WEST END

and hemlock bark produces tannin, so a major tannery operated at Hutton from 1893 to 1925. And we will show that still another logging line reached B&O at Rinard.

At Terra Alta the B&O reached the end of the Glades. The railroad named this spot Cranberry Summit Station on 2 February 1852 and, under pressure from local residents, accepted the new name Terra Alta in September of 1883.

But for seventy feet, Terra Alta would be the highest point on the B&O ... at 2,558 feet it is, locals insist, the highest point on the B&O within a municipality.

Another military axiom states, "If your attack is really going well, it's an ambush."

The ambush on the Glades was, of course, the Weather. B&O had to operate through this blissful land 24 hours a day, 365 days a year, year after year after year ... not for them going home at the end of the summer season.

One last weather reference ... there was a cold snap in the winter of 1936. Number 2 *National Limited* made a station stop at Terra Alta and promptly froze to the rails. Poor Mr. Latrobe and his descendants were not the first to learn that a night with Venus too often ends with a dose.

Thus the Glades. Only 24 miles to go.

C. S. Roberts Collection

DEER PARK, about three-and-a-half miles west of Altamont, ultimately became one of the most exclusive and luxurious resort locations in the United States. Shown here in its glory, the Deer Park Hotel was opened by the B&O on 4 July 1873 with 104 sleeping rooms and a price tag of over $100,000. The hotel was an instant success ... its elite and moneyed clientele arrived in such droves that a thousand applicants were turned away in 1881. In 1882 two connected annexes were added (shown on this drawing) to double the capacity ... ultimately the complex boasted a golf course, two glass-covered swimming pools and a large nearby lake. The latter, incidentally, was used to make ice in the winter which was shipped to metropolitan areas by the carload before the advent of mechanical refrigeration ... in fact, solid ice trains were run on the B&O from this area for many years. A cottage colony also blossomed. John Work Garrett, who was enamoured with the area and was the moving force behind its development, died 26 September 1884 ... appropriately, in his cottage ... we cannot help but note that it is given to few of us to expire in a county named for us. In a wry twist of fate, his son Robert and successor president of the B&O, died in a nearby cottage 29 July 1896.

THE GLADES

DEER PARK HOTEL showing B&O rails and station. The Hepburn Railway Act of 1906 prohibited railroads from subsidizing hotels, so ownership passed to various operators until the hotel was foreclosed and shut down in 1929 ... it was dismantled for materials in 1944. The Deer Park area was the fiefdom of Henry Gassaway Davis, a nineteenth century magnate who was into just about everything in the region including the West Virginia Central. Mr. Davis was a summer resident from 1867-1892 and owned much land in the area ... in fact, he sold the hotel parcel to B&O. He also made a fortune lumbering the area ... his tramroads laced the central part of the county and offloaded into B&O cars at Deer Park. He was not as gentle as the Bond brothers ... his woodcutters denuded the area to such an extent that, in the end, the State of Maryland had to replant vast acreage.

B&OHS

WE SEE AGAIN our valuation photographer with the faulty shutter in this shot of the station at Deer Park Hotel, painted red in this era. The hotel was not owned by B&O by this time, but the station was still spiffy and neat.

B&O Museum

ONE OF THE SNAKES in the lovely Glades was the Deer Park Grade ... while "only" .92% and about four miles long, it faced eastbound tonnage and was still another helper grade on the West End. In fact, Deer Park Hotel (DE) was a helper station and this photo shows the coal tipple, built in 1901 and a rather large installation. DE was open day/night until the early 1920s, when we assume Mountain Lake Park to the west took control. We have found a vague reference that the first true interlocking plant on the West End was installed at DE. We cannot help but wonder how the privileged guests at the hotel regarded all this around the clock activity at their doorstep.

B&OHS

WEST END

Howard N. Barr, Sr.

THE HOTEL WAS GONE by 25 July 1950, but not the activity. Here we see EL1a 7113 with a drag waiting in the passing siding for QD Timesaver East 196 to pass with F7 DH1 190 on the head-end. On the rear of the drag is Q4 4407 to give a shove to Altamont. Note that the switch is hand-operated and that the brakeman should be on the other side away from the throw. You can never find a trainmaster when you really need one.

SOLUTIONS CREATE new problems and B&O was bitten by a snake on the "minor" Deer Park Grade. More powerful locomotives and stronger cars meant longer trains, which was good. Unfortunately, it also meant that some helper stations had to be moved because the lead engine could not get its train far enough up some grades to clear the rear-end for the helpers. This was the case at Deer Park, so a new helper station had to be built c. 1916 about 2½ miles west near Mountain Lake Park. This station was complete with rest house, callers, coal, water, sand and usually four Mikado engines permanently assigned. About two-thirds of a mile east of the road crossing at Mountain Lake Park on the south side of the tracks, this facility was in service until the mid-1950s when diesels had completely replaced steam power. One of the many advantages of the diesel is its capability of overloading traction motors for limited periods of time and this finally killed the snake on the short Deer Park Grade. This out-of-focus valuation photo is the only one we could locate ... it shows the coal tipple, sand bin, sand elevator and engine house in the background. There were two 50,000 gallon water tubs and two penstocks serving both nos. 1 and 2 tracks. Form work on the locomotives was done in Cumberland. Longer trains also meant longer sidings, so a passing siding was

B&O Museum

built in 1903 and extended to Deer Park by 1911. The helpers backed west past the tower at Mountain Lake Park and coupled-up about a mile west of the helper station.

THE GLADES

C. S. Roberts Collection

THE DELIGHTFUL GLADES spawned still another resort and recreation center at Mountain Lake Park, this time on both sides of the B&O main line. Here we see the eclectic station (finished in 1885), waiting shed and original tower looking eastward early in this century. Mountain Lake Park is to the left of these scenes ... just to the right is Loch Lynn, also a resort center with a slightly different persona than its mate. We believe the tower was built c. 1903 when the eastward passing siding was built and we have some evidence that it was destroyed by fire c. 1927 ... in any event, a new tower was built west of the scene and is extant. Note in one view that the train is really a local working the commercial siding just east of the station.

C. S. Roberts Collection

WEST END

Mountain Lake Hotel, Mountain Lake Park, Md.

C. S. Roberts Collection

NORTH OF THE B&O Station, a "summer resort founded upon Christian principles" was created, a bit different than the worship of creature comforts practiced at Deer Park. Founded in 1881 and flourishing until decline started in the early 1900s, Mountain Lake Park became a thriving summer colony ... by the turn of the century it boasted nine hotels and numerous other facilities. The summer "Chautauqua" was a major attraction with a program of guest speakers, musicians and evangelists of national fame. At its height, thirteen B&O passenger trains stopped and disgorged thousands of visitors daily ... many reports spoke of "standing room only" in the cars, about the only way any railroad could make money out of carrying passengers. It was great while it lasted.

LOCH LYNN HEIGHTS, on the south side of the B&O main line at Mountain Lake Park, developed into a resort area with more worldly attractions ... casinos, billiards and liquid refreshment. Pictured here above the B&O Station, the Loch Lynn Hotel was opened in 1895 ... it burned down in 1918. Rednose or bluenose, as long as you paid your fare it was all the same to the B&O.

C. S. Roberts Collection

THE GLADES

REBORN C. 1990, the Mountain Lake Park Station is seen here in May 1991 completely restored except for an abbreviated tower and is host to several shops which face on the other side of the structure.

C. S. Roberts

MOUNTAIN LAKE PARK (MK) is seen here in April 1945 with the ubiquitous Q4 on the siding waiting for the next train. This view is looking westward. This tower is a twin of Halethorpe (HX) near Baltimore and both were built from the same blueprints ... the date for MK, however, is not so clear. One source suggests 1916, another 1929 ... we suspect the earlier date is correct. The tower lost her call letters to a new tower at M&K Junction in the mid-1950s, one of those changes made by the railroad for the sole purpose of confusing historians. The tower stayed open for some time after helper service ceased ... it was Day/Monday to Friday as late as 1960 and was closed in 1961. A grand, but temporary, reopening occurred during the Great Coal Boom ... it functioned as a temporary train order station with call letters PK. Tragedy struck east of the tower on 10 September 1959 ... No. 4 *Diplomat* struck a school bus stalled on a road crossing at about 45 mph, killing seven and injuring twelve children. While no fault of the railroad, the operator on duty witnessed the entire incident and told us of his nightmares for years after the sad event.

E. L. Thompson/B&OHS

WEST END

OAKLAND VILLAGE.

A LITTLE OVER TWO MILES west of Mountain Lake Park, B&O reached Oakland (OA) in 1851 and a village was created which would ultimately become the county seat of Garrett County. Much property in the area was owned by an early settler named Isaac McCarty. His cooperative attitude toward the railroad led B&O to suggest that the town be named McCartysville. Mr. McCarty declined and left the naming of the town to his daughter, Ingaba. This gracious lady chose "Oakland" as the name, a relief to those who feared she might choose "Ingabaville" or some such … call letters IG or IB or BA would not have been welcome. Naturally, a grog shop appeared for the railroad's Irish laborers, and one old-timer recalled a brawl in which 25 or so simply swarmed into the street and started a free-for-all "with no friends or foes" as could be distinguished. We must be fair, even if Mr. Latrobe probably would not, and point out that many of the Irish who survived the early years stayed and became solid citizens as well as hardworking employees of the railroad. This etching of Oakland was rendered in the early 1880s.

C. S. Roberts Collection

THE GLADES HOTEL in Oakland, reputedly the first mountaintop resort hotel in the world to be served by a railroad, was built in 1858 and is shown c. 1872, just two years before it burned down in 1874. Rebuilt in the same year, it continued to serve guests until being torn down in 1908. Located on the south side of B&O tracks opposite the present-day station, the hotel was host to many distinguished guests over its span.

B&O Museum

THE GLADES

C. S. Roberts Collection

B&O DID EVERYTHING in good taste throughout its history and the Oakland Hotel was no exception ... opened in 1876 behind the Glades Hotel, it was built with 110 "chambers" ... even more than the 104 at Deer Park Hotel. Overwhelmed by demand, two wings were added in 1882 and the hotel prospered ... for awhile at least. It was closed in 1907 and razed in 1911.

C. S. Roberts

THE FAMOUS OAKLAND STATION, a national historic landmark, is pictured here in the spring of 1991. Designed by E. Francis Baldwin, B&O's principal architect for most of the latter part of the last century, Oakland Station was opened in 1885 and remains a jewel along B&O rails. While taking this photograph, we were startled by the sounds of a flutist playing some delightful airs and wondered if we had entered the Promised Land. With some relief, we found the source to be a rather disheveled young man playing for no visible audience. Further inquiries developed that this modern-day Pan has been roaming about Oakland for some months, startling and pleasing the residents with his music albeit at some odd hours of day and night. We re-read Greek mythology and feel obligated to report that we saw no evidence of horns.

WEST END

![Railroad St. and Depot, Oakland, Md.]

C. S. Roberts Collection

OAKLAND STATION looking westward around the turn of the century, this postcard view postmarked 1909 shows an early style water jug next to the station and an active commercial section along the line of road. A more modern tank was built later and water was available at Oakland until c. 1927.

Warren Somerville

AN EARLY OAKLAND STATION that moved about a bit. Apparently B&O used the Glades Hotel as a station until c. 1871 when this small structure was built. With the opening of the new station in 1885, this building was moved to Altamont and later purchased by a nearby farmer for use as a utility building in which use it is shown. The building seems rather small for a station and we wonder if it might have been a telegraph office. B&O definitely reported a new station at Oakland in 1871 and a new telegraph office at Altamont in 1877, the measurements of the latter matching this building.

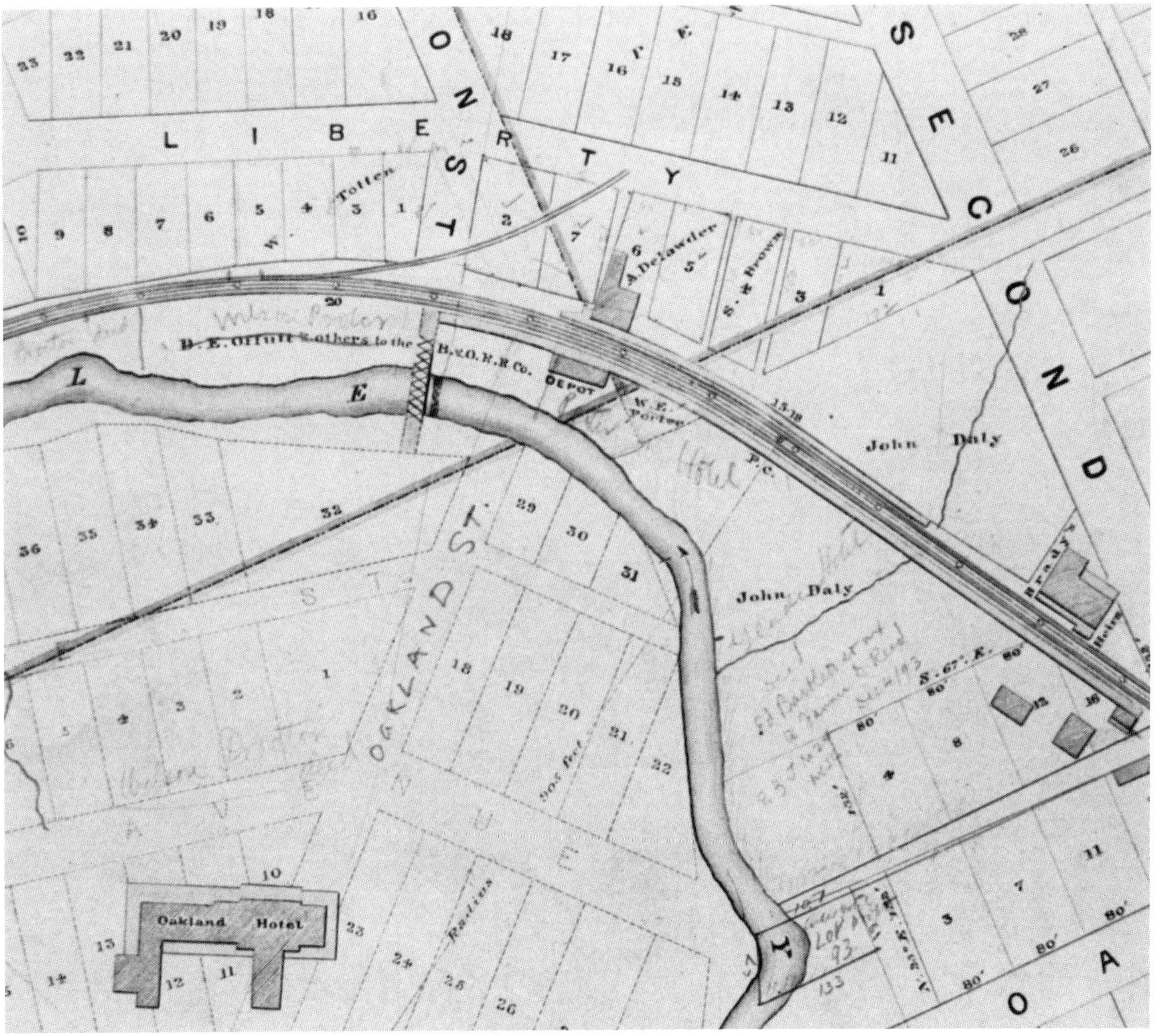

THE GLADES

OAKLAND C. 1874 according to the B&O, this company map shows the depot on the south side of the tracks with a platform leading to a substantial bridge and thence to the Oakland Hotel. The depot shown here appears to be too large for the previously shown station and too small for the Glades Hotel. Note how long the platform and the small building at the eastern end lower right ... perhaps this little fellow is the one.

B&OHS

Baltimore & Ohio

WEST END

B&O FOUND another snake in the Glades about five miles west of Oakland at the towns of Hutton and Corinth, twin towns straddling the Maryland-West Virginia boundary. As you can see on the drawing, the original line through 58 Section Cut had sharp curves and short but sharp grades just nasty enough to require helper service from Terra Alta. With longer trains coming into play after the turn of the century, B&O solved the problem by straightening the line and easing the grades. This improvement was completed in 1911 and eliminated the need for helpers, thus stomping the head of the snake. The name endured, however ... to this day the new cut is still called "58 Cut." Hutton, incidentally, was an interchange point for many years with The Preston Railroad, first a logging and then a coal road that reached deep into the hills.

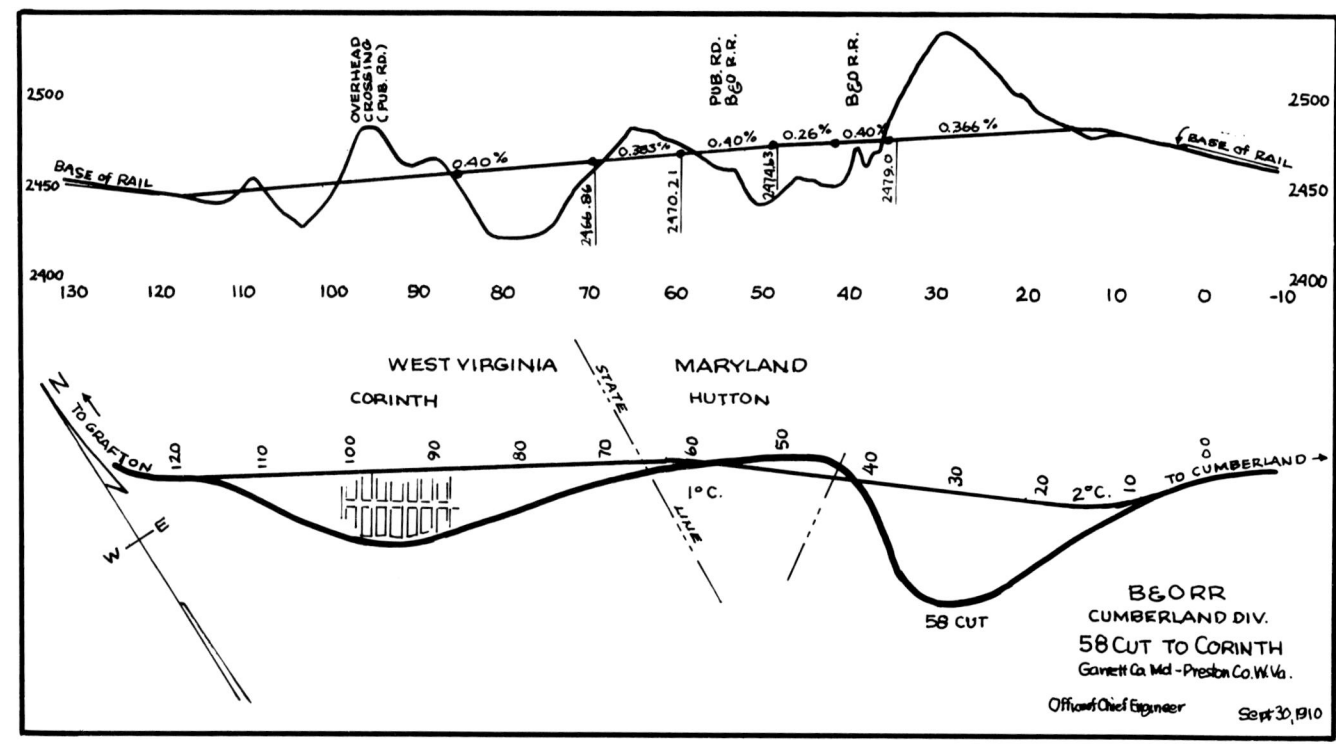

THE WELCOME SIGHT of tangent on the West End ... this photo of the new alignment was taken from the Corinth road bridge on 22 October 1978 with an eastbound drag and Gateway 97 racing west.

C. S. Roberts

THE GLADES

E. L. Thompson/B&OHS

RINARD (RX) just east of Terra Alta was a major interlocker on the West End until c. 1921. Rinard yard, which reached east from Terra Alta for about a mile, was a "fill-out" yard for eastbound drags coming off Cranberry Grade ... the pattern was to double-up at Rinard for passage east. Until the 1911 improvement at 58 Cut, helpers were also attached at RX. The tower was active at least as early as 1902 and probably was older. A logging railroad, the Snowy Creek and Cranesville, met the B&O just east of Rinard at what is now Hopemont and was active turn-of-century ... a Sylvester Rinard was a part owner, hence the name. Hopemont derives its name from the Hopemont Sanitarium, opened in 1913. This photo of Extra East 7604 with 50 cars was taken 16 August 1947 with the headend in the middle of the "yard," which was by this time merely a passing siding ... the westbound passing siding is the track on the far right and the two middle tracks are main line. Note the water jug over the middle of the train at the left ... this spot marks the wye at Terra Alta. Only the two main line tracks remain today.

LOOKING WEST from the station area 10 August 1947, CA tower is in view. Built c. 1923 with a flat roof, CA was one of the hottest interlockers on the entire B&O system from the early years until the mid-1980s. Eastbound trains flooded into CA, almost all with helpers to be returned ... westbound traffic was also heavy and complicated by station, brake test and retainer stops. In the triple track era on Cranberry Grade, the eastbound line went back to double track at RX and drags, QD and passenger trains had to be woven together. Operators earned their pay at CA.

WEST END

C. S. Roberts

SINCE THE MID-1980s, CA has been merely a location name for B&O ... the only thing left in this scene taken 4 May 1991 is the tower building with nothing left to control. While some helpers still occasionally cut-off at CA, they simply return on No. 2 track. Note the "new" roof on the tower. There is a National Weather Service station at Terra Alta and following are some snowfall reports: Winter 1976-77, 237 inches; 1985-86, 180 inches; 1987-88, 163 inches. We admit that we would like to interview the architect who designed CA tower and ask him what he had in mind when he specified a flat roof.

B&OHS

THE ORIGINAL wooden CA interlocking tower shows clearly in this view of Terra Alta looking west c. 1920 ... note the Q7f 4800 Mikado locomotive just west of the tower and the station just to the left of the tender. This tower dates to at least 1903, burned in 1923 and was replaced by the brick tower.

THE GLADES

LOOKING EAST from the wye area at Terra Alta, Tommy caught what is probably No. 11 *Metropolitan Special* leaning into the curve with two Q4s providing the power. This photo dates from the mid-1920s and shows two jugs at the wye as well as a semaphore home signal ... automatic color position light signals were not installed on the West End until 1929-30.

E. L. Thompson/B&OHS

THE "NEW" STATION at Terra Alta was opened c. 1883 and is seen in this view looking east in the mid 1940s ... the jug at the wye can be seen in the background. Water was either scarce or expensive at Terra Alta ... employee timetables in the late steam era carried the admonition "take water at Terra Alta only if absolutely necessary." The station still stands ... the jug and the wye are gone.

WEST END

James D. Bennett/H. H. Harwood Collection

TWO SMALL VICTORIES against The Hill in the late 1940s are apparent in this view looking westward just west of the Main Street road crossing in Terra Alta. No. 76 *Cincinnatian* Engine 5303 has made it up Cranberry Grade and the drag pulled by an EM1 7600 looks like it just might.

THE GLADES

THE 1868 DEPOT at Terra Alta shows in this valuation photo, or so the label claims. Even if the recordation is correct, by the time of this photo it was long out of service as a station yet must have still been a company structure. Whatever the story, it's gone now.

B&O Museum

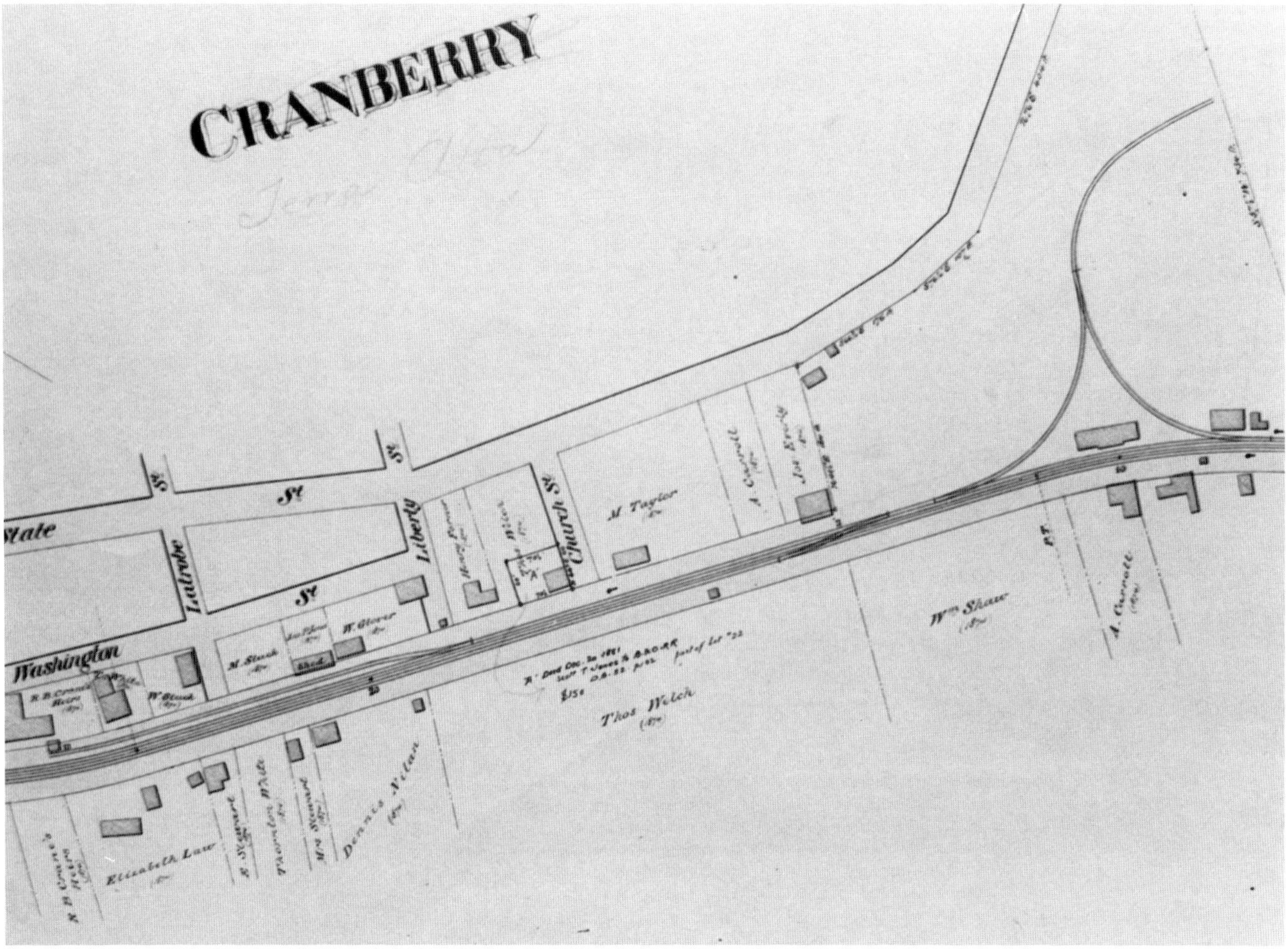

WEST END

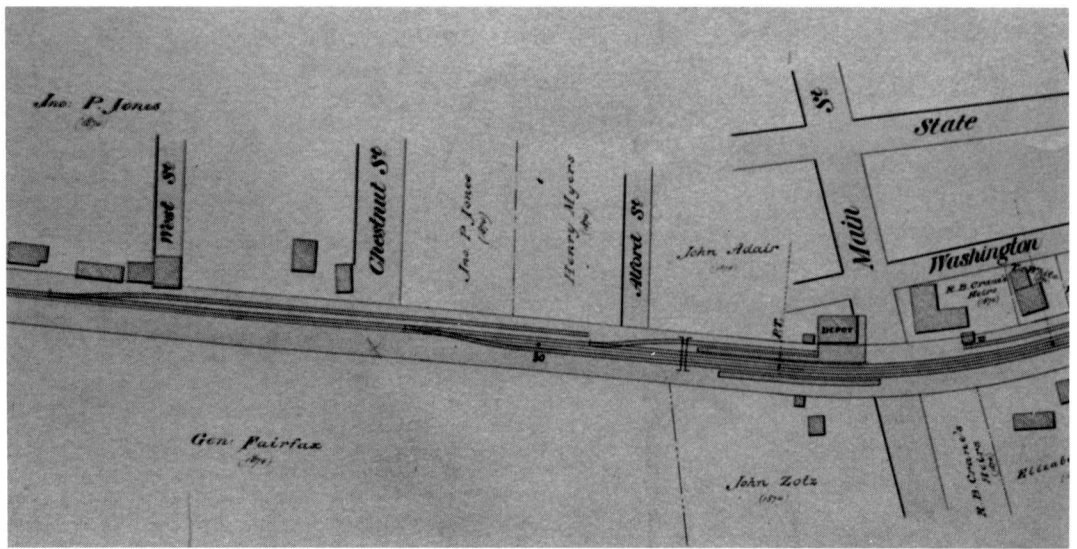

TERRA ALTA c. 1872 east of the Main Street grade crossing shows in the above photograph of a company map. The wye was installed when the railroad first reached what was then Cranberry Summit on the railroad ... note the pencilled name change at the top. The photograph below, from the same map, shows the 1868 B&O Depot at the Main Street crossing. This depot was later turned around and moved to the next lot westward, where it survived until the spring of 1991. Note that the main line coming off Cranberry Grade is still single track ... it was double tracked in 1875. Livestock pens were installed at the upper end of the wye in 1879 and remained until the mid-twentieth century.

B&OHS

B&OHS

Chapter 5

Cranberry Grade

Terra Alta to M&K Junction

THE NOSE-DIVE down Cranberry Grade began just west of Terra Alta ... a zig-zag path then ensued through a summit cut, across Salt Lick Creek, down the side of Briery Mountain past famous Salt Lick Curve to McGuire Tunnel and dizzying Graveyard Curve. The line then left Salt Lick Canyon and descended along Spruce Run to Rodemer Tunnel ... from there it spiraled down to Amblersburg and recrossed Salt Lick Creek on a viaduct. From there, the railroad followed Salt Lick Creek through McMillan to what would become M&K Junction and then met the Cheat River ... all in all, a tumble of about 1200 ear-popping feet in eleven miles.

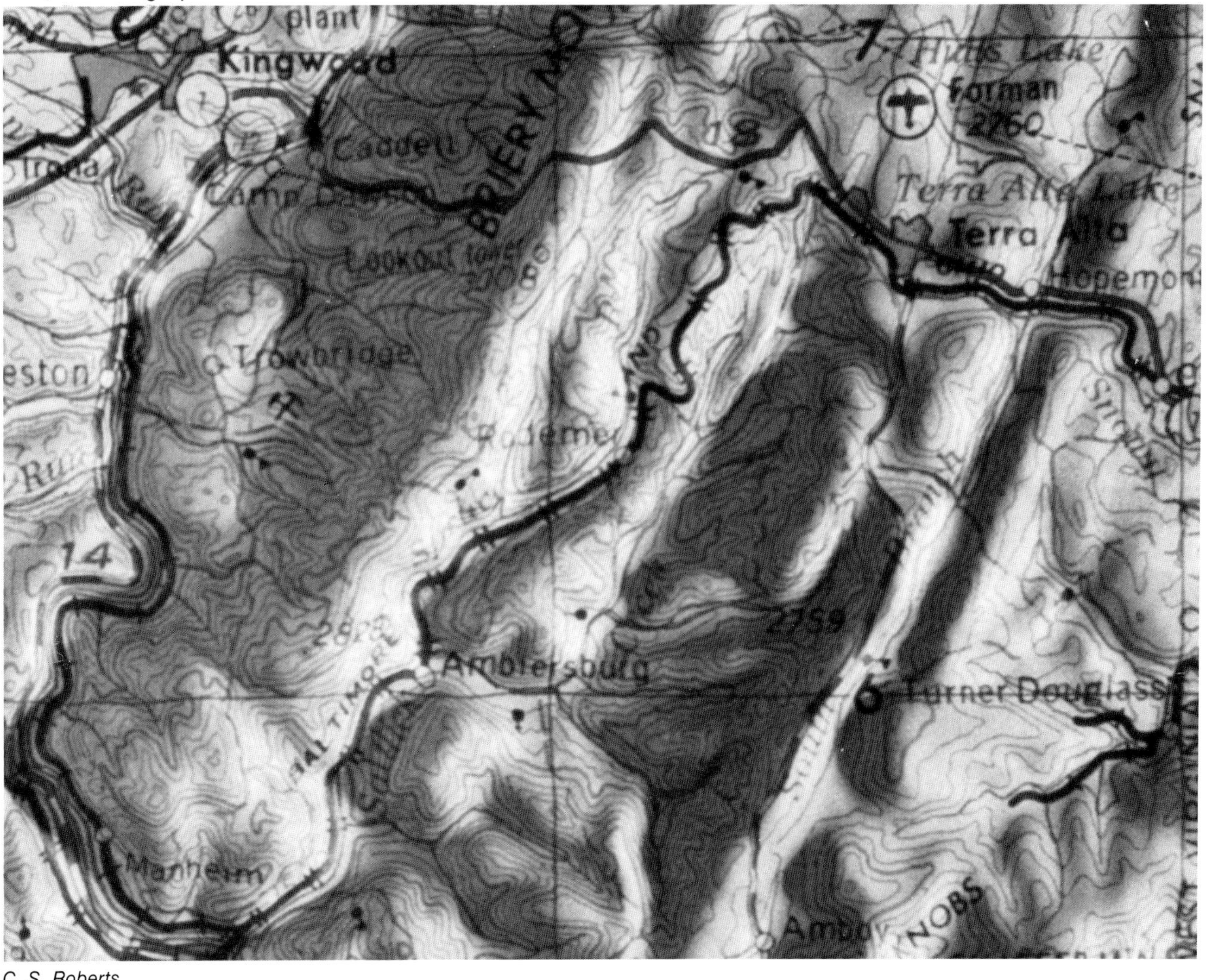

C. S. Roberts

WEST END

Whatever the attributes of paradise that may be ascribed to the glorious Glades, there is no question that paradise was lost on Cranberry Grade.

Comparisons with Seventeen Mile Grade are facile for one simple reason ... Cranberry faced the *tonnage*.

Mr. Latrobe could see certain similarities between the two ... rotten rock, two tunnels, extreme curvature, bad weather and so on. At eleven miles, Cranberry was even shorter. Unfortunately, it was also more steep.

The ruling grade on Seventeen Mile is 2.28% ... on Cranberry 2.40%. And Cranberry's Briery Mountain was not a docile cousin of Backbone Mountain ... it, too, had so arranged itself in such a defensive posture that Mr. Latrobe had no choice but to assault "right up the middle."

We have tried to second-guess Mr. Latrobe by looking for alternate paths to the summit so as to ease the climb by making it longer ... to no avail. There was only one way to get there and that was straight up.

Even "compensation" wasn't possible to any significant extent. To a railroader, compensation means the amelioration of curve resistance to trains by lessening the grade on curves and stiffen-

C. S. Roberts

E. L. Thompson/B&OHS

THE SUMMITS of all West End grades poised on precipitous declines, but none were so visually apparent as the drop-off just west of Terra Alta at the start of Cranberry. Ancient man thought the world was flat and if you traveled too far you would fall over the edge ... we can pardon B&O engineers if they briefly thought the myth might be true when they saw the railroad disappear in front of their eyes. At least eastbound engineers did not have to behold that grim sight ... we see Extra East 7622 on 28 July 1949 with 53 cars draped over the summit's vertical curve and the smoke from helpers 7159 and 7115 far down the grade. Just behind the 7622 the grade is 2.06% ... the middle of the train is on a 2.31% grade. Behind the helpers it was worse. The single-lane girder bridge across the tracks seen here was built in 1927, replacing an earlier through-truss named the Crane Bridge for a local citizen.

ing it on tangent. To do that you have to have some tangent ... on Cranberry tangent was measured in such short lengths that little solace could be found with this technique.

Another military aphorism states, "The important things are very simple and the simple things are very hard."

On Cranberry, getting tonnage up The Hill was very hard indeed ... hard in 1853 and hard in 1991. Hard and expensive.

We have been a student of the West End for almost a third of a century and will have to say that one of the most puzzling discoveries we have made is that William Prescott Smith, in both his 1853 and 1858 works, devoted exactly one paragraph in each to Cranberry Grade. "The descent of twelve miles to Cheat River presents a rapid succession of very heavy excavations and embankments, and two tunnels ... also a viaduct over Salt Lick Creek ... it passes through a dense forest of fir and oak trees in its approach to the river."

THE FIRST CUT west of Terra Alta looking eastward c. 1872 shortly before double-tracking efforts removed most of the glob of rock on the right ... later triple-tracking removed even more. Salt Lick Creek lies just behind the photographer ... initially Mr. Latrobe bridged the creek with a 50′ iron span which rested about 50 feet above the water. Just north of the track on the hillside is Salt Lick Falls, a very high waterfall of great charm that is impossible to photograph today because of overgrowth. The grade at the falls is 2.31% and, yes, is about to get steeper. A masonry support wall was built at this spot in preparation for double track in 1874 and we believe the bridge was removed and filled-in at that time. Certainly the location was a fill-cum-culvert when triple-tracked in 1910.

B&O Museum

FAMOUS SALT LICK CURVE c. 1872 looking westward with the hallmark cut just in view ... note the accumulation of rotten rock at the bottom of the cut about to interfere with the railroad. The remnant of the hillside on the left would be removed when double tracking was completed by 1875, thus opening up the scene which would become a mecca for photographers in a later time. The grade is now 2.65%!

WEST END

That was all he had to say about that backbreaking grade, the existence of which would prove to be the heaviest cross of crosses for B&O to bear in its long and glorious history. It was good that Mr. Smith was not a witness on, say, the Beaches of Normandy 6 June 1944. "The landing was across a wide beach with high and charming embankments overlooking the ocean with just a few entrances to the rolling tableland above ... there were many trees and picturesque hedgerows."

Whatever the reason for Mr. Smith's myopia about Cranberry Grade, generations of B&O operating men had to battle The Hill without rose-colored glasses. If they ever had time to admire the hemlock trees, it surely would have tempted them to think of hemlock tea.

As we have reported, traffic on the West End soared beyond expectations upon opening of the road and double tracking was the highest of priorities. It is hard to imagine today how they coped with a single track railroad on Cranberry ... somehow they muddled through until a second track was completed from Terra Alta to Rowlesburg in 1875. By 1902 a third track was completed from Rowlesburg to Rodemer and by 1911 it was extended to the summit at Terra Alta. Even with three tracks, operations were difficult as we shall show.

In 1973, diesel efficiency and effectiveness ... and the annulment of most passenger trains ... enabled the railroad to remove the third track. Two tracks remain today ... rumors abound that single tracking is being considered.

We have followed a traditional pattern of working from east to west in this narrative, including this chapter. In the case of Cranberry Grade, it would be more instructive to reverse the approach beginning on the east bank of the Cheat River for a few paragraphs. The reader should note that M&K Junction as a helper station was not completed until April 1913 and will be treated in the next chapter. The reader should also be informed that heavy-traffic grades exceeding 1.5% are regarded as being almost prohibitively severe.

SALT LICK CANYON in the mid-1880s presented a spectacular view to travelers ... the West End was and is scenic if nothing else. Notice the eastbound train moving into Salt Lick Curve from what would become known as Salt Lick Water Tub Curve ... a jug would be built just west of the last car in view. The grade just behind the train is a staggering 2.80% ... almost, but not quite, the worst on the West End.

ON CRANBERRY GRADE.

C. S. Roberts Collection

CRANBERRY GRADE

Howard N. Barr, Sr.

LOOKING WESTWARD from the top of the distant signal bridge for CA, the helpers of Extra East 7603 claw for the summit on 14 November 1948 and give meaning to the expression "on hands and knees." Salt Lick Falls is to the right of the last loop in the train just ahead of the helpers. A few minutes after this shot, a coal car train dropped down the grade.

WEST END

From the river to the road bridge just east of the engine house at M&K the grade was eased by filling to .07% ... from there to McMillan 1.08%. The following are all in percentages as we move upgrade from there: 1.06, 1.32, 1.83, 2.26, 2.27 (Amblersburg), 2.75, 2.45, 2.32, 2.23, 2.37, 2.34, 2.44, 2.47, 2.16, 1.94 (Rodemer), 2.40, 2.52, 2.80, 1.53, 2.84, 2.23, 2.45, 2.24, 1.96, 2.24, 2.66, 2.80 (Salt Lick Curve), 2.65, 2.31 and 2.06 to the summit just west of Terra Alta. Atlas is supposed to have held up the world, but we suspect even he would have declined a commission to carry it up such a grade.

Reverting to westward movement from Terra Alta, following are the names given to certain of the more vicious curves: Salt Lick, Salt Lick Water Tub, Bradshaw, Muddy Cut, Seymour, Shaffers, Graveyard, Burkes Cinder Fill, McVickers and Grahams. Unnamed curves totaled an additional thirteen.

Mercifully, little traffic originated on Cranberry Grade over the years so B&O avoided the agony of making pickups and setouts with consequent interference with mainline traffic. There were two tanners' sidings at Rodemer, a lumbering siding at Amblersburg and a commercial siding at McMillan ... all gone by the middle of this century. Cranberry Grade is located deep in moonshine territory, however, a subject of worry to crews, railfans and historians. Since revenuers wisely avoid forays into this wild country, it is just as well that the shiners do not require rail transport.

We recall reading an investment analysis comparing the nation's three trunkline railroads (PRR, NYC, B&O) some years ago that cautioned investors not to expect comparable results from B&O because of its heavy helper expenses. Cranberry Grade was the principal ... and, sadly, not the only ... cause of this warning. The grade, of course, took its name from Cranberry Summit which in turn was named for cranberry bogs in the area. B&O found the fruit to be very bitter.

Only 12 miles to go.

E. L. Thompson/B&OHS

SUBLIMITY ON SALT LICK CURVE on 28 May 1950 ... Tommy regarded this photo as his favorite. Extra East 7610 with 53 loads and DH1 190 on the rear is passed by QD No. 96 with 50 cars and DH1 192 shoving. Tommy was standing in the middle of No. 1 track spinning his head like a top to be sure a coal car train didn't catch him.

CRANBERRY GRADE

THE LAST HALF-CENTURY of B&O passenger service on the West End involved two premier feature trains ... the *National Limited* and the *Diplomat*, Nos. 1, 2, 3 and 4. All save No. 4, the eastbound *Diplomat*, went through at night and spared the passengers from some frightening vistas. Here we see No. 4 entering Salt Lick Curve in the rain on 17 August 1947 with the sun just coming up. B&O's first E7 (DP4) is against the twelve cars of the train and enjoys the assistance of Q4s 4416 and 4405 ahead. The lead Q4 will cut-off during the station stop at Terra Alta and either run ahead to Keyser or return to home base at M&K Junction. The *Cincinnatian*, of course, was a daylight feature train but its tenure was less than five years on the West End.

E. L. Thompson/B&OHS

WEST END

E. L. Thompson Collection/B&OHS

SALT LICK CURVE must have viewed this train with astonishment on 16 June 1956 ... Santa Fe ran its new Hi-Level train over the West End on a press run and so startled The Hill that the passage was uneventful.

C. S. Roberts

IT WAS JUST LATE DECEMBER in 1978 when this photo in the Salt Lick Curve area was taken to give insight to the frigidity and beauty of the West End.

CRANBERRY GRADE

E. L. Thompson/B&OHS

A TANK AND A TALE at Salt Lick Water Tub on 17 August 1947. This jug was installed in 1911 and lasted until 1954 ... it was an emergency water station located between No. 42 below Rodemer to the west and the Terra Alta wye tank at the summit of Cranberry to the east. The engineer on drag Extra East 7210 (EL2a) with 53 cars and two mallets on the rear apparently thought he had it "made in the shade" on a hot, dry August day and passed No. 42. Whatever his reasoning, he was wrong and The Hill smiled as he put his fireman on the tank with a penstock hook to catch a tankful at Salt Lick. He got the water all right, but his train was stopped on a 2.80% grade and there it intended to stay. Now, dear reader, we must give you an important sidenote in the history of the West End. The poor engineer's road foreman of engines at this time was one "Wild Bill" Henry who had a perfectly consistent personality ... he was *always* mad. And he was tough ... so tough that his grandson, not associated with the railroad, was also known as "Wild Bill," which says something about inherited genes. We will refrain from relating other stories about this fiery road foreman at this time ... it is sufficient to say that the engineer on the 7210 had a very large problem indeed.

DRIVEN BY DESPERATION, the engineer on the 7210 tried everything and Tommy was his witness ... even the helper engineers, in terror at the thought of being even indirectly associated with this unpleasantness, slammed and rammed the train. All to no avail ... the train had decided to rest and that was that. There was nothing for it but to go to the next drag and borrow EL3a 7143 from the headend. Here we see three mallets (the helpers were EL5 7163, compound as built, and EL3a 7127) shoving the train up to the summit. Even Tommy decided it would be the better part of wisdom to disappear at this point. There is no doubt that the engineer of the 7210 faced crucifixion when he got to Keyser ... if he got that far. It is entirely possible that Wild Bill chased the train so as to get his hands on the engineer's throat that much sooner.

E. L. Thompson/B&OHS

WEST END

THE CINCINNATIAN on the middle (#2) track is about to pass the rear helper of QD No. 96 on #4 track in a winter scene on Cranberry Grade 22 January 1947. Normally QD trains used the middle track ... in this case the dispatcher did not wish to take the slightest chance of stabbing No. 76 and his caution was justified ... they passed below Salt Lick Curve.

E. L. Thompson/B&OHS

ANOTHER CROSS for Mr. Latrobe to bear was the McGuire Tunnel, less than a mile west of Salt Lick Water Tub Curve. McGuire was originally built 22 feet wide for double track and immediately suffered from the West End tunnel disease. The usual drill ... collapse, timber lining, brick lining and reduction to single track. The 572 foot long tunnel is seen here looking westward c. 1872 ... in 1874 B&O widened it to 26 feet and re-arched it still another time with cut stone for double track. With the coming of mallet locomotives and the urgent need for a third track, B&O bit the bullet and tore the roof off, completing the project by July 1911 and removing 290,000 cubic yards of rotten rock in the process. An early water tub, located west of the tunnel, was closed at this time.

B&O Museum

CRANBERRY GRADE

Howard N. Barr, Sr.

EXPRESS TRAIN No. 30 is about to enter the McGuire Tunnel Cut on 10 June 1949 on a 9 degree curve and 2.24% grade ... the latter is about to stiffen to 2.66%. The 4459 and a P1d provide the power as the train passes the McGuire road crossing. This photo emphasizes another serious problem which plagued West End operations ... sand, brake lining residue and cinders. Rails are held in place and cushioned by ties which in turn are suspended by ballast ... the latter also provides drainage. A case could be made that B&O used almost as much sand as coal and water to combat ferocious West End grades. Locomotives poured sand on the rails to maintain adhesion and then blew it off with rail washers ... the sand clogged the roadbed, reducing drainage and hardening the cushion. Downgrade, the bad actor was brake lining residue. Cinders by the ton rained down on the whole mess with the net result that the West End was a maintenance-of-way nightmare ... and all this was in addition to the perpetual rock scaling in cuts and rail replacement on curves. In this scene it is easy to tell which is the upgrade tonnage track, the upgrade high speed track and the downgrade track ... whitest, white and brown. Even superelevation was a bugbear on West End curvature. It should be high for QD, passenger and downgrade movements but low for drags ... a contradiction that almost killed your writer as we shall see.

"THE BEST WAY"

"The Quickest Way"

WEST END

B&OHS

THE HISTORY of Rodemer Tunnel, about a mile east of Rodemer and just below Graveyard Curve, is a near-duplicate of McGuire's Tunnel ... built 22 feet wide, reduced to single track, widened to 26 feet and re-arched in 1874, top torn off by August 1911. Rodemer Tunnel was somewhat shorter ... 477 feet ... and "only" 250,000 cubic yards of rock was removed. This scene looks eastward while the deroofing was in progress ... note the steam shovel at upper left. If the reader will study the map at the beginning of this chapter, an almost 180 degree curve will be seen east of Rodemer ... this is Graveyard Curve. Lore has it that the site for the graveyard that gave the curve its name was given by B&O to the Catholic Church in Rowlesburg for burial of Irish-Catholic casualties incurred during the building of the road. We have not visited the graveyard (for fear of rattlesnakes, not ghosts) but have heard the story that someone periodically tends the graves. For a short stretch just east of Graveyard Curve the grade reaches record steepness for the West End ... 2.84%. And another dubious honor occurred on the railroad near here 8 December 1868. An eastbound passenger train was snowbound to the extent that local residents had to carry food and drink to the trapped passengers while B&O figured out a way to rescue the train, thus giving B&O another "first" long before the Donner Pass incident in this century.

B&O TOOK VENGEANCE on The Hill when they deroofed Rodemer Tunnel ... sixty years of frustration culminated in a crescendo of violence that solved the problem once and for all. Here we see Train No. 11 *Metropolitan Special* drifting through Rodemer Tunnel Cut in May 1951 with the 4481 on the point. The cut is wide, the slopes gentle ... B&O even left ample room for incoming. Briery Mountain took serious defeats at McGuire and Rodemer ... the tunnels were never heard from again.

Pontin/C. S. Roberts Collection

CRANBERRY GRADE

Pontin/C. S. Roberts Collection

RODEMER TOWER (RO) in September 1950 with Extra East 7124 pounding upgrade ... the only photo of the tower we have found. There was a siding at Rodemer as early as 1853 and two additional ones west before Rowlesburg, one of which was at Amblersburg. The earliest reference to Rodemer as an operating point appeared in an 1884 Employee Timetable ... certainly it was a major choke-point when triple tracking was completed from Rodemer to Rowlesburg in 1902 because drags had to be woven into the double track main from here to Terra Alta. This arrangement was not joyous because drags had to stop on grades ranging from 2.16 to 2.47% until B&O finally deroofed Rodemer and McGuire Tunnels and completed triple tracking all the way to the top in 1911. RO continued to be an important interlocker for another forty years ... its location in the approximate middle of Cranberry Grade gave dispatchers a great deal of flexibility. The tower was still Day/Night when this photo was taken ... diesels made RO unnecessary and it was closed by the mid-1950s. Even the third track became redundant ... #4 track (the southernmost) was removed in 1973.

89

WEST END

Howard N. Barr, Sr.

NUMBER 42 WATER STATION had a customer on 2 April 1950 ... the 7619 on the point of this QD train had just replenished. That DH1 helper 182 will not have to make a stop is a harbinger of the future. B&O's numbering of water stations is confusing ... sometimes reference is made to original sections as in No. 37, but that doesn't explain No. 42. We have noted that No. 42 was 342.3 miles west of Park Junction in Philadelphia ... perhaps that is the origin of the name. This train, of course, is eastbound ... the water tank is on the hillside to the right of the penstock and Spruce Run flows downhill on the left of the line of road. This location is about one-and-a-half miles west of Rodemer, giving ample room for drags to park in the steam era. There was a water station here as early as 1889 and probably much earlier. General Orders announced that No. 42 was out-of-service 1 July 1953 ... the site is still referred to by its original name.

THE DISTANCE from No. 42 to Amblersburg is about 2½ miles ... in this stretch are nine curves and grades ranging from 2.23 to 2.75%. This classic c. 1950 scene clearly shows the Amblersburg Viaduct in the middle of the photo crossing Salt Lick Creek, which is about to join Spruce Run to the left. Hundreds and perhaps thousands of photos have been taken from the hillock by the house at upper right, in both directions, to the extent that the scene has become a cliche. Just west of Amblersburg and the power seen here is the true beginning of Cranberry Grade ... all eastbound trains maximize speed when leaving M&K Junction and McMillan to the west to obtain as much momentum as possible. There was a siding here when the railroad was built ... the earliest evidence we have of Amblersburg as a place name on the road is 1884.

Howard N. Barr, Sr.

CRANBERRY GRADE

STILL ANOTHER DRAG on 20 March 1948 at Amblersburg, the only unusual aspect being that the train is on the middle (#2) track. The helper against the train is on the viaduct ... the waiting shelter for local residents would disappear by 1950.

Bob's Photo

UNUSUAL, to say the least, is this road bridge under the Amblersburg Viaduct ... notice that it is supported by cables as well as crossbeams. This photo was taken looking northward in October 1977 ... the bridge still exists.

C. S. Roberts

WEST END

C. S. Roberts

C. S. Roberts

THE PARAPET on the Amblersburg Viaduct was raised in 1986 ... these photos were taken 11 September 1987. Note the new wing wall on the north side and the substantial vertical support beams and horizontal tension bars. After a century and a third of doing without, B&O decided to put a railing on the north side ... on the south side you have to continue to take your chances.

Chapter 6

M&K Junction

B&OHS

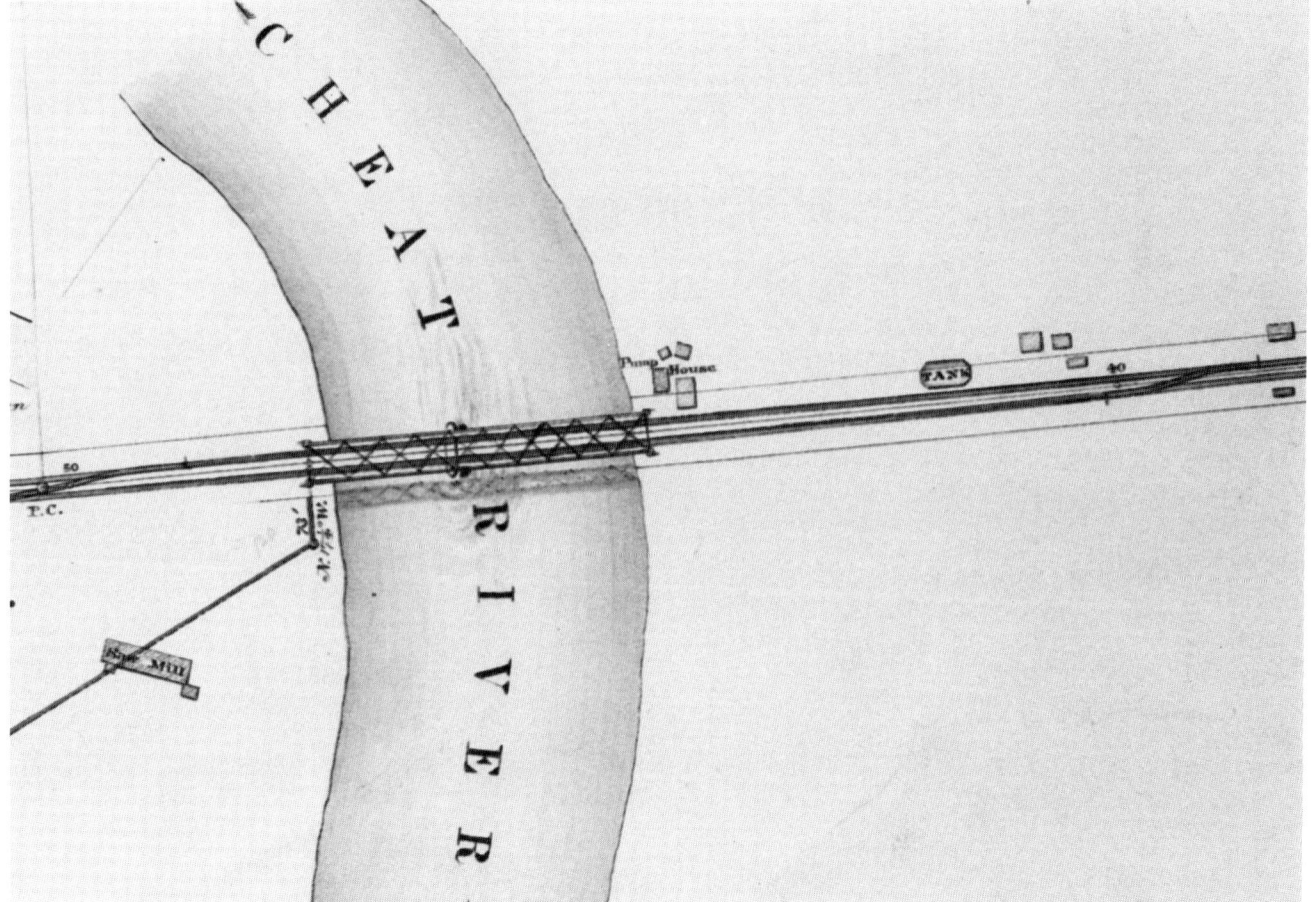

THE SITE of what would become M&K Junction is shown on this c. 1875 company map to the right, or eastern, side of the Cheat River. Note the pump houses by the river and the water jug ... apparently steam locomotives watered on the eastern side throughout history. Salt Lick Creek is not shown ... it enters the river from the right just above and parallel with the railroad. The town of Rowlesburg is just out of the picture to the left. As we shall show in the next chapter, by the late 1870s a helper station would be built there ... until then, the best evidence indicates that sufficient road power would be added at Newburg to the west and Terra Alta to the east to surmount the grades on either side of the river. The railroad, and the Cheat River Bridge, is double tracked through this area at this time ... the double track continues up Cranberry Grade to the right to Terra Alta, but becomes single track to the left up the Cheat River Grade. The two crossovers facilitate movement.

93

WEST END

As Jerusalem is to Christendom, so the B&O is to railroading. As Rome is to Jerusalem, so M&K Junction is to the B&O. As the Sistine Chapel is to Rome, so the engine house is to M&K Junction.

Even the unwashed who lack the faith to accept the premises in this creed must acknowledge that M&K Junction and its engine house has become a Shrine over the 78 years of its existence.

This Holy City, if you will, owes its creation to the coming of the mallet locomotive. B&O pioneered the use of the mallet (literally two engines under one boiler) and saw in it an important weapon in its battle against The Hill. The mallet (pronounced *malley*) doubled power for the same crew cost, a huge step forward.

The West End, of course, had to be completely rebuilt to accommodate this revolutionary development. Doubled power meant doubled

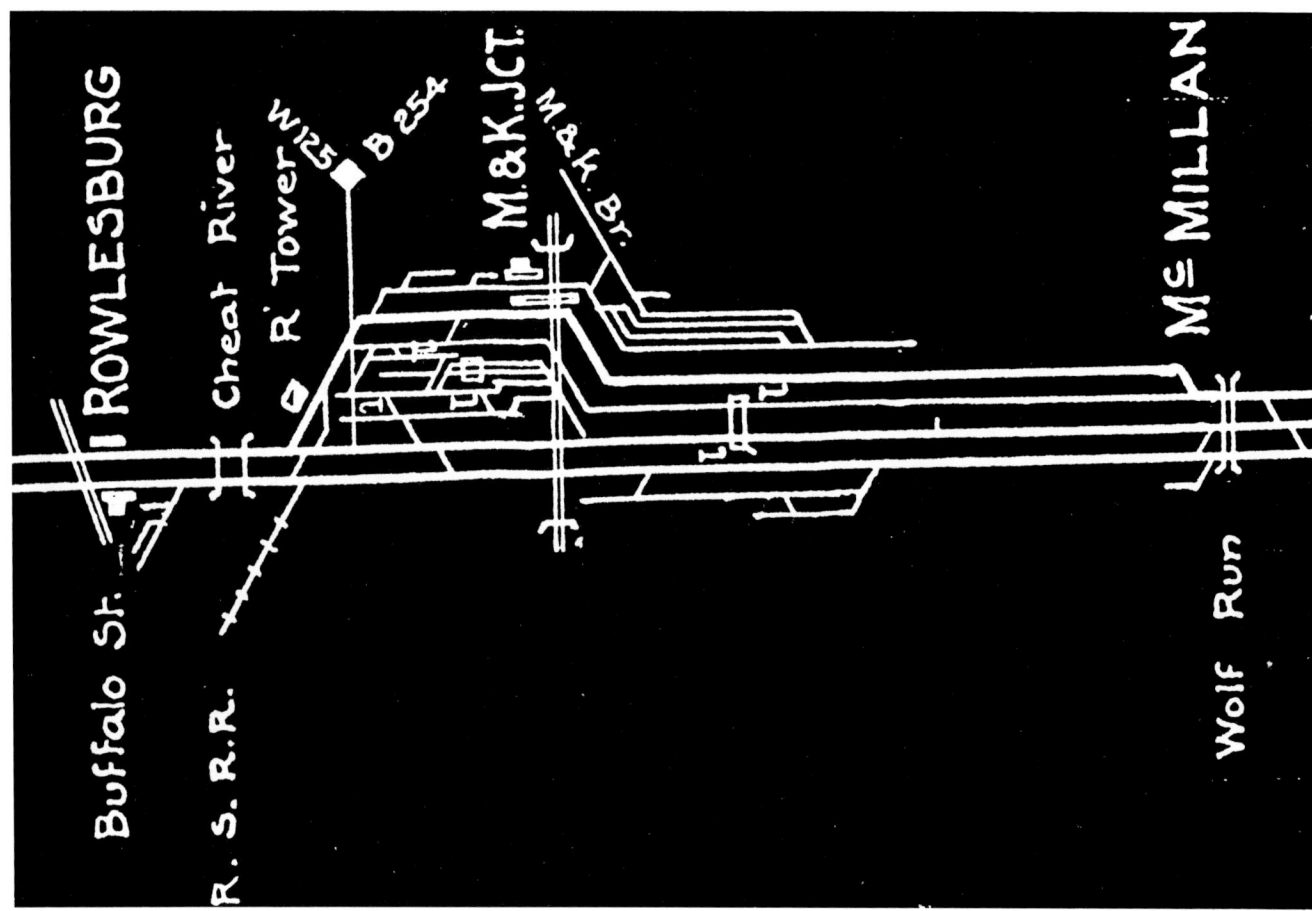

THIS TRACK CHART of M&K Junction in 1931 presents a splendid schematic summary of all the essential facilities in this storied helper station. The interlocker at McMillan (MC) on the right was installed late in the last century before the other facilities were constructed. MC tower, a standard B&O frame affair, was on the south side of the tracks and was built in 1907 ... prior to that date a telegraph office was on the site. The tower was active until c. 1915 when its functions were taken over by R Tower near the Cheat River bridge. For some reason it was reopened in 1920, but was gone by 1922. Moving left from MC, we find the massive coaling dock with support tracks on the south and the M&K subdivision yard on the north (at a lower level). Next we see the road bridge over the yard, then the engine house complex, R tower and Cheat River Bridge 92. Rowlesburg is shown with its station, small yard and Buffalo Street grade crossing. The "R.S.R.R." caption marks the junction with the Rowlesburg Southern Railroad, which we will explore later. Going back to the cross-yard road bridge in the middle of this scene, on the north side we see the M&K subdivision line leaving to the northwest and, just to the left, the original M&K station. Until the 1900s, a wye ran from the M&K sub tracks to the vicinity of R tower. Note the plethora of penstocks. The milepost marker just east of R tower translates "Wheeling 125 miles/Baltimore 254 miles." The grade from Buffalo Street to the road bridge is a mere .07% ... from there to MC 1.08%. Curvature is slight. At MC, from top to bottom, the four tracks are as follows: No. 1 westbound main, westbound passing, No. 2 eastbound high speed, No. 4 eastbound slow speed. When the third mainline track was removed in 1973, No. 2 became No. 1, No. 4 became No. 2 and the old No. 1 was converted to a passing and storage track. All in all, a well laid out and efficient facility.

M&K JUNCTION

train length. Doubled train length meant the helper station at Rowlesburg, among many other things, was inadequate and so in April 1911 B&O authorized the construction of M&K Junction and a near-twin at Hardman at the base of Newburg Grade to the west.

We will treat Hardman and other aspects of this revolution in later chapters. The name M&K Junction evolved simply enough on 8 July 1907 when the Morgantown and Kingwood Railroad was completed from Morgantown through Kingwood to a junction with B&O at this location ... actually a two-plus mile branch to a stone mine at Manheim had existed for some years prior to that date.

So the site had a name in 1907. It opened for operations as the citadel of helper operations on the West End in April of 1913 at a cost, to be exact, of $391,106.

In a bowl at the bottom of Cranberry Grade and Cheat River Grade to the west, M&K was the focal point of West End helper operations and it had everything it needed to fulfill that mission. The details of this magnificent facility will be

B&OHS

COAL, WATER AND SAND were supplied in profusion and with despatch at this outstanding 600-ton facility installed in 1913. This view looks westward in May 1921 ... vaguely, in the distance, the auto bridge and original M&KRR station can be seen. Under pressure of World War II traffic, this dock serviced about 150 road and helper locomotives in a 24-hour period and as many as 60 in an eight-hour shift. Average turnaround time was about forty minutes.

WEST END

EXTRA WEST 7608 with 90 coal cars is about to eat and drink on 22 April 1945 ... this view of the massive dock looks eastward. The train has stopped ... the locomotive will uncouple and move forward into position. To attempt to position with the train attached on a downgrade is too risky. If the engineer does not stop in time, he might not be able to back the train upgrade far enough and then he'll really be in a hole ... an unpleasant prospect with Wild Bill Henry somewhere on the subdivision! Nine years later almost to the day, this facility was closed, and blown down shortly thereafter ... by odd chance, we met the engineering type in charge of demolition some sixteen years later at a party.

E. L. Thompson/B&OHS

given in captions to photographs ... the reader shall see that M&K was, in short, *compleat*.

For various reasons which shall be treated, it took a number of years for M&K to reach its full potential as a helper station. By the early 1920s the drill had settled into a pattern that would hold until the end of steam.

Eastbound drags of about 52 cars would drop down Cheat River Grade and stop just west of Buffalo Street in Rowlesburg to turn down retainers. When cleared by the distant signal at the west end of Bridge 92, they would release brakes and immediately work steam to cross the river and enter No. 4 track (actually a straight-through movement) on the east side of the river, using momentum from the Cheat River Grade as well as power to get the head-end to the coal dock between M&K and McMillan. The caboose would be just east of the engine house ... while the road locomotive replenished with coal, water and sand, a pair of mallets would cross over at M&K and couple up. The conductor would flip a switch on a pole which would flash a "helper-on-train" light within sight of the road engine crew.

All this was accomplished with the sound effects of a great whistle storm ... the reader must remember that there were no radio communications in those days.

When the road engine stopped, the engineer would blow a long and three shorts to send out his flagman. As the helper moved forward, the engineer would blow a short and two longs to acknowledge that he saw the flagman. When coupled up, the helper would blow a long to tell the road engine to test the air. The road engine would blow a long to announce a service reduction. The helper would blow two longs to suggest that the road engine release the train brakes (engine brakes would hold, but not stop, a drag). The road engine would call in his flag ... four longs and four shorts if on track 4, four longs and two shorts if on track 2. The helper would blow two longs, saying "release engine brakes ... I am shoving." The road engine would answer with two longs... "I have released brakes and am pulling."

And then everyone involved in this drama would look toward Heaven and issue forth the West End prayer, "Please, God, let the train start to move."

Eastbound QD trains moved more quickly... retainers were turned down *while moving* at the bottom of Cheat River Grade, thus demonstrating the axiom that brakemen were not paid for what they knew but for taking a chance with their lives and limbs. Not all that much had changed from the pre-air brake days of hand brakes.

The train would usually enter track 2 and a drill similar to that for drags would follow except with more expedition... get it out of here *now* was the command. Of course, QD trains typically ran to about 40 cars and were much lighter... the same amount of power was used, front and rear, to insure speed.

Eastbound passenger trains usually had sufficient power added at Grafton or Hardman to the west to breast Newburg and Cranberry Grades... they went straight through, almost invariably on track 2. The passenger helpers, however, were out of M&K. For example, an M&K-based Q4 would back to Grafton for Train No. 2, help to Terra Alta, cut-off and back to Grafton for Train No. 4, cut-off again at Terra Alta and either run ahead to Keyser or back to M&K depending upon circumstances.

All eastbound freight helpers cut-off on the fly at Terra Alta and returned to M&K on tracks 1 or 2 depending upon the decision of the "Hill Supervisor" at M&K. When automatic signals were installed in 1930, track 2 was signalled in both directions to facilitate such movements.

Westbound the pattern was similar. Coal car trains of 60-90 cars would stop at the coal dock to replenish and turn down retainers. On signal, they would then race across Bridge 92 and ascend the

IN CLASSIC FORM, two 7000s shove the rear of an eastward QD train and build up momentum for Cranberry in the late 1940s. The 7000 against the train is a "second group" LL1 or EL4 with a curved-top tender... the other is sporting a short Vanderbilt tender, an unusual but not rare configuration. Note the water tank just ahead of the exhaust of the rear engine... this is a 200,000 gallon steel jug built in 1931 and is extant. The helpers would have been serviced after their last shove... the road engine while waiting for the helpers to couple up to the west. In this vicinity are two "Helper-on-train" lights, one each for tracks 2 and 4 facing west ... another light is located east of the dock on track 4. When helpers coupled-up, the conductor would turn on the appropriate light by a pole-mounted switch to inform the road engineer. A similar light was located west of Rowlesburg which we will show in the next chapter.

William Hoffman II Collection

WEST END

Cheat River Grade as far as possible until they slipped... hopefully the rear end was clear of Buffalo Street in Rowlesburg. Helpers would follow and couple-up, then shove. Cut-off on the fly was accomplished at Blaser and return was made on either track 1 or 2 as convenient... in 1956 track 1 was signaled in both directions to speed the return.

Westbound helper power varied... one mallet, two mallets, one or two Mikes, or any combination as needed. Many times these helpers shoved backwards if necessary... there were no turning facilities at M&K and a steam engine could shove in either direction without problem.

Westbound QD trains... and they were principally the famous 97s... followed the same drill except, of course, retainers were turned down while moving.

Westbound passenger trains might pick up a helper at M&K if needed, put on the head end at the engine house and taken off at Blaser. If a diesel-powered passenger train had more than twelve cars, a helper was always added at M&K in either direction to keep speed above 25 mph and avoid problems with traction motor overheating.

M&K was a busy place in the steam era and it functioned with efficiency and effectiveness. For example, on 16 November 1945 only fourteen mallets (13 7000s and 7147) and six Mikados (all Q4s) were stationed at M&K... these locomotives handled 21 eastbound and 17 westbound shoves plus numerous passenger assignments and local work on the M&K subdivision. Another ten mallets (7100s and 7200s) were assigned to Hardman for Newburg Grade. In 1949 Hardman was closed and the mallets were transferred to M&K in preparation for the dieselization effected in that year which would prove to be another major revolution in the history of the West End in general and M&K in particular.

The DH1 F7 diesels arrived in late summer of 1949 and everything changed. Steam at M&K lasted until 8 February 1953 when the last one was dispatched. Steam helpers did not entirely disappear in the interregnum, however... EM1 7600s shoved out of M&K in the early 1950s and a few Q4s remained for mine runs.

THIS SINGLE-LANE road bridge over M&K Junction trackage was built in 1914 and is extant... for railfans and historians it is a perfect platform for photography. The "station" for M&K was probably the smallest on the B&O system and was actually a station stop for a few passenger trains. The I12 caboose is on the rear of an eastbounder awaiting helpers on 13 October 1946.

E. L. Thompson/B&OHS

M&K JUNCTION

The impact of dieselization was so profound on the West End that we will discuss it in more detail later in the book. M&K Junction remained a major helper station and was even converted to a diesel maintenance facility, but its days were numbered. B&O learned that a very few diesel sets could handle all the grades and later generation diesels were even more efficient.

Most shop work was moved to Cumberland over the years ... by the mid-1970s only limited running repairs were effected at M&K and even that small function disappeared.

M&K remained a helper station until 1986 ... on 16 August servicing was moved to Grafton and in October the helpers themselves were stationed at that point. The use of end-of-train devices and other factors led B&O to decide to put helpers on at Grafton or Hardman and run them to or through the Glades without stopping. After 73 years, M&K was no longer a helper station. B&O people had nicknames for operating personnel ... West Enders were known as Snakies and crews out of M&K as River Rats. There are no more River Rats and, for that matter, no more M&K Junction ... it is now just Rowlesburg.

B&O Museum

THE ENGINE HOUSE at M&K on 17 May 1921, in all its grimy glory, gives little evidence that it would become a shrine to students of the B&O. On this date, B&O owned the Morgantown and Kingwood Railroad so the station on the right is B&O property ... the connection track dips behind the station. The water jug is probably ex-M&K. The brick engine house itself was completed in 1913 and at this stage in its life is 148′ 6″ long and 61′ 3″ wide at its widest point ... the two-track bay is 45 feet wide. Two LL1 mallets are sitting in front of the entrance doors, which are roller-type as built ... swinging doors would come later. The EL4 in the foreground still has its road pilot. Note the tall engine house stack from the boiler room and the coal hopper on the ramp ... in 1946 the ramp would be moved easterly and the east wall of the boiler room extended flush with the bay wall. In the bay were two drop-tables for changing driver tires ... the grades and curves on the West End chewed-up both steam and diesel wheels as well as rail, causing B&O still more expense. And the four-wheel bobber K1 caboose introduces another problem ... two mallets on the rear would crush wooden cabooses against the train, so they had to be switched to the rear of the helpers until B&O finally developed steel underframe and all steel cabooses. B&O saved a few bucks in 1930, however ... needing a new boiler in the engine house, they used the boiler from retired H4 4-4-0 757. Since the 757 was built in the mid-1880s and retired in 1918, one would have to say B&O got its money out of that one.

WEST END

The Morgantown and Kingwood Railroad gave M&K Junction its name and the B&O a lot of loads, so a brief summary of this line is in order. Construction of this railroad was completed in 1907 ... it took over the short switching line from M&K to Manheim (MD) for its final link to B&O. B&O purchased the railroad in 1920 and incorporated it into the system by making it a subdivision of the West End shortly thereafter.

From M&K, it ran about 14 miles to Albright down the Cheat River, which it crossed enroute. It then started climbing for eleven miles to Kingwood (county seat of Preston County) and a summit at Manown with grades hovering around two percent. The M&K then descended for another 27 miles to Morgantown and a connection with the B&O FM&P line, again with two percent grades.

VALUATION photographers did not worry too much about mundane things like focus, so this foggy early 1920s photo is the only one we can offer of the M&K station. A mudslide from Lantz Ridge in front of the station in 1919 ruined some platforms, but spared the station until 1935 when it was closed and demolished.

B&O Museum

E. L. Thompson/B&OHS

BY 13 OCTOBER 1946, our shrine has incorporated a few changes. The boiler room has been extended and the coal ramp moved back; swinging doors have been installed; the stack has been shortened; a long ramp for boiler room ash has been installed to a raised platform by the gondola. Note the two hoppers right middle to the right of the caboose ... they are company ash-service hoppers. Steam locomotives in general and M&K helpers in particular produced mountains of ash, an expensive disposal proposition. The white panels on the hoppers identify them as being in ash service and lettering on the sides indicate the routing. Elimination of the ash problem was another unsung benefit to dieselization. Ash, however, has returned to M&K. Coal off the M&K is shipped to Baltimore, barged to a northeastern utility, resultant ash barged to Baltimore and returned in hoppers to M&K to be dumped near Albright on the M&K sub (now Kingwood Branch). Local residents are not happy with this arrangement ... early in 1991 persons unknown released the brakes on a string of ash hoppers at Albright which, among other things, took down a number of telephone poles. And B&O has learned that water-soaked ash will freeze, expand and rearrange the side panels on hoppers ... apparently utility ash is very fine and soaks up a lot of water.

M&K JUNCTION

E. L. Thompson/B&OHS

TRAIN NUMBER 30, Engines 4464-5086 and 9 cars, is slowing on 16 August 1947 to take water at a penstock just east of the auto bridge as workmen are completing a 35 foot extension to the engine house and installing glass-block windows ... ash from the boiler room is still hauled by hand, however. Notice the MOW people and hoppers on No. 4 track. Cinders rained down on M&K Junction in volcanic proportions and had to be cleaned from roadbed, ditches and hillsides in an ongoing battle that would not end until dieselization. The two wooden cabooses on the far right were used on M&K sub runs ... steel wagontop cabs were standard in mainline service on the West End by this time.

COAL GAS from steam locomotives had at least one socially productive use ... it kept foliage away from the railroad so that it was possible to get photographs like this beauty of the south side of the engine house on 13 October 1946. The LL1 with extended rectangular tender by the house is the 7047, an example of the very first fleet of mallets the B&O purchased which revolutionized West End operations and made necessary the extensive 1910-1913 improvements. In this view you can see the completed boiler room extension now flush with the east wall. Just out of sight to the left and north of the westbound main, a 61 by 19 foot single-story Rest House was built in 1913 and it lasted until the mid-1950s. Of the hundreds of photos taken of M&K Junction, we have not seen one that shows this Rectory to the Shrine.

E. L. Thompson/B&OHS

WEST END

The M&K was built to tap vast coal resources along its line of road. As late as the mid-1940s there were 15 coal mines along the railroad with a daily capacity of 235 cars. B&O would send daily turns from M&K Junction and Morgantown to service these mines ... the trains would meet at Bretz (which had a wye) at the foot of the west slope and trade cars for many years. Just west of Bretz was Oak Park, a recreation center in the early years. Passenger service was minimal, with two through trains each day until the early 1930s ... the last few years of such service was accomplished with Brill motor cars. Service for the two miles from Morgantown to Sabraton continued until the mid-1950s, apparently as employee runs.

As mines were worked out in the hinterlands, B&O severed the M&K in the early 1970s from Kingwood to Reedsville ... the west end became the Morgantown subdivision and the east end the Kingwood subdivision. By 1987 the east end was cut back to Albright and became the Kingwood Branch, which it is today.

Today there are only two active mines on the Kingwood, but they are major producers giving B&O about 75 cars a day of Tide Coal east and, as we shall show, a lot of ash west.

In fact, the M&K has always produced a lot of coal loads for B&O ... they have always been assembled into trains at M&K Junction and sent east to Keyser and beyond daily. In the steam era Mikados would service the line. When you see a diesel set at M&K Junction today, they are not helpers but rather power to work the branch.

A LOT OF THINGS changed when the seven sets of four-unit DH1 F7 diesels arrived at M&K Junction in the late summer of 1949, not the least of which was the need for a large machine shop on the south side of the engine house, completed by early 1950. Diesels were not exempt from wheel wear, so a diesel drop table was installed in the engine house (and the steam tables removed) in the summer of 1949 via the simple expedient of knocking a hole in the south wall. Steam was not gone, however; we see Extra East 7102 with 52 cars on 18 June 1950 moving into position to receive helpers. *E. L. Thompson/B&OHS*

M&K JUNCTION

The Rowlesburg Southern Railroad also connected with B&O at M&K Junction. A lumbering line opened in 1913, it ran about seven miles along the east bank of the Cheat River upstream to a base at Erwin where it had a shop, band mill and company store. A spiderweb of lines for logging crisscrossed Cheat Mountain ... if you travel down the Route 50 grade to Erwin in winter you can see the traces of this archetypal logging line. In the brush at Erwin one can find the footings and foundations of the railroad's base.

The RSRR operated with two or three two-truck shays and apparently had no cars, let alone cabooses, of their own ... they would deliver one or two loads in foreign cars to B&O once or twice a week, usually cut wood in boxcars. Predictably, there was a tannery at Macomber which RSRR reached with a bridge across the Cheat River. Locals say the effluent from this tannery poisoned the river for fish for a quarter of a century. The Rowlesburg Southern stopped operations and was torn up in the early 1950s ... legend has it that there is a Shay rusting away somewhere along the line of road.

As we prepare to leave M&K Junction to claw up the Cheat River Grade, we should point out that M&K was the lair of Wild Bill Henry from the early 1940s to the summer of 1948. That fact alone qualifies M&K Junction as a Shrine.

B&OHS

THE NEW MACHINE SHOP in 1950 from the west ... note that the old oil house is now joined with the engine house. The penstock gives notice that steam is not gone, but new DH1 184 hints that the end is in sight. New ventilators on the roof over the bays also signal change is in the wind.

Safety Above Everything

CUMBERLAND DIVISION

WEST END

THE COMING of the DH1s involved more than engine house improvements ... a new sand and fuel oil facility was built in late 1949 between the house and the Cheat River. On the left we see the new ash hoist built in 1947, and over the cab of the 184, the top of a penstock. Steam would stay another four years. The two service tracks lead east to two new inspection pits, built in 1947 ... the hoppers on the left are for ash service. Fuel for this complex was supplied from a 260,000 gallon tank built just north of the engine house in 1949. The DH1s were not the first diesels to be seen at M&K ... passenger E units appeared on the *National Limited* in 1938 and FTs powered QD Trains 94 and 97 in the mid-1940s. Only westbound diesels fueled at M&K, and that from a tank car-cum-pump until this installation was made. All diesel fueling and servicing was transferred to Grafton on 16 August 1986 and this facility was cut-up for steel scrap in late April 1991, just short of its 42nd birthday.

B&OHS

M&K JUNCTION

E. L. Thompson/B&OHS

THE READY TRACK at M&K on 13 October 1946 bespeaks power! As usual, most of the power based at M&K is out on the line of road ... in steamy ambience, others await the call. Over the second Q4 from the left, please note the frame of the original ash hoist at M&K ... a replacement would be installed in 1947 along with track and inspection pit improvements. The cantilever signal is the eastbound home signal ... the water jug on the right serves the engine house complex.

THE BRAIN CENTER of M&K Junction operations for over forty years was R Tower, seen here from the side of Lantz Ridge 13 October 1946. Salt Lick Creek meanders behind the tower to the Cheat River ... there was a dam just before the river at one time although it is not clear if it served the company or supplied Rowlesburg with water. The road bridge in the background was replaced in 1958 with a concrete span which was washed away in the 1985 flood. The M&K sub can be seen on the right of the river as it starts its path down the Cheat River to Kingwood and Morgantown. Part of the town of Rowlesburg is seen on the left ... in the center distance is the beginning of the Cheat River Grade with No. 76 (Section) Fill bridging Kyers Run. Rather obviously, R was a rod plant.

E. L. Thompson/B&OHS

WEST END

E. L. Thompson/B&OHS

R TOWER IN RED on 13 October 1946 dominates the entrance to M&K Junction. Possibly the widest B&O standard tower, R housed 68 levers and required three men to function ... operator, leverman and "Hill Supervisor." The latter, probably a unique position on B&O, was responsible for scheduling returning helpers on Cranberry, Cheat River and Newburg Grades ... there were so many such movements that the Cumberland Dispatcher could not handle them all and the duty devolved to R. Built c. 1913, the call letters were originally MJ as there was a tower at Rowlesburg called R. The Rowlesburg R was destroyed by a runaway train c. 1916 and was not replaced, so the call letters were transferred. Oddly, letters MJ were retained for M&K sub operations and remained in use until 1954. This tower was replaced by a nearby new one c. 1954 and torn down shortly thereafter.

MK TOWER, the replacement for R and seen 14 September 1985, was opened in 1954 along with a modernized interlocking system and call letters stolen from Mountain Lake Park to the east, a transfer that confused your writer in his early years as a student of the West End. When CSX centralized systemwide dispatching in Jacksonville, FL in the late 1980s, call letters confused the computer so the few remaining towers on the West End were given names ... Rowlesburg in this case as well as Viaduct Junction, West Keyser, Altamont and Hardman. We must not do anything to upset our new masters.

C. S. Roberts

M&K JUNCTION

B&O Museum

THE CHEAT RIVER was crossed with a "viaduct," reported Mr. Latrobe in early 1853, consisting of "two spans, one of 180 and one of 132 feet; elevation of floor from low water, 27 feet. Pier and abutments of blue freestone of remarkably fine quality ... superstructure, timber and iron, Fink's truss." We believe this c. 1870 photograph shows the original bridge looking eastward and also believe the building next to the track on the east shore was the original telegraph office and waiting room for passengers ... if the latter is correct, both functions were transferred to the west side of the river in 1879. The bridge has an iron roof to protect the wooden structure from the weather. Note that Mr. Latrobe built the central pier for two tracks.

THE CHEAT RIVER crossing was "doubled" c. 1872 with a two-span Bollman truss built on the downstream side of the original covered Fink truss. The Fink was then replaced with a Bollman truss in 1873. Both these bridge designs were very similar. The Fink used fewer diagonal supports and was more economical to construct ... the Bollman was stronger and more expensive.

B&O Museum

WEST END

THE TWIN BOLLMAN bridges over the Cheat River c. 1890 are seen in this illustration. Lack of evidence to the contrary indicates that these spans survived until 1910 ... if so, they must have been a source of concern to B&O as power and trains got heavier.

C. S. Roberts Collection

IN 1910 B&O built this magnificent Warren Truss over the Cheat River and removed all worry about bridge loading in this location. This photograph was taken in the 1920s and shows the tracks of the Rowlesburg Southern at lower left ... on the far side of the river to the left of the railroad it also shows an open area where the Rowlesburg shops had been located. By this time, the structure was simply known as Bridge 92.

B&OHS

M&K JUNCTION

AFTER SEVENTY-FIVE YEARS of gazing at Bridge 92, The Hill called upon its ally Weather and together they produced a 10,000-year rainstorm in the region. First it rained for about a week to load the soil and then up to 12 inches of rain was dumped on 4 November 1985. At 1:15 a.m. on 5 November, with a roar that residents will always remember, both spans of Bridge 92 went out ... one span was flung on the Rowlesburg shore and the other was pushed downstream to take out the road bridge, which virtually disappeared. The Hill also took out about 60 homes in Rowlesburg, thus extending the war to the childrens' children ... upstream, Parsons WV was wiped out (the wreckage piled up on 92) and downstream Albright received its share of fury. This photo looks upstream from M&K sub rails on 9 November ... the east abutment of 92 is in the center. When you have secured an area, be sure to inform the enemy.

THE TWO SPANS of Bridge 92 on 9 November 1985 give testimony to the vehemence of the counterattack.

C. S. Roberts

WEST END

FOR ALL THE GOOD IT DID, The Hill might as well not have tried. B&O "combat engineers" had a new deck plate girder bridge in place and open for traffic 28 November 1985 ... here we see five units with coal cars westbound on 29 November and evidence that the old spans are being cut up for scrap. B&O could be implacable, too. The new Bridge 92 rested on pilings, which would be encased in concrete over the next few years.

THE NEW BRIDGE 92 on 4 May 1991 ... only single track but that was good enough. Both of these photos were taken from the western shore and serve as a warning to The Hill ... try it again and we'll build it again.

C. S. Roberts

THIS PHOTOGRAPH of M&K Junction was taken in October 1977 from a hill west of Rowlesburg through a lot of glass and is included to make a point ... it is not intended as a testimonial to the writer's lens skill. Lantz Ridge is on the right and it originally extended to the general area of the left wall of the engine house ... the mainline circled around it prior to 1913. The fill taken from the side of the hill was used to raise the level of the junction area so as to ease the grade from M&K to McMillan and give drags a fighting chance to move east far enough to enable helpers to tie-on the rear ... a good plan and it worked with 52 car drags. As drags grew longer in the diesel era, we suspect that it did not work as well and this may be one of the reasons helpers came to be left on from Hardman all the way east to Terra Alta. In the F7 diesel era, drags were limited to about 65 cars with help added at M&K ... this adds credence, but not proof, to our theory.

C. S. Roberts

M&K JUNCTION

C. S. Roberts

ON THE M&K SUBDIVISION, about 2.2 miles downstream from M&K Junction, lies one of the more obvious and interesting mines on the B&O ... obvious because it is in clear view from the Cheat River Grade (as this photo taken 14 September 1985 attests) and interesting because the mine itself is near the top of the mountain. The limestone from this mine is apparently of very high quality and there is plenty up there ... mine owners told us in 1977 that man had been taking out stone for almost a century and there was another century's worth left. A short railroad hauled stone and cement to a B&O connection at present day M&K Junction before the railroad was built from Morgantown through Kingwood to connect at Manheim, the name of the town near the mine. In this scene the stone is dropped in a chute to the facilities at the bottom ... in earlier years tramway railroads lowered the stone. Study the woods to the left of the chute and you will see the various paths used in the past ... new mine entrances have been proceeding from left to right. Known as the Alpha Portland Cement Company for years, B&O received a lot of limestone tonnage for use in Pittsburgh steelmaking which moved to M&K to Cumberland and west. Developers of the lush limestone beds near Frederick, MD captured this business in the late 1940s ... the haul from Frederick to Pittsburgh was cheaper because of easier grades; thus the famous B&O Stone and Dolomite Specials. The mine is still active, although rail service has not been used for many years.

WEST END

THE OWNERS of the mine at Manheim were kind enough to take us up a hairpin, switchback road to the mine mouth in October 1977. The entrance to the latest mine is shown ... inside it is light and airy and boasts a year-round temperature of about 70 degrees. Stone is blasted into chunks, hauled by truck to the crusher and then sent down the chute with a rattle that can be heard for miles. The chute was originally built without lids, but they lost so much stone enroute that cover was mandatory.

C. S. Roberts

Chapter 7

Cheat River Grade

M&K Junction to Tunnelton

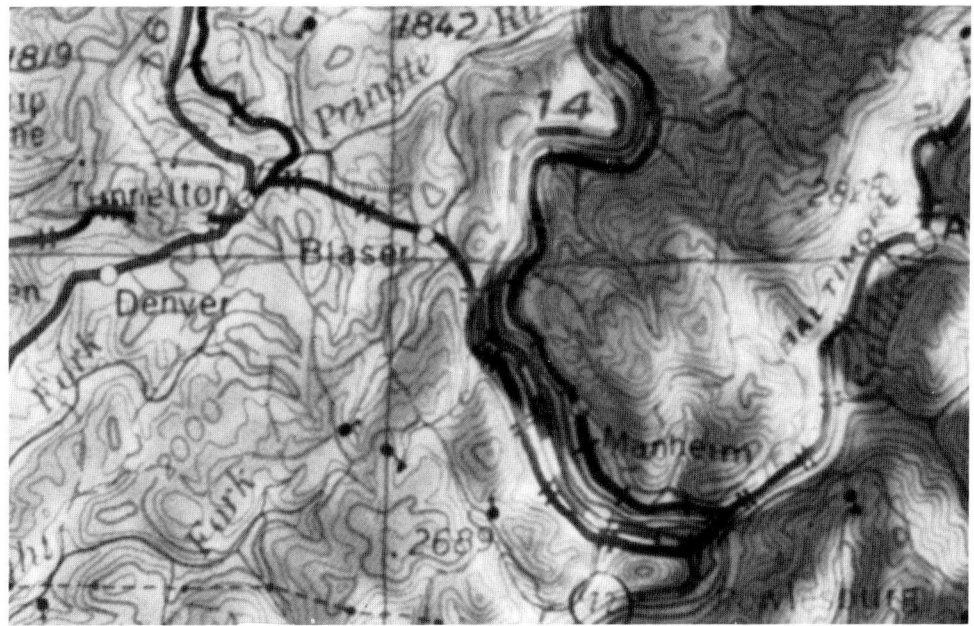

C. S. Roberts

CHEAT RIVER GRADE proper is only about four miles long ... it begins at Rowlesburg at lower right, clings to the side of Laurel Mountain on the west side of the Cheat River for about three miles and then leaves the river for about a mile to Blaser at the summit. The line then runs for about two miles on a slight downgrade through Tunnelton to the mouth of the horrid Kingwood Tunnel. The line on the east side of the river is the M&K subdivision, which follows the river course through Manheim (with its mountaintop mine) and continues along the river downstream on its course westward. This grade is B&O's second crossing of the Great Barrier on the West End.

WEST END

A cursory glance at B&Os second crossing of the Great Barrier, after the agonies of Seventeen Mile and Cranberry, gives the impression that it was anti-climactic. The Cheat River Grade was short, did not face the tonnage, was relatively straight by West End standards except in one place, had only 454 feet to rise, was uncursed with tunnels and ended up with a 2.10% ruling grade only four miles long ... it was and is the shortest of the four major grades on the West End.

The Canyon of the Cheat River was also breathtakingly beautiful. Since beauty is always a splendid painkiller for man, this grandeur must be counted as a palliative.

To be sure, Laurel Mountain was just as vicious as Backbone and Briery and in no mood to live and let live. Yet four miles is a short distance and most of The Hill would be untouched.

Why, then, did the Cheat River Grade turn out to be a "stupendous work of engineering," as a mid-1850s civil engineer put it? Why did three of the four miles turn out to be, in all probability, one of the most expensive works of man to that date?

The reason has to do with just four creeks, or "runs" ... by name Kyers, Buckeye, Tray and Buckhorn. They are short runs and do not drain a lot of water ... in fact, if B&O were building a river line they would have been crossed with a few minor culverts. Unfortunately, B&O had to climb the side of Laurel Mountain and the nature of these runs made them major impediments.

At one time in geologic history these runs must have been waterfalls because they cut very deep, narrow and steep ravines. And the Cheat River (named, some say, because it cheats men of their

E. L. Thompson/B&OHS

THE MAIN LINE crosses the Cheat River on Bridge 92 and curves to the right through Rowlesburg to the Buffalo Street crossing by the cluster of buildings left center. Buffalo Street marks the beginning of the Cheat River Grade ... the gradient hits 2.00% at the cut just west of the crossing. Buffalo Street continues upstream to the left for about three miles to meet modern-day Route 50, originally the Northwestern Turnpike which provided B&O with ingress during construction. The Rowlesburg shop and helper station was located in the open area just to the left of the line. The first opening in the bulk of Laurel Mountain is crossed by 76 Fill ... originally Kyers Run, now simply known as Fill Hollow. Up to this point it was easy. Notice the slope just to the right of 76 ... the amount of rock that was removed here must have set a record. The next gash in the mountain is Buckeye Run, initially crossed with a viaduct and then filled ... the beginning of the massive Buckeye Wall can just be seen at upper right. The grade eases briefly to 1.63% over 76, increases to 2.34% by the slope and then settles to 2.01%. This poor photo, taken in the mid-1940s, hints at the scenic beauty of the Cheat Canyon.

CHEAT RIVER GRADE

lives) had scoured the sides of the mountains containing it with so much vigor that the flanks were quite steep between the runs.

The Cheat River Grade really begins at Buffalo Street in Rowlesburg, a town chartered in 1858 and named for one Thomas Rowles, an assistant engineer for B&O who surveyed this part of the railroad. With photos and captions to follow, we will take the reader up the flank of Laurel Mountain and demonstrate the severity of each succeeding crossing of each ravine. Briefly, the higher B&O climbed the more challenging each crossing became and the more expensive the solution. The grade was topped at Cassidy Summit Ridge, named Anderson and later Blaser on the railroad. The line then actually descended with many curves for two miles through a mountaintop tableland to Tunnelton where it met the spine of Laurel

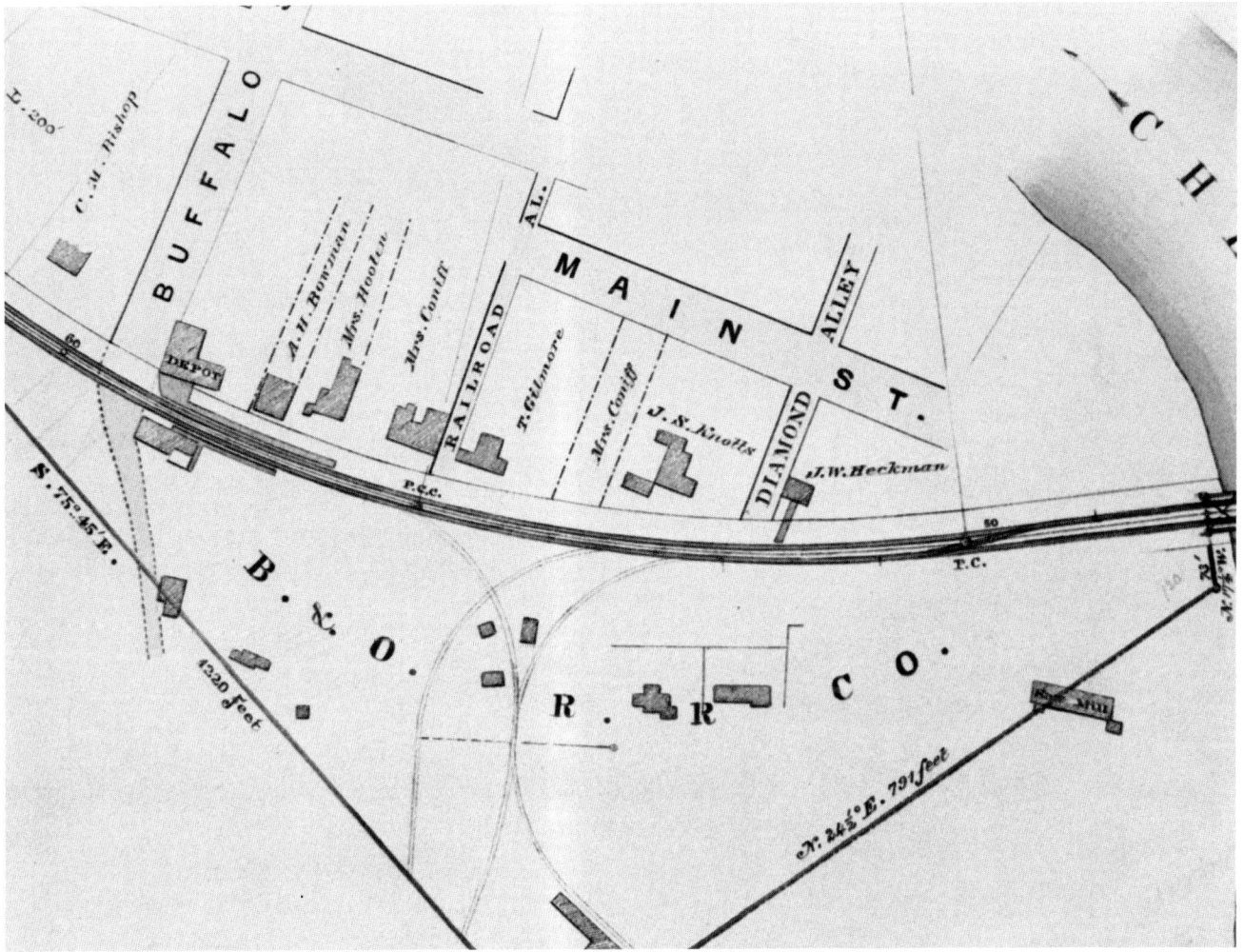

B&OHS

THE ORIGINAL PLAN by Mr. Latrobe in 1850 called for an engine house and repair shop to be built at Rowlesburg, but we have found no evidence that they were actually constructed ... our guess is that it was decided to put the facility at Newburg to the west. A wye was also reported at Rowlesburg in 1855 ... if it existed, it must not have lasted very long. In 1853 a 1320′ siding was installed, which is probably correct. This photo of a mid-1870s company map shows a wye and other tracks sketched in pencil, indicating preliminary planning for the engine house, engine pits and coal chutes known to have been constructed in 1880. We have good proof that helpers were *first* dispatched to Rowlesburg from Newburg in 1879, which gives credence to our theory (which will be developed later under Operations) that shoving did not start until late in the last century and that help was either on the front end or trains were shortened on grades with single power up front. Note the depot on the northeast corner of Buffalo Street and the railroad as well as the small structure across the tracks ... we are quite sure (and so are local residents) that the structure on this site today is *not* the original depot. The small structure, however, was apparently built in 1873 and enlarged in 1879 to become a combined freight and passenger station ... it is almost certainly the extant building on this site today. The third building to the right of the depot is Mrs. Hooten's Tavern, predecessor to the eminent New Howard Hotel.

WEST END

AGING SLANT-NOSE DP3 57 on Train No. 11 with seven cars slows for a mob of passengers on 21 July 1951. This view, of course, is looking east and just behind the engine and through the trees can be seen Mrs. Howard's New Howard Hotel, Rowlesburg's claim to world renown.

E. L. Thompson/B&OHS

TRAIN NO. 12, the *Metropolitan Special* Engines 4417-5085, eases its eleven cars into position for a stop at Rowlesburg on a dreary day in June 1947 and allows Tommy time to record the venerable station in its new buff and brown livery.

E. L. Thompson/B&OHS

CHEAT RIVER GRADE

Mountain which would be breached with the malign Kingwood Tunnel... that bitter story will be told in the next chapter. At this point the B&O had reached the Great Western Coalfields, as they were called in those days... from Anderson west vast beds of coal lay on all sides of the B&O which, to this day, would provide B&O and industry with a torrent of black diamonds.

The tableau of scenic elegance viewed from the line of road up the side of Laurel Mountain enraptured early travelers to the point that they were running out of superlatives: "Enraptured... grandest and most boldly picturesque scenery to be found... midway between heaven and earth... glorious views... truly inspiring... emotions inspired by the scene... solemn poetry of nature... wealth of wilderness solitude." These and other paeans, we can assure the reader, are substantially true... it is sad that the disappearance of the passenger train has made impossible public access to this stunning scenery.

In March 1853 some B&O passengers on the grade made the trip from earth to Heaven rather abruptly. A two-car train apparently collapsed some temporary wooden trestlework over one of the runs... one car rolled down the grade for a hundred or so feet and the other ended up on its side about halfway down. About ten of forty passengers were killed and many others injured.

Mr. Latrobe referred to this accident in B&O's 1853 Annual Report, angry at the rhetorical mileage being made by rival railroads over this unpleasantness. "The fears of the public which have been excited by the unscrupulous assertions of the agents of other lines must soon subside, and this magnificent route over the mountains (will) become as popular a highway for travel as any of its competitors." B&O did not handle this one very well... as late as 1857 B&O *promotional* literature asserted, "The safety of this line is a strong feature in its claims to public support. With the exception of one occasion in March, 1853, (when the road was first opened to the Ohio River) no accident to the trains has occurred on the roads of this Company, by which a passenger has been killed or seriously injured." All that is another way of saying "we haven't killed anybody lately, so trust us."

ROWLESBURG evolved into a major helper station on the West End and served for 33 years until M&K Junction was opened across the Cheat River. This drawing, taken from a photograph, shows what we believe is the "new" engine house built in 1892. Coal chutes paralleled the eastbound main and were located just to the right of this scene. The tower is the original R, destroyed by a runaway train c. 1916. After the 1985 flood, B&O generously gave away most of the land in the old shop area to local residents needing new homes. Since the flood waters did not reach this site, the homeowners must sleep well at night, no doubt confident that there won't be any more runaways.

Warren Somerville

WEST END

E. L. Thompson/B&OHS

THIS IS THE "NEW HOWARD HOTEL" in Rowlesburg 13 April 1947, hard by the tracks and across from the station. Whether or not one accepts M&K Junction as a shrine to stoicism, there is no question that this hostelry was a temple to epicurism. The rear portion of the building was "The Hooten Tavern" from the building of the railroad until well after the Civil War ... it then became "The Commercial House." The front of the hotel with the mansard roof was added in 1900. On 1 November 1925, Mrs. Annette Howard and her husband, a medical doctor, purchased the hotel and a new era dawned. Actually, Dr. and Mrs. Howard planned to use the first floor as an office and the balance as a home ... the boarders, however, begged Mrs. Howard to allow them to stay and Mrs. Howard relented. Soon other B&O people prayed for admittance and in short order Mrs. Howard was proprietress of what rapidly became the most revered "home away from home" on the entire B&O system. She acquired linen and china from the Howard Hotel in Baltimore, which prompted the name "New Howard Hotel." It soon became simply "Mrs. Howard's," a spotless hotel with thirteen rooms, dining room, lounge, two kitchens, fresh flowers, marble-topped dressers and even her early China collection on display with some pieces over 200 years old. Mrs. Howard's international fame, however, came from those two kitchens. Steaks, country sausages, baked cabbage (her specialty), buckwheat cakes, deep-dish pie, homemade vegetable soup and other goodies sated the hunger of guests for fifty years ... her baked cabbage was served at the Waldorf-Astoria in New York and the Drake in Chicago. While perhaps eighty percent of her patrons were B&O people, the names of railfans, historians, local residents and foreign visitors made her guest book a text in geography. The dining room seated eighty people and was filled frequently. For many years she was assisted in her illustrious kitchen by two assistants, Virginia McCabe and Irene Buckingham. Mrs. Howard never forgot a name or favorite dish ... as B&O men advanced in rank they made pilgrimages to visit her temple. Tommy was among her devoted servants ... he always reserved a room in front by the tracks where "the trains came right through the room." No one left Mrs. Howard's hungry or penniless ... as late as 1973 "steak and bed" was a mere $9.50. Mrs. Howard retired to a nursing home in Kingwood c. 1975 where she became a vibrant personality ... she died in the 1980s and her thousands of mourners must have faith that there is a kitchen in Heaven. Only after the "New Howard Hotel" was demolished c. 1986 did the residents of Rowlesburg wonder if perhaps they had lost their most historic structure. One last story to come back to railroad operations ... a young assistant road foreman of engines had been assigned to M&K from a midwestern flatland division and arrived at Mrs. Howard's late in the evening. After dinner, he walked to Buffalo Street and saw his first drag descending Cheat River Grade. Every wheel and brake shoe on every car was rimmed in red ... he later related that he briefly thought he had just seen his first train "with one hundred percent hotboxes."

CHEAT RIVER GRADE

LOOKING EAST from 76 Fill on 4 May 1991, we see track 2 joining track 1 on the approach to the new single-track Bridge 92 erected in 1985. Farther up the grade, track 1 was severed by a derailment in 1989 and taken out of service, so this junction is not active. Note the two dead rounds ... since incoming always has the right of way, we tried to look unimportant. Laurel Mountain just might be low on ammo.

C. S. Roberts

Students in Public Relations 101 are enjoined that buttoning one's lip is the first rule with bad news. There are probably some people out there who haven't heard about it ... don't go out of your way to tell them and don't remind the others. B&O must have gotten the message ... this incident is the only one B&O every publicly acknowledged. To be fair, the accident must have been traumatic because B&O rapidly became a fierce advocate of safety and set an enviable record for passenger safety over the 160 years of its life.

Lest the reader forget the perils of the downgrade leg, let us remind him that the tonnage went *down* the Cheat River Grade and did not always arrive in one piece. As has been seen, the original R Tower in Rowlesburg was taken out by a runaway. In the Fall of 1979, a grain drag started down and the engineer made the startling discovery that he could not apply the brakes ... a fault in the brakestand was responsible for this ugly turn of events.

Actually, this problem had manifested itself in an earlier incident and was supposed to have been corrected.

We interviewed the conductor, wondering why he didn't activate the emergency brake valve in the caboose. His explanation was simple ... the cab was bucking and tossing so wildly he couldn't stand up to reach the valve!

The crew and residents of Rowlesburg got lucky that day ... the helper was still on the rear and its engineer was the late G. T. Jackson, a veteran with whom we had ridden for a number of shoves the year before. He did not panic and throw the train into emergency, which almost certainly would have smeared it all over the valley. With tender, loving care (from the *rear*, now) he made a series of light reductions that first slowed the train and then stopped it at 76 Fill.

An incident with a coal drag did not turn out as well. With four units on the front, three on the

WEST END

rear, 74 cars in the middle and *all four* of the headend crew sound asleep, the train went over the top at Blaser and started down the grade with the lead units still pulling. The rear man could not raise the headend on the radio, saw the speed leap to 40 mph and pulled the plug. The shock wave tore the train apart, flinging some 36 cars all over the landscape and closing both tracks.

The damage totaled about a million dollars and B&O decided to retire rather than repair track two. For 136 years The Hill had tried to take out the railroad without success... a sleepy crew took out half of it at 2:05 a.m. 11 February 1989.

The erosion process over eons of time had left the West End mountains unwashed and mean, as we have reported. The silver lining was coal... it was still in place and at Tunnelton the railroad reached the first massive deposits. Aside from some mines contiguous to B&O tracks, large de-

LOOKING WESTWARD at 76 Fill c. 1872 from the bed of a country road crossing, one can clearly see the steepness of the grade and have an appreciation for the large amount of fill needed to avoid a viaduct... note the individual standing next to the track right center. This was merely the first (and lowest) chasm that B&O would encounter on the Cheat River Grade... around the curve in the center of the photo is the approach to Buckeye Run.

B&O Museum

CHEAT RIVER GRADE

posits lie north of Tunnelton to Kingwood and a short railroad was built to tap them. By 1889 a TK&PRR joined B&O at Tunnelton ... it would become the West Virginia Northern by 1904. The WVN meanders through the coalfields to Kingwood (although it did not actually connect with the M&K sub at that point) ... for many years thousands of cars were handed to B&O for forwarding. By the mid-1940s there were 19 mines on the WVN, capable of producing over two hundred cars of coal a day. A typical day would produce about forty loads ... west and lake coal would be tacked onto a convenient coal car train; tide coal would be picked up and taken to M&K Junction where it would be forwarded east with M&K loads on a Keyser turn.

The WVN, which had shops at its terminus at Kingwood, had four Consolidations until dieselization c. 1950 ... two of the Consols were sold to the Preston Railroad at Hutton and reportedly still exist in a quarry near Hyndman PA.

WVN ceased operations in March 1991, purportedly because of financial problems at its parent company.

Of Mr. Latrobe's "central sixty miles," only seven miles remained when Tunnelton was reached. The first of those miles would prove to be the worst on the West End.

Pontin/C. S. Roberts Collection

AN EASTBOUND DRAG appears to have made it most of the way down the grade in one piece May 1951 as it crosses 76 Fill. The fill was widened and second track installed c. 1875. In the center of the photo we see the "Helper-on-train" light facing in both directions and just beyond in line with the fourth hopper a post-mounted sign that gives westbound engineers a car count to Buffalo Street in Rowlesburg. Rail and tie replacement, a perennial occupation on the West End, is about to begin. The country road that crosses the railroad here is just behind the photographer ... railroaders call it "Carrico Crossing" for the owner of contiguous property. If a reader should note on a geodetic map that this road leads to Tunnelton and is tempted to use it, we beg him to forget it. We tried it in May 1991, and while we ultimately got there, we did so only because God is kind to fools and historians.

WEST END

C. S. Roberts Collection

THE NEXT CHASM on the Cheat River Grade was Buckeye Hollow ... this view looks westward c. 1872. A stone wall was built across the base of the ravine and Mr. Latrobe originally planned to continue that wall to track level. Since there probably wasn't that much stone in the world, he decided on this handsome viaduct (a near-twin of more famous Tray Run Viaduct a mile or so to the west). Both structures were of cast iron connected by wrought iron bolts and rods ... the track was supported by heavy wooden beams. Buckeye was 340 feet long, straight and rose 46 feet from the stone wall. Platforms were extended for passengers to alight and admire the view of the canyon, which was becoming spectacular at this point. The blockhouse on the western side was built during the Civil War for protection from Rebel raiders ... it was probably being used as a telegraph office and shelter for track walkers at this time. It would go when Buckeye Hollow was filled.

TO BUILD A SINGLE TRACK railroad up the side of Laurel Mountain was an expensive engineering challenge ... to double track it was worse. At Buckeye Hollow, the choice between a walled fill or another viaduct was decided in favor of the former in 1882 and the project was completed in 1884. The wall approach was probably chosen for Buckeye because it could be built next to the viaduct while keeping it open for traffic ... there does not appear to have been any room next to The Hill for a new structure. This wall has been described as being "stupendous" and it certainly was that. This view, used frequently in B&O promotional literature, became immortalized when it graced the celery tray of B&O's famed Blue China in 1927. The stone mine at Manheim is visible on the right and the deep cuttings west of Tray Run Viaduct in the center. The shack is a telegraph office and track walkers' abode.

CHEAT RIVER GRADE

C. S. Roberts Collection

THIS EASTWARD SCENE from the top of Buckeye Wall gives visual evidence of its height simply because it towers over the treetops! At this point the railroad is only one and a half miles west of Rowlesburg and yet the view of the canyon is already magnificent. Lantz Ridge is the background mountain and Rowlesburg lies in the center of the photo. Many have testified, and we will confirm, that a westward trip up the Cheat River Grade is akin to the takeoff of a jet ... one seems to be soaring above the river at a steep angle and breathtaking pace. From here, the best is yet to come.

C. S. Roberts

THE CENTER OF BUCKEYE WALL began to subside in the early 1930s and by 1932 B&O had to do something about it. Strapped for money because of the Great Depression, B&O moved the mainline closer to the mountain with fill to get away from the wall ... the wiggle in the line of road is still apparent. This photo was taken from the other side of the river in late December 1978 in a snowstorm and clearly shows the subsidence. At one time or another, perhaps in 1932, B&O compensated the grade by raising the track through this rare piece of tangent ... the result is obvious. Let us caution students of the West End ... the wall is buried in scrub growth at the top and we found it one day by almost stepping over the edge. As this photo indicates, B&O has dumped a lot of fill by the wall over the years but it is still quite high ... your first step would be a long one.

WEST END

THE NEXT GASH in the side of Laurel Mountain is Tray Run and it is a big one, deep and steep. The taking of this photo from Lantz Ridge in late December 1978 involved your writer in adventures we will relate later ... as our nerves have long since stopped quivering, we now gaze upon it with equanimity and pride for it dramatically epitomizes Cheat River Grade and its three principal obstacles; Buckeye, Tray Run and Buckhorn. Moving from left to right, we first see Buckeye Hollow and its wall. Tray Run Viaduct in the center is obvious ... follow the dark line of the right of way to the far right and one will see the horseshoe trace over Buckhorn Wall which is just out of sight. The slices in the side of the mountain are apparent, numerous and so high that they dwarf the railroad. Not seen are the retaining walls *below* the line of road ... they total eight just between Tray Run and Buckhorn and some are quite high and wide. With full knowledge of all the tribulations on the grades east and west of this scene, we must say that the Cheat River Grade gives the ultimate tribute to the courage, determination and resourcefulness of Mr. Latrobe and his men who built this stretch of road with picks, shovels, black powder, horses, strong backs and guts.

FROM ANY ANGLE, the original Tray Run Viaduct was comely ... this eastward view dates from c. 1872. We do not know its exact completion date (or that of Buckeye) because these hollows were originally spanned by temporary wooden trestles, but it was definitely opened for traffic by the summer of 1856. The back of the seal of the State of West Virginia features this viaduct, proving that even feisty mountaineers knew sublimity when they beheld it.

B&O Museum

CHEAT RIVER GRADE

B&O Museum

THE GREAT TRAY RUN VIADUCT, seen here c. 1872, would receive our nomination as the most beautiful viaduct ever constructed by man. Form may follow function, as engineers love to say ... in this case they are as of one. One grants that Buckeye Viaduct was a near twin, but it was straight ... the curve of Tray Run gives it the touch of grace that makes it a work of splendor. The span of Tray Run was 445 feet and it rose 58 feet from the top of its supporting wall. It cost $36,049 ... its inherent elegance made it worth every penny.

THE PLATFORMS on both Buckeye and Tray Run Viaducts were built for the viewing pleasure of passengers ... at least through the late 1850s day trains would stop for ten minutes weather permitting. We doubt if this nice touch survived the pressure of the Civil War and traffic growth. The blockhouse is a war relic, built to the same plan as the one at Buckeye ... the small shack is a telegraph office. Mr. Latrobe gave Albert Fink credit for the twin viaducts, although we suspect it was a joint project. This photo was taken c. 1872.

B&O Museum

WEST END

E. L. Thompson/B&OHS

FOR ALL ITS BEAUTY, the original Tray Run Viaduct's days were numbered when double tracking of the West End began ... as it turned out, the viaduct was the last impediment to that project. Construction of the replacement viaduct began in 1885 and was completed by early 1888. The new viaduct is not an eyesore as we see from this photo taken 8 June 1947 ... it has its own symmetry and stolid style and even boasts some pink stone trimming not apparent in colorless photos. The new viaduct was built next to the original on the hill side ... at lower right portions of the original support wall are all that remain.

C. S. Roberts Collection

THE NEW VIADUCT, officially Bridge 94, consists of four 90 foot arches, is 443 feet long and on a grade of 1.92%. This view of the statuesque structure was taken shortly after completion in 1888. Laurel Mountain was just as vicious as Backbone and Briery ... rock scaling on the Cheat River Grade was a career for generations of B&O personnel. By 1940 B&O had to install a 532 foot trailing point siding off track 1 just the other side of the viaduct to hold cars and equipment in aid of this ongoing activity. For at least six years MOW crews blasted the first cut east of the viaduct and then switched to the west cut for another ten years ... the siding was not removed until February of 1957. Track 2 had to be closed during these operations, which explains why so many photographers recorded eastbound trains on the westbound track.

CHEAT RIVER GRADE

A WESTBOUND QD EXTRA with a 7600 on the point is working hard on the viaduct in the late 1940s. This shot was taken from the east bank of the Cheat River near Manheim and would not be possible today because trees block the view.
William Hoffman II Collection

THE GRADE swings westward to leave the Cheat River Canyon at Clements Fountain (known simply as the Flower Garden to B&O people) and in the doing presents viewers with a last dramatic view of the valley of the Cheat. This photo shows the garden and fountain on 8 June 1947 ... Buckhorn Wall begins just beyond the curve. We suspect that the Flower Garden was created in the 1850s ... we know it was there in the late 1880s, complete with fountain. There was a telegraph office at Buckhorn until 1904 and a track walker's shack nearby for many years thereafter ... the garden was maintained by the walker until that job was eliminated and, surprisingly, was kept up by MOW personnel as late as 1950. The ravine B&O crosses is Buckhorn Run, but the stream does not run under the wall. B&O dammed the stream and diverted it into a stone-lined channel which ran to a culvert under the tracks to the left and fed the fountain by gravity ... excess water was simply fed over the edge to the right. The dam and channel are extant but impossible to photograph because of overgrowth.

E. L. Thompson/B&OHS

WEST END

THE FOUNTAIN at the Flower Garden 21 October 1945 is still functional and invites the eye to the overlook of the valley. A track supervisor told us that the concrete pool and fountain were bulldozed over the edge in the early 1950s and a search by him for the remnants was unsuccessful. Interestingly, he was also searching for some sign of a locomotive that reportedly went down the ravine around the turn-of-the-century and was abandoned ... again without success even though he scoured the area with a metal detector.

E. L. Thompson/B&OHS

C. S. Roberts Collection

THE CHEAT RIVER GORGE from Clements Fountain in the 1880s was, for the westward passenger, his last glance at this majestic valley. From this vantage point over four hundred feet above the river, the typical traveler in that century regarded the Cheat as the "American Alps" and ranked it with Niagara Falls as one of the two sights all must see.

THE ONLY CHANGE in the view from the Flower Garden by 8 June 1947 has to do with intrusion by man ... the M&K subdivision track on the east bank and a road on the west bank. Today, even in the dead of winter, tree growth has curtained this inspiring tableau from the eyes of man.

E. L. Thompson/B&OHS

CHEAT RIVER GRADE

B&O Museum

THE BALTIMORE AND OHIO RAILROAD COMPANY
EASTERN REGION
Safety Above Everything

CUMBERLAND DIVISION

IMMEDIATELY WEST of Clements Fountain, the railroad crossed Buckhorn Run on a very deep fill buttressed by an enormous stone retaining wall named, naturally enough, Buckhorn Wall. It lies in such a position that it is impossible for a photographer to get a perspective on it that portrays just how gigantic a structure B&O had to build. The downhill slope at this point is at an angle of about 20-25% for over four hundred feet to the Cheat River ... the wall itself at its deepest point is about 100 feet, the equivalent of a ten-story building. Tree growth in this mid-1870's view has hidden most of the wall and gives the erroneous impression that it is a minor affair. Over the years B&O has dumped fill over the side to the extent that most of the wall is underground. The top of the wall was raised several feet in 1875 and the roadbed widened toward the hill in 1891 ... the roadbed has also been heightened and shifted hillwards several times. As late as 1979 the roadbed was lifted about three feet, an action that probably saved your writer's life as we shall see. Lore has it that the stone for Buckhorn Wall came from the quarry of one Jack Frock near Fairmont, although that seems like a long haul for such a quantity of stone. At right center of this photo one can see the stone channel that directs the waters of Buckhorn Run to the fountain in the Flower Garden. The grade here is typically severe, ranging from 2.00% on the wall to 2.25% near the camera. There is a "Little Buckhorn" Run and Wall several curves downgrade from here ... it was realigned in 1908 and should not be confused with the "real" Buckhorn Wall.

WEST END

WE MARCHED the two miles from Blaser to the Wall on 28 December 1979 with the hope that snow cover and lack of foliage would enable us to study the area. We snapped Gateway 97 Engine 4097 at 2:40 p.m. almost as an afterthought and recocked our camera. As the tenth or so car came into sight at the east end of the Wall, we saw a lot of smoke and assumed we were looking at a hotbox. As the car reached the west end of the Wall, we saw with horror that the sideframe of the car's leading truck was riding on the rail and the leading wheel on the ties ... mercifully, as events unfolded, the wheel had dropped on the *inside* of the rail. With a cocked camera on our chest, we confess that taking the photo of the century did not enter our mind and confirm the reader's suspicion that as photographers we would make excellent plumbers. Our first frenzied thought was to roll down the slope for several hundred feet to get away from the train, which was now grinding car after car onto the ground with a sound that we would not care to hear again. At least one brain cell was functioning and informed us that the train would get to the bottom first, so we dove for the wall below the closest telephone pole and hugged it with a fervor that the most passionless woman would find exciting, hoping that the falling cars would pass over us. After what seemed to us to be several lifetimes, the grinding stopped ... we risked an infantryman's peek, saw the cars were still upright and had a new unpleasant thought. The headend was out of sight and the helper might assume that the train was simply hung up and would give that whole mess a maximum effort shove to our detriment. (It turned out there was no helper, a contributory cause of the derailment.) We decided to run to the west to the cover of a hillock and did so with a speed that would have qualified us for the Olympics. From cover, we saw that sixteen cars were on the ground and we leisurely walked to the headend and informed a chagrined engineer that he had a problem. Our fly-fly friends have a delightful expression to the effect that "any landing you can walk away from is a good one," which would paraphrase nicely to derailments. B&O Historical Society members familiar with this episode refer to this spot as a piece of West Virginia that shall remain forever green. Technically they are wrong, but we will have to say that we have not noticed any problem with constipation since this event.

C. S. Roberts

CHEAT RIVER GRADE

C. S. Roberts

HAVING FORTIFIED ourselves with a few wee drams, we returned to the site the next day and had the good fortune to meet the late Mr. Snyder (his first name escapes us), track supervisor, and his splendid crew. The cars had been rerailed and pulled out by 1:00 a.m. ... the line was open by 3:00 p.m. Gateway 97 passed on track 2, this time with a helper. The entire crew had heard of our experience and *each one* touched us for luck ... apparently we have joined our relative Thomas Swann as part of the heritage of the West End. Amazingly, only one of this crew of about ten men had ever experienced a derailment even though they worked next to moving trains every day. We learned that the basic cause of the derailment was an overloaded gondola with steel beams improperly distributed ... on a severe curve still superelevated for Amtrak trains, the rail rolled over. As one can see from these photos, our luck had held because the trucks either rode the web or dropped inside the rail. Mr. Snyder informed us that he had just raised the roadbed within the year and replaced the inner rail ... he flatly stated we would have been in deep trouble had this not occurred. He added that we owed a debt to continuous rail ... had it been jointed, our show would have been over. The lack of a helper aggravated the situation. He also informed us that unbalanced loads were a problem only with QD trains ... the load in drags is so evenly distributed that rail rollover is rare. *Gateway 97/Almost Charley's/Gateway to Heaven*. Seven years later we slipped on a stone and almost fell off the wall. Eight years later we exposed our most precious part to relieve ourselves over the wall and the largest wasp in the world alighted thereon for a stay of interminable length. We are sure that the reader will understand with sympathy our Oath not to return to Buckhorn Wall again.

C. S. Roberts

WEST END

BUCKHORN WALL started to subside over the years and B&O reacted by inching the roadbed closer to The Hill ... compare the distance from the wall to the inner rail in these photos and the 1870's view shown earlier. The amount of fill dumped over the years is also apparent ... only about one quarter of the wall is now above the surface. During 1986-87, B&O invested in major repairs. Liquid concrete was pumped into the fitted stones to make the entire visible wall a solid mass ... stones were removed from the center of the wall and buttresses installed as shown. Numerous horizontal tension bars reinforce the repair ... notice the platform on the hill side which provides access to the through-bolts. Also note the thickness of the wall in the slice and keep in mind only the top quarter is shown ... the massiveness of the entire structure boggles the imagination, particularly when one recalls that it was built in the early 1850s. These photos were taken in October 1987 when the project was just about completed and commemorate the Day of the Giant Wasp.

C. S. Roberts

C. S. Roberts

C. S. Roberts

CHEAT RIVER GRADE

WATER was available just west of Buckhorn Wall in the early years ... this photo from the early 1870s looks down the Cheat River. The jug is rather solidly constructed of stone, as were most of Mr. Latrobe's early installations. Cheat River Grade is short and does not face the prevailing tonnage. As tender capacity increased, it was found unnecessary to provide water on this grade ... by 1889 water was available only at Rowlesburg to the east and Newburg to the west.

B&O Museum

C. S. Roberts

THE TOP of the Cheat River Grade is a few feet in front of the engine on this coal car train ... the locomotive is on the vertical curve. This summit cut was opened c. 1912 along with other substantial improvements on the line of road west of this point, which we will detail shortly. The original line looped around this hill on the left ... its roadbed is now a public road. This photo was taken 28 December 1979, a few hours before we met Gateway 97 on Buckhorn Wall. Blaser interlocker is a few hundred yards to the west at the exit from the cut.

WEST END

E. L. Thompson/B&OHS

BLASER (K) on 19 October 1947 as Extra West 7200 with 95 coal cars pounds by with a stack clean enough to satisfy even Wild Bill Henry. The original line met the new line from the left at this point, although it was known as Anderson until 1912. We are quite sure this tower was built c. 1912 when the line was relocated. The call letter K was used at Anderson, however, for many years prior to that date ... the name Blaser (for a B&O official) was substituted c. 1910. K was closed 18 December 1956 and handled remotely from West

E. L. Thompson/B&OHS

End ... in the mid-1980s West End was closed and K handled remotely from MK. There was also a tower KN at Tunnelton to the west for many years as we shall see ... it closed in late 1912 or early 1913.

QD 196 Engine 7610 and 49 cars rolls by K on 19 October 1947 in this view looking westward toward Tunnelton. The road just to the right of the tower traces the original line. This plant was modernized during 1957 in conjunction with control transfer to West End.

CHEAT RIVER GRADE

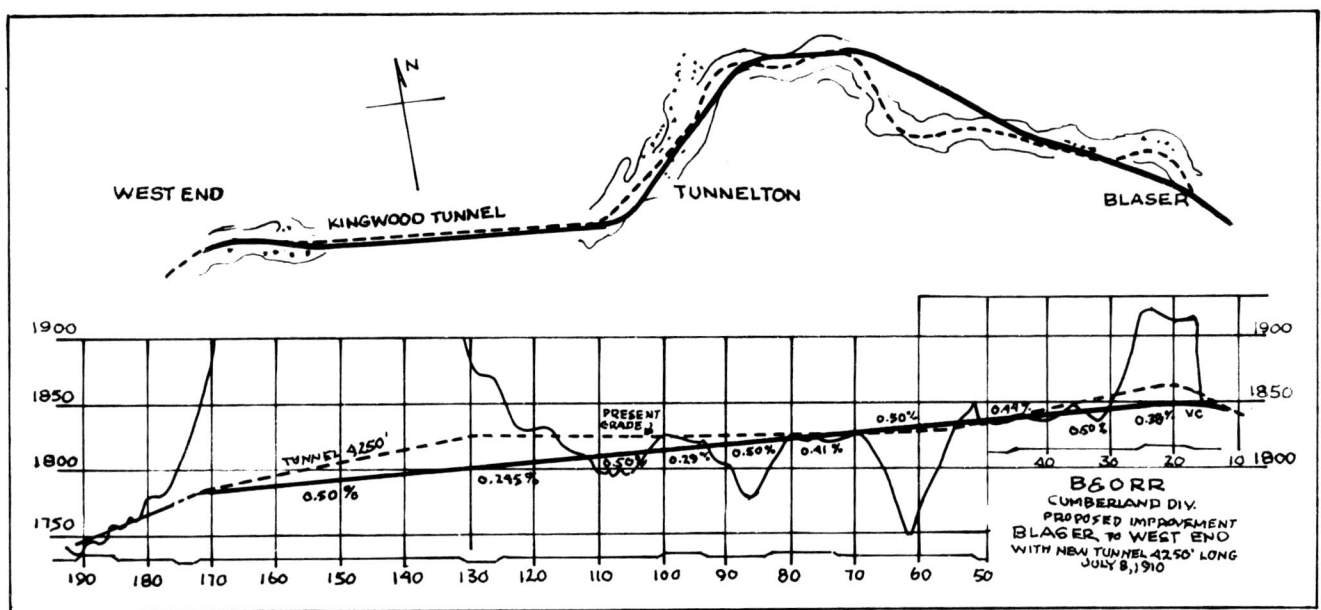

THE WEST END was literally rebuilt, at great expense, in the 1910-1913 period as we have reported. The most urgent, and most costly, improvements were made at Tunnelton ... more exactly, from Blaser to West End. This drawing, taken from a company proposal dated 8 July 1910, gives an excellent summary of the problem and the solution. Monstrous Kingwood Tunnel (which will be treated in detail in the next chapter on Newburg Grade) was 4,250 feet long on a 1.00% grade facing the tonnage ... helpers had to stay on to the east portal. Worse, the tunnel was in effect single track ... that it was a gauntlet track was of little solace. Eastward trains enjoyed a slight dip to Tunnelton, but then hit a sharp and curvy climb to Blaser before the plunge down the Cheat River Grade. The solution was draconian, expensive and effective ... bore a new twin-track tunnel on a lesser grade (.50%), eliminate almost all the curves and, through extensive filling, reduce and compensate the gradient to Blaser to under .50%. In less than two years from proposal to fruition, the new alignment was open ... B&O now had three tracks from Hardman at the foot of Newburg Grade to Blaser at a cost of almost two million dollars for the Tunnelton improvement alone. The money was well spent. In 1926 B&O engineers summarized the dollar savings over the preceding fourteen years and they were impressive. In addition, the line was ready for mallet locomotives, longer trains and increased traffic.

B&O COALED directly from the mine mouth at Tunnelton for many years ... this facility predates the 1910-1912 improvements and is connected directly to the tipple. While this scene looks eastward with a westbound train, most coaling activity at Tunnelton was for eastbound trains. The mainline was moved left and lowered during the improvements so the overhead conveyor was extended to the left. As this photo implies, the West End is now in the heart of the vast coal beds underlying the region. As coal operators are wont to point out, almost all of the cost of coal is transportation ... cheap fuel was one of the few advantages B&O gained with the West End.

B&O Museum

WEST END

Gary Schlerf Collection

THE NEW "TIPPLE" at Tunnelton in the late 1940s services Extra East 7617 ... the carriage under the conveyor will move into position over the tender and give a refill. Sand was also available if needed. The cinder mound at the bottom of this photo indicates that ballast cleaning was recently accomplished. More modern steam power had sufficient coal and water capacity to load at Grafton and make it to M&K Junction and the reverse. Newburg Grade helpers would also coal here ... the helper station at Hardman only had a clamshell capability. This facility was gone in the early 1950s, a victim of dieselization.

B&OHS

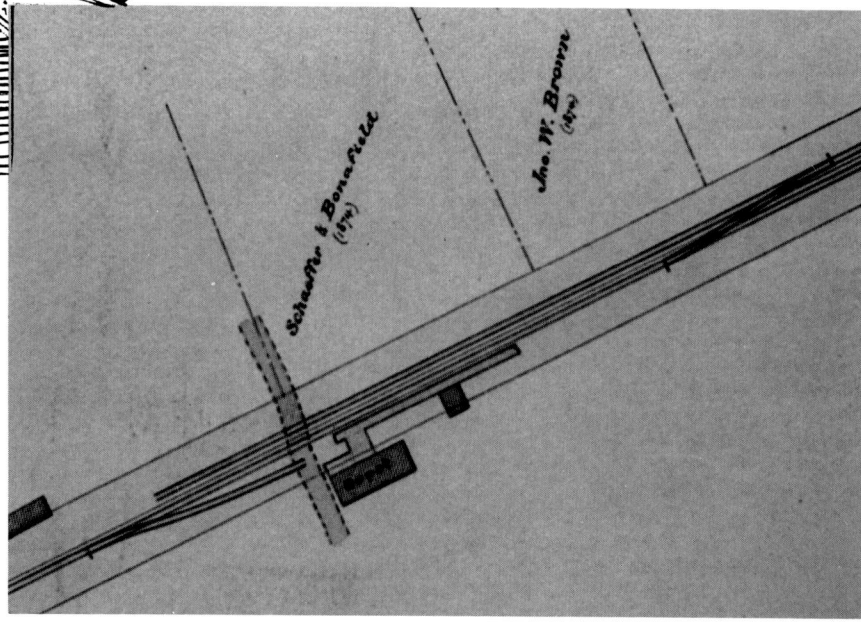

TUNNELTON c. 1873 was something less than a thriving town although it did boast a depot. The single track to the left approaches the horrendous Kingwood Tunnel, named for the county seat of West Virginia's Preston County which lies about six miles to the north as the crow flies. This town, rather obviously, acquired its name from the tunnel. Future coal mining in the region would spur development.

CHEAT RIVER GRADE

C. S. Roberts Collection

TUNNELTON was booming by the time of this photo c. 1909. The new 1907 depot can be seen on the left, a train at full strain in the center and some narrow-gauge mine cars being pulled by a dinky locomotive on the right. We suspect that this view looks westward, but we are not positive. The whole town in general and this area in particular was devastated for the 1910-12 realignment. Interlockers were installed at each end of Kingwood Tunnel in 1896 and we believe this tower was built then ... since a more modern interlocker was installed at Tunnelton in 1902, the tower may date from that year. Certainly it was gone, as reported, in late 1912 or early 1913.

Gary Schlerf Collection

SURELY ONE of the shortest-lived stations in history, this attractive brick depot was finished in 1907 and gone by 1913, if not sooner.

THE LATEST AND LAST station at Tunnelton is this distinctive structure, opened in early 1913 along with the freight house in the distance. Pictured looking eastward in December 1977, both buildings survive.

C. S. Roberts

WEST END

C. S. Roberts

ERECTION of this pedestrian overpass was part of the 1910-12 improvement and, if nothing else, provided an excellent platform for photographers as will be shown. This photo was taken in October of 1987 ... the structure is extant.

THE VIEW east from the overpass c. 1920 ... the white slash in the center of the photo marks the location of an underpass installed as part of the great improvement. The track on the left is the old line to the old tunnel ... the two on the right lead to the new tunnel.

Gary Schlerf Collection

CHEAT RIVER GRADE

BY 4 MAY 1991, the scene from the overpass hasn't changed all that much over three-quarters of a century. The building beyond the signal bridge is the "new" station. The line to the old tunnel, long since closed, has been assigned for the use of the West Virginia Northern since at least 1981.
C. S. Roberts

STILL PERCHED on the overpass, we spun 180 degrees and took this westward view 4 May 1991. Around the curve will be found the Kingwood Tunnels ... the road on the extreme right was originally the path of the 1850's shoofly over the ridge to West End.
C. S. Roberts

Chapter 8

Newburg Grade

Tunnelton to East Grafton

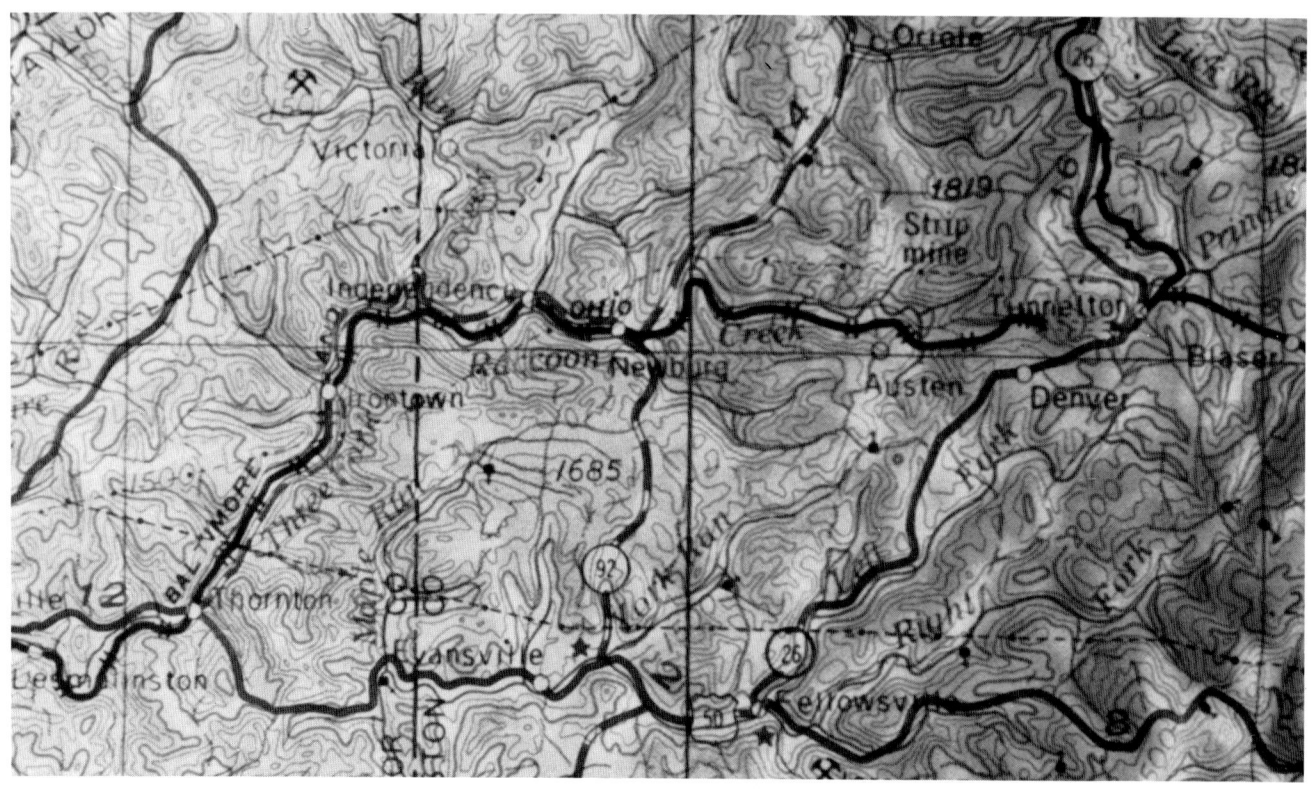

C. S. Roberts

THE WEST END'S final descent from the Great Barrier begins at Blaser, drops through the Kingwood Tunnels at Tunnelton, slides downhill through Austen to Newburg (the end of Mr. Latrobe's "central sixty miles") and then continues the decline on easier gradients through Independence, Irontown, Thornton and Lesmalinston. The Hardman Helper Station is at the "d" in Independence. A few hundred yards west of Lesmalinston the post-1911 West End Subdivision ends at GN Tower ... prior to that year the old Third Division continued to the eastern outskirts of Grafton to meet the old Fourth Division.

NEWBURG GRADE

Early travelers and chroniclers of the West End progressing from east to west were running out of words and energy once they left Tunnelton and started downhill to Grafton. They would wearily acknowledge the Kingwood Tunnel, issue a few words about Newburg Grade, note the helper station at Newburg and then come back to life when Grafton was reached, no doubt refreshed by the thought of food and drink. Cranberry Grade at least merited a full paragraph ... Newburg Grade had to make do with a sentence or so. Mr. Latrobe's "central sixty miles" ended at Newburg and so did their prose.

We assume their literary somnolence was related to the fact that their locomotive was silently drifting down these two grades and they concluded that they were enjoying interludes in the main performance.

We have made the reader painfully aware of the nature of Cranberry Grade. Newburg Grade was almost as bad and in some ways worse. If Cranberry did not exist, Newburg would be regarded as the most arduous mainline tonnage grade in the world of railroading.

Parenthetically, we should note that we have taken some poetic license by treating the road from Tunnelton to Blaser as part of the chapter on the Cheat River Grade. Actually, the original Newburg Grade began at Newburg and ended at Blaser (Anderson), a distance of some nine miles ... operationally, however, Newburg Grade ended at the Kingwood Tunnel at the west end of Tunnelton.

When the helper station was moved back from Newburg to Hardman early in this century, the official grade was eleven miles long. This contrasted with Cranberry's length of eleven and a half miles from Bridge 92 to Terra Alta.

A more valid comparison would be to measure those portions of each climb with gradients exceeding 1.9%. From east of McMillan to Terra Alta, this works out to eight and a half miles; from east of Newburg to West End, five miles. With Cranberry's ruling gradient of 2.40% and Newburg's 2.00%, the former wins the dubious title of the worst grade on the West End. Newburg, then, has always been a bridesmaid, never a bride.

Maiden or not, Newburg Grade lost her virginity at birth. Her original Kingwood Tunnel was the longest and most malicious of the six on the West End, relieved only in degree by Murray Tunnel in the middle of the grade. Newburg has curves galore, including the near-horseshoe Brains Curve, and numerous deep fills ... Fill 83 is one hundred feet deep. Her approaches from Grafton to Newburg involved over twelve miles of .6% uncompensated gradient, enough to make this stretch still another helper grade for over a half-century.

And the scenery on Newburg was uninspiring in the early days; it became downright bleak as mining and coke-making flourished. Even today the scars mar the landscape and make it easy to see why Newburg Grade never found a husband.

As always, we will tell the detailed story of the building and evolution of Newburg Grade in captions to illustrations, presenting only an overview in the following paragraphs.

Newburg Grade was built as a single track line ... double-tracking was, in comparison to some other sections of the West End, somewhat less burdensome because much of the line of road passed around lower, more rounded hills and along creek beds. The process was completed in the 1870s ... completed, that is, except for the old Kingwood Tunnel. The best B&O could manage was a double-track gauntlet through that bore.

The 1910-12 improvements on the West End in preparation for mallet locomotives involved a staggering dollar expenditure and a very large portion was spent on the line between Grafton and Blaser.

First, an entirely new yard was built at Grafton ... it winds along Three Forks Creek for over two miles toward Newburg and was opened in 1912. It was built as a flat yard with ten forty-car eastbound class tracks and seven sixty-car westbound tracks. The new yard became part of the Monongah Division and the western boundary of the West End was moved east to new GN Tower.

The seven and a half mile line from GN to a new helper station at Hardman was fully compensated and the ruling gradient reduced to .5%. This improvement was very significant because it eliminated helper service in this district and also enabled road locomotives to handle full-rated tonnage from Fairmont as well as Grafton ... it went into service in July of 1911.

And a desperately needed eleven miles of third track was installed between Hardman and Blaser. Murray Tunnel was deroofed and widened for three tracks. Most important of all, a new two-track Kingwood Tunnel was punched through Laurel Mountain parallel to the old tunnel but on an easier gradient which enabled helpers to cut off

WEST END

at West End. The grand opening was in May 1912.

In physical form, Newburg Grade and approaches remained unchanged until 1973 when the third track was removed . . . as of this date, it is still double-tracked.

Our guided tour from Cumberland and Patterson Creek on the east to GN Tower on the west will be completed at the end of this chapter . . . the reader will have seen the West End in all its glory and agony and witnessed 142 years of its history.

From a height above sea level at Cumberland of 640 feet to 999 feet at Grafton involves a rise of only 359 feet in about one hundred miles. For what B&O had to do to get and stay there, it certainly doesn't seem like very much was gained.

Now, dear reader, we will take you to the meat of the story. Gaze at those monstrous grades from west to east where the tonnage flows and recall Mr. Latrobe's comment, "that they require some increase in motive power was known."

Mr. Latrobe and his successor engineers prepared the battlefield. Now B&O's infantry, if you will, had to fight the war. And to do that, they needed *power*.

C. S. Roberts Collection

OF ALL THE ADVERSITIES that B&O faced in the construction and operation of the West End, the most ruinous was the original Kingwood Tunnel. Construction of the 4,100+ foot long tunnel began in 1849 and by the Spring of 1850 Mr. Latrobe happily reported that "the tunnel is generally in compact slate rock favorable for excavation . . . promising to stand, for a time at least, without artificial support. There is little or no water thus far in the trunk of the tunnel, a very favorable circumstance." The standard width of 22 feet for double track appeared ample. In short order, Mr. Latrobe began to learn the wisdom implicit in the military warning "never underestimate the enemy." At this location, Laurel Mountain consisted almost entirely of porous shale. As tunneling progressed, The Hill sucked in air, mixed it with water and then began belching. And Laurel Mountain was very flatulent . . . when it unloaded, Mr. Latrobe learned, it "frequently fall(s) in such large masses as to block up the tunnel for a considerable distance, to a depth of 8 or 10 feet." Timber supports fared no better than at other tunnels on the West End and removal was perilous. In the end, arching of stone and brick with cast iron ribs was the only answer and it was not until the Spring of 1857 that it was completed. Since the railroad opened in 1853, the interim four years was marked by sporadic operations, to say the least. In 1854-55 the tunnel was closed twice, once for two-three weeks and again for ten days. In early 1855, it was decided to run a railroad over the hill for two miles at about a ten percent grade . . . it is a measure of B&O's desperation that it was completed in three weeks. Locomotives could only handle *one car at a time* over this bypass and, in wet weather, frequently slid backwards with locked wheels. (There is some question just when this bypass was built . . . some sources imply that it was constructed several years earlier to move rails and construction materials.) Even after B&O managed to keep the tunnel open, it was a serious chokepoint . . . the most that B&O could fit into the tunnel was a double track gauntlet. Technically the West End was entirely double tracked with the completion of the second Tray Run Viaduct in 1888 . . . if one winks at Kingwood Tunnel. The tunnel was also on a 1.0% grade facing the tonnage . . . notice the ventilator shaft at the top of the ridge which Mr. Latrobe had the foresight to install. The approach cut, as one can see, was no small project . . . 90,000 cubic yards were removed from the shaft and another 110,000 from the cut. The cast iron ribs had to be replaced constantly and drainage was always a problem. On 18 December 1956, when Blaser Tower was closed and operated remotely from West End, B&O stopped using the tunnel and it was plugged at both ends in 1962. Both Mr. Latrobe's Shade and Laurel Mountain cheered.

THE NEW KINGWOOD TUNNEL exits on the east side about 24 feet below the old bore, thus allowing a reduction in gradient to .5% and enabling helpers to cut off before entering the tunnel. These advantages came at a price of extensive excavation as can be seen in this photo taken 27 July 1949 as EL5a 7154 leads 52 cars with the assistance of LL1 7041 and EL1a 7102 on the rear. The road across the top of the photo follows the path of the ancient bypass and should be taken by the West End student as a history lesson. This slice of Laurel Mountain graphically illustrates the unstable composition of The Hill in this locale. The new tunnel is about 4,250 feet long and was opened in May 1912 with, you can be sure, very thick sidewalls and arches of concrete and brick. Drainage problems were worsened by the lesser gradient ... we have rarely visited this area without finding crews working in the tunnel cleaning out muck and reballasting. And the reader should not assume that The Hill has given up ... the *new* bore had to be extensively relined in 1945.

E. L. Thompson/B&OHS

Gary Schlerf Collection

WEST END c. 1912 just after the opening of the new tunnel, looking west from over the tunnel portals with the new tower (WS) in the distance on the right ... note the helper pocket between the two new lefthand tracks. The original track is on the right, of course, and would only be used for westbound traffic in the future. The bypass road can be seen at upper left ... it wanders around the curve and crosses the railroad just beyond. There are coal mines on the hillside just behind the tower.

THE WEST PORTALS of the two tunnels are at almost the same elevation as can be seen on 17 October 1947 as Train 29 Engines 4026-5093 with 22 cars and two cabooses drifts downhill through the old bore. The old portal has been soaked in gunite by this time. The original WS interlocking tower was located just to the right of the old portal and had to be protected from blasting when the new tunnel was under construction. The operator in the old tower must have been a busy man in the gauntlet track era ... not only did he have to squeeze together eastward and westward traffic, he also had to get helpers back through the tunnel. West End has been called just that for many years ... we have seen references as early as 1884. A coaling facility served the two eastward tracks for a number of years after 1912 ... we assume the fuel came from a nearby mine.

E. L. Thompson/B&OHS

WEST END

WEST END (WS) Tower was still active and in good condition in December 1977, but it was closed c. 1985 and the interlocking plant taken out shortly thereafter. When B&O decided to keep helpers attached to the Glades and beyond, WS lost its mission. The tower, which is very similar to but not a twin of Mountain Lake Park, still stands.

C. S. Roberts

ABOUT ONE MILE downgrade from West End, B&O met the Greenbrier, Cheat and Elk Railroad, a coal line that reached into the hills via three switchbacks and was serviced by Shay No. 6 which laid over on the tracks in the foreground. Here, on 19 June 1951, DF5 F7 287 leads a drag upgrade.

H. N. Barr, Sr.

SHAY NO. 6 of the GC&ERR was left in the hills when the rails were taken up, but that wasn't the end of her story. A gentleman from Kingwood somehow dragged her down to B&O rails and was negotiating with the railroad to haul her out when B&O ended the discussions by derailing a train at the site and customizing her. We found her in December 1977 a bit the worse for wear and noticed that a wag had spray painted "Penn Central" on her boiler. She was gone by the following October, reportedly to the Cass Scenic Railroad. Some years later, by an odd twist of fate, we happened to meet the engineer of the train involved.

C. S. Roberts

NEWBURG GRADE

B&O Museum

THE SIXTH and last tunnel on the West End was Murrays at Austen, about two miles downgrade from Kingwood Tunnel. By the time of construction of this bore, Mr. Latrobe was a veteran and ordered a width of 24 feet so the inevitable arching would not preclude two tracks. This c. 1872 view looks eastward with two tracks in place and ineluctable rock scaling in progress. This 310 foot tunnel wasn't quite as bad as the others ... it was daylighted for triple-tracking in early 1911. Early travelers noted that the rails lay on a bed of coal ... if it wasn't mistaken for shale, one wonders if the tunnel floor ever caught fire.

EXCAVATION at Murrays Tunnel in the Fall of 1910 hints at the method generally used on the West End to daylight bores. First a shoofly was cut around the tunnel and rails laid to keep traffic moving. Then the top of the tunnel was removed to the arch ... explosives blew down the arch, the rubble was cleared and the side wall cut through to the shoofly.

C. S. Roberts Collection

WEST END

E. L. Thompson/B&OHS

MURRAYS TUNNEL CUT can be seen behind helpers 7153-7133 as they shove 54 cars on Extra East 7170 on 27 July 1949. Austen Tower (WA) was located in this vicinity ... it was closed when the tunnel was deroofed.

NEWBURG GRADE

C. S. Roberts

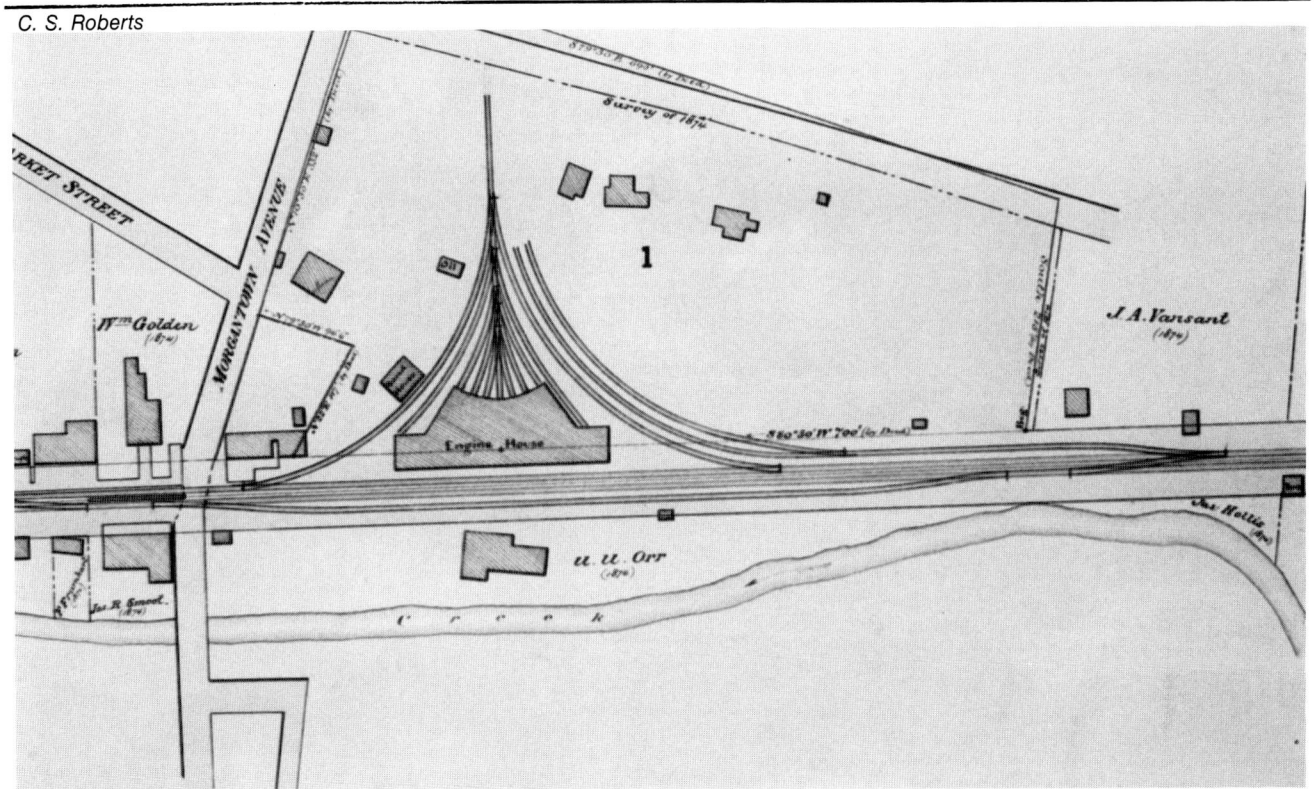

THE VERY FIRST major helper station on the West End was Newburg, shown on this company map in the late 1870s. Newburg faced the tonnage, unlike Piedmont on the east end of the Great Barrier, and was the west end of Mr. Latrobe's "central sixty miles." Since B&O was open to Fairmont west of Grafton by 22 June 1852 and we believe Rowlesburg did not become a helper station until 1879, Newburg was for 27 years the main base for assaults on The Hill. This site was Simpson's Water Station when the line opened, but was renamed Newburg by mid-1854 ... we do not know the source of the name. The first engine house at Newburg burned down in 1854-55 and the second was destroyed by Rebels in 1863 ... the one shown here was presumably the third one. The grade stiffened to 2.18% just east of the water jugs shown at extreme right and was severe for six miles to the east end of Kingwood Tunnel. We know that a new passenger station was built c. 1869 in the vicinity of the crossing of Morgantown Avenue and the railroad and believe it was in the northeastern corner, but we are not sure. Raccoon Creek parallels the railroad in this view, but shortly turns northerly and goes under the railroad.

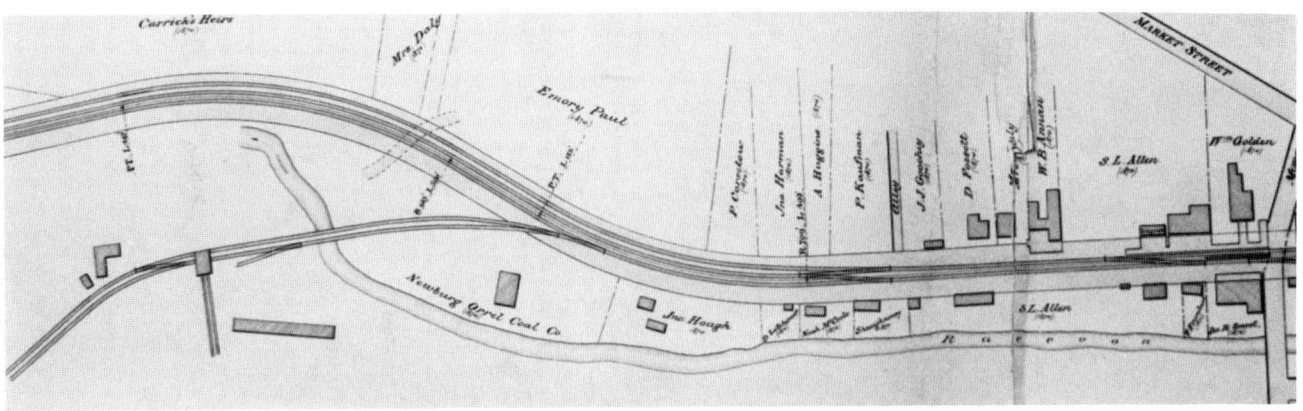

C. S. Roberts

THIS VIEW of Newburg, again in the late 1870s, shows the railroad west of the engine house area ... note the numerous crossovers and the triple track which continues for about a mile to Independence to the west. The Newburg Orrel Coal Company has an impressive facility at this time and apparently was giving B&O some nice loadings.

WEST END

LOOKING TO THE WEST in the early 1870s, this photo shows an early hexagonal stone water jug and the Newburg engine house complex in the distance. The town is obviously thriving and paying the smoky price of being a helper station. Curiously, the penstock serves the westbound, downgrade track.

B&O Museum

NEWBURG GRADE

A COMPANION photo to the preceding one, and apparently taken on the same day in the early 1870s, this view looks eastward and provides the eager historian with a classic dichotomy. We know the wooden, topless water jug was built in 1869. We notice the wooden rail joint bars, the replacement frog, the stub-rail switch and what is apparently the equivalent of "blue flag" warning blocks on the westbound track near the closest car ... one assumes the latter is to protect the photographer. We are quite sure water was available to the west at the engine house. Yet there are no water spouts or penstocks serving the eastbound, upgrade main line. The grade here is about .74% and Newburg Grade proper does not begin for another half-mile. In the Operations chapter to come, your servant will happily practice the historian's perogative of taking a few tiny clues and producing a Great Tome of conclusions, studiously avoiding small errors while sweeping forward to what cynics would call the grand fallacy. *Why no water service here for eastbound tonnage?* Joy or peril for our theory?

B&O Museum

WEST END

THE MESSAGE on the back of this postcard dated 6 October 1910 opines, "I find this a dirty town." The Mother Hubbard center-cab Consolidation ("Snapper" on the B&O) taking water at the west end of the engine house dates this northward-looking view of Newburg c. 1905. The mainline penstock by the fourth car from the caboose on the westbound train will not harm your historian's theory of early operations. Notice that the wye tracks have been removed and a metal-roofed reservoir built on the hill above the engine house. The Newburg (NE) telegraph office and depot is in clear view behind the sixth and seventh cars from the rear of the train.

OUR VALUATION photographer with the bad shutter and no sense of composition recorded the metal-roofed reservoir at Newburg ... it was built in 1875 with a diameter of 64 feet and a bowl 17 feet deep. Supplying water was a constant problem on the West End and Newburg was one of the most troublesome spots. Constant well drilling at Newburg never completely alleviated the situation and B&O actually had to haul water in tank car trains during dry summers. With mallets coming into service, B&O built a 34′ high dam on Raccoon Creek with a 1200 acre watershed and a capacity of over twenty million gallons ... it was finished in February 1912 at a cost of $134,910 and piped water from Newburg to the new helper station at Hardman. Even then there were shortages, e.g. in 1937 crews were warned that water was short.

NEWBURG GRADE

THE NEWBURG station and engine house around the turn of the century was an active place ... passengers boarding trains and pedestrians had to dodge helper moves as well as dig cinders from their eyes.

Gary Schlerf Collection

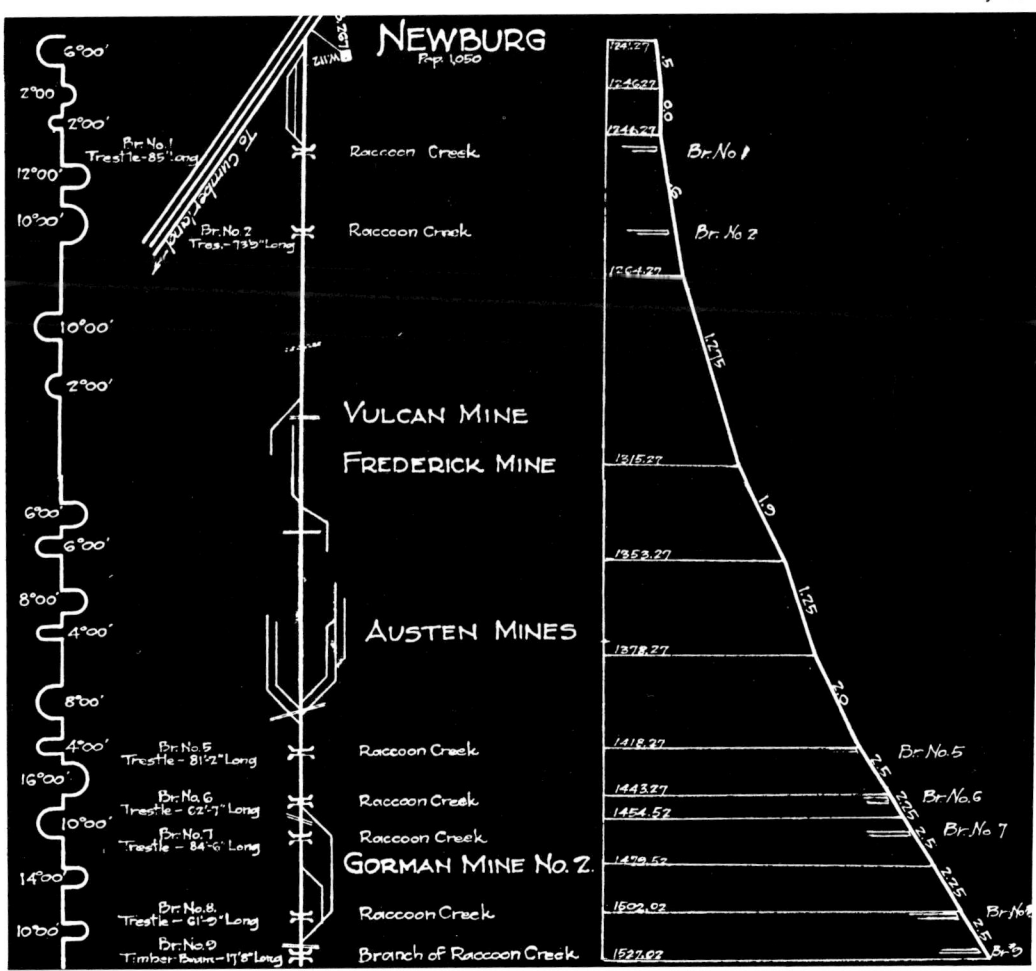

JUST EAST of Newburg was the Raccoon Valley Branch, a four mile long line that served numerous coal mines and coke ovens for many years ... when one drives from West End to Newburg in winter, the ruins of scores of ovens and slag piles are quite evident. By c. 1940 most of the deposits were worked out and the branch was closed.

WEST END

C. S. Roberts

THE 1910-12 improvements in preparation for the introduction of mallet power spelled the end for Newburg as a helper station simply because Newburg Grade started just east of the engine house ... doubled train length meant that trains could not ascend the grade for a sufficient distance to allow helpers to tie on. B&O built a new helper station at Hardman about two miles west and Newburg's day in the sun was over ... actually, residents probably first saw the sun when the station closed. This view, taken 4 May 1991, looks west from an auto bridge ... three turnouts handled remotely from Hardman and a signal bridge are the only indications that something important may have been here in the past. The shops and depot were right center ... no trace remains. Even the telegraph office was closed by 1915 ... the depot remained for some years, however.

NEWBURG GRADE

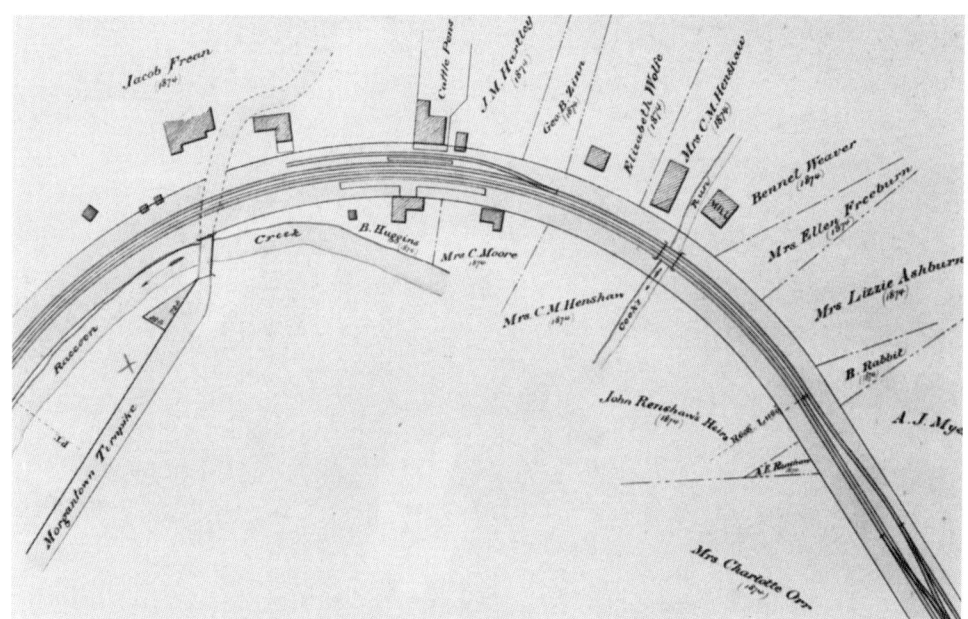

E. L. Thompson/B&OHS C. S. Roberts

INDEPENDENCE, a tiny town about a mile west of Newburg, did not play an important role in the history of the West End but did warrant a page in the company's map album in the mid-1870s. At lower right one can see the end of the three tracks from Newburg ... surely there must have been a telegraph office here but we have found no record. Note the crossing of the Morgantown Turnpike and the "B. Huggins" depot just to the right. In later years a standard B&O depot was built in this spot and was moved across the tracks to the north side in 1924.

HARDMAN (Q) on 25 May 1946 was in full service, dispatching pairs of mallets to shove up Newburg Grade. This view looks eastward and is the only one we have ever found which shows the entire installation. The engine house in the center was built from the same plans used for the M&K Junction Shrine. The tipple is for sand ... the two tracks on the right are mainline Nos. 2 and 4 which, by this date, ran the eleven miles to Blaser. Westbound track 1 is on the left. The ash dump and hoist lies just below and to the left of the signal bridge followed by the crane-cum-clamshell for emergency coaling. Q Tower, built in 1907, appears at the bottom of the photo. This facility was opened in September 1912, was closed during the Great Depression and was reopened in 1942. Helper servicing was transferred to M&K in 1949 and the buildings were demolished during the 1950s ... they were definitely gone by 1960. There was a siding at Hardman as early as 1889 and a telegraph office at least as early as 1904. A branch which left the main just to the west of the tower served a couple of mines and was active as late as 1954. The creek, of course, is the Raccoon. Notice the evidence of a mine line on the right hillside.

WEST END

ECOLOGICAL considerations were not a factor during the steam era ... this scene at Hardman 16 May 1921 shows a hillside devastated by coal gas and cinders. The building just east of the engine house is a rest house, again built to the same plans used at M&K Junction. The two jugs on the hill are fed from the Newburg Dam ... notice the pipeline on poles and the pump house by the railroad. We assume flow kept the pipe from freezing. The ash hoist is evident ... the water problem at Hardman is not. Diesel era railfans refer to steam locomotives as "water burners," with some justice. On the West End consumption of water was prodigious and the supply erratic, particularly on Newburg Grade. Apparently the Newburg Dam did not fully solve the problem as the history of Hardman and Newburg is studded with references to lack of or shortages of the essential fluid.

C. S. Roberts Collection

THIS WESTWARD view of the Hardman Engine House on 16 May 1921 emphasizes that it is a twin of the Shrine. We have shown that many installations and locations on the West End are remote ... Hardman tops the list. Until Hardman Branch rails were taken up and the third track removed in 1973, you literally could not get to Hardman except by rail or foot. Even Tommy was never on the ground at Hardman.

NEWBURG GRADE

JUST THREE YEARS before closure, the Hardman engine house was improved with an addition to join the oil house and office (on the left) to the main building and replacement of windows with glass block. This upgrading actually occurred in 1946 ... the year *before* similar work at M&K Junction. This rehabilitation epitomizes our longstanding puzzlement with the reasoning of the highest B&O management. Quite often they improve something only to tear it down. For example, on Cranberry Grade the third track was removed in 1973 (as indeed it was on Newburg Grade). Yet they removed track 4 which boasted continuous rail and left track 2 with old jointed rail. With all goodwill, we venture to suggest that an introduction between left and right hands is in order.

Q TOWER is framed by a rather bleak landscape on 16 May 1921 in this westward view. The Hardman Branch left the main through the cleft in the hills at middle left.

C. S. Roberts Collection

E. L. Thompson Collection/B&OHS

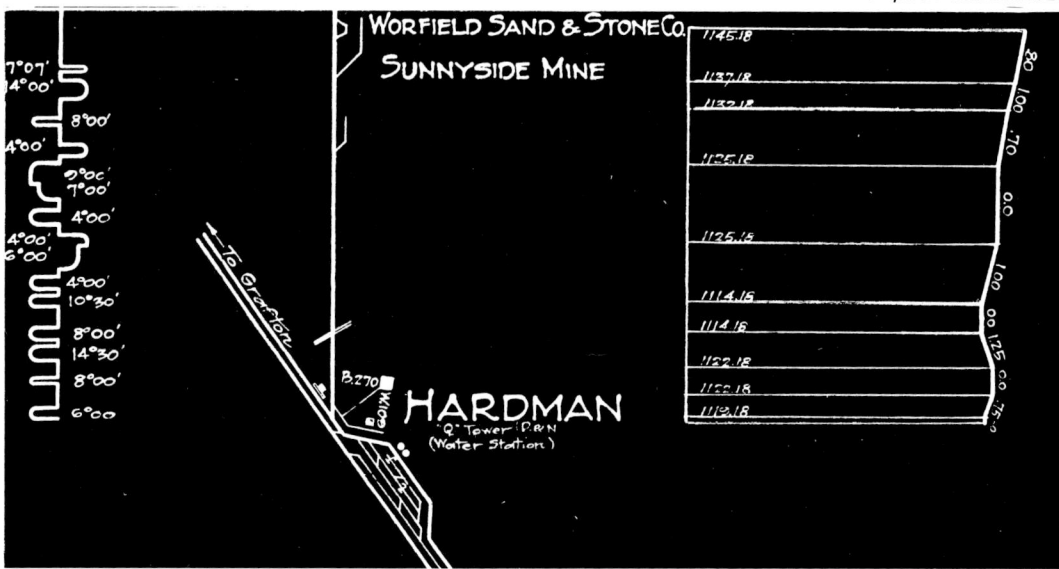

THE HARDMAN BRANCH, from a c. 1916 track chart, shows a rather tortuous path to two mines. The roadbed from a public road to the tower is the famous Hardman Expressway, providing ingress and egress to Q. The potholes are notorious ... a few are so deep that one wonders if his vehicle will disappear. They are particularly dangerous when filled with water because the depth is not apparent ... in May 1991 we hit one at about 2 mph that literally threw us across the cab of our truck.

WEST END

STILL ACTIVE IN 1991, Q Tower presented a rather dilapidated appearance when this photo was taken in April 1984 and we assure the reader that no visible improvements have been made as of May of 1991. The operators serving this tower hope that none will ever be made ... they, too, have noticed the tendency of B&O to fix up and tear down.

C. S. Roberts

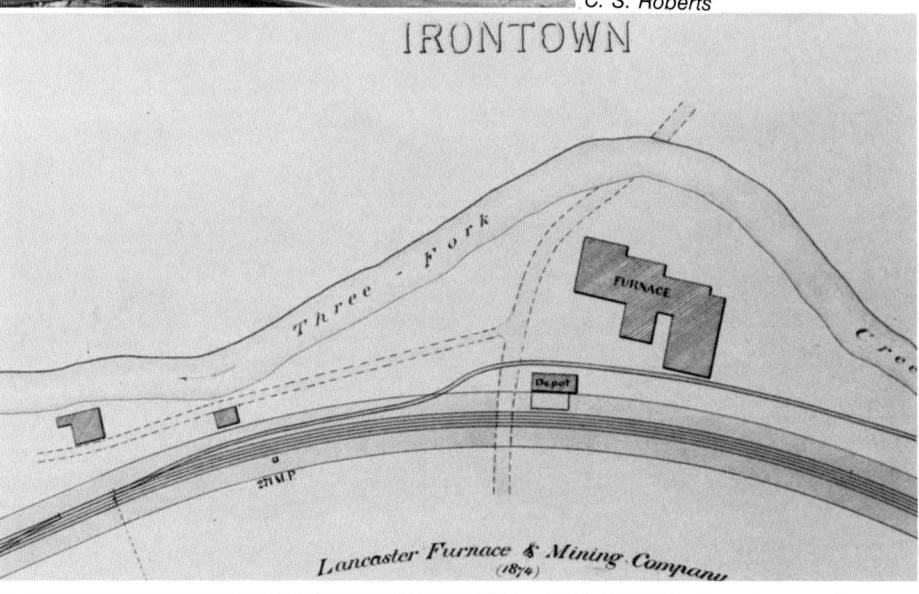

DOWNTOWN IRONTOWN is located slightly less than two miles west of Hardman and in the mid-1870s was living up to the promise of its name with a rather sizeable furnace, a long siding and even a depot. Note that Raccoon Creek has joined Three Forks Creek which the railroad will follow to Grafton. Irontown remains a place name on the railroad and that's about all.

C. S. Roberts

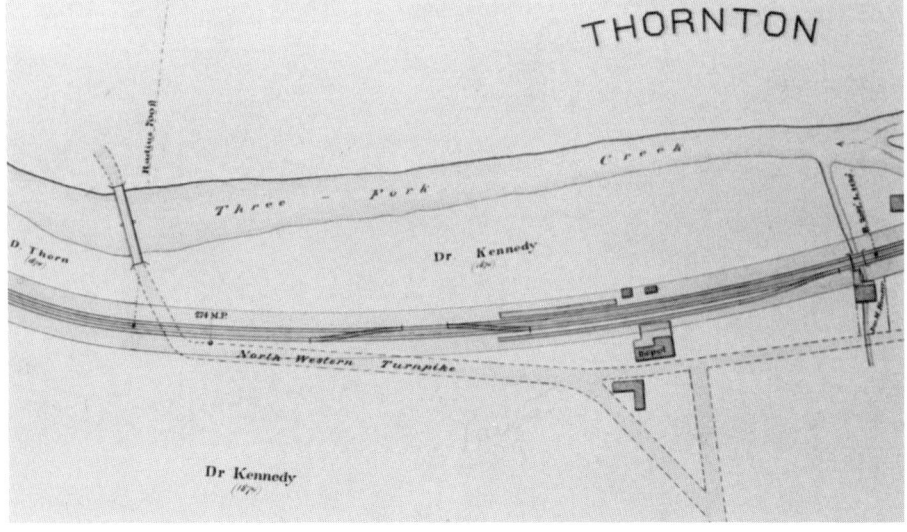

THORNTON lies three miles west of Irontown and marked the crossing of the Northwestern Turnpike with the B&O as seen in this mid-1870s company map ... modern-day Route 50 crosses slightly to the west of the original bridge. The town was apparently named for the Thorn family and was active on the railroad as early as 1855. A depot shows on this map ... a new combination station was built in 1905. B&O maintained a telegraph office here (UN) until c. 1916 and a siding at least as late as 1964.

C. S. Roberts

NEWBURG GRADE

H. N. Barr, Sr.

THE LAST "TOWN" on the post-1910 West End is Lesmalinston and Mr. Barr caught Train No. 30 Engine T3t 5579 on 9 June 1955 at that location in one of his most spectacular photographs. Just around the curve behind the train is GN Tower, the official end of the West End ... cars can barely be seen in the Grafton East Yard. T3 and EM1 locomotives were the only modern post-1940 steam power to ride B&O rails. The EM1s were built specifically for West End service ... the T3s, however, were built (rebuilt, actually, from old Pacifics and Mikados) for midwestern flatland service and only appeared on the West End late in the diesel-steam transition era. The long tank behind the 5579, however, is pure West End. The premier West End power before the EM1s were the outstanding EL6a 7300s ... in the 1920s B&O took a number of S1-S1a tenders, lengthened them and put them on the 7300s. The "t" in T3t signifies that an ex-7300 long tank is attached, giving the old girl a last few months of life on her hometown railroad.

Roberta Poling

THE WEST END OF THE WEST END is GN Tower, shown here in December 1984. The original Third Division ended west of here at the outskirts of Grafton. The 1912 yard improvements east of Grafton pushed the boundary to this location. The tower was opened by April 1911 and continued in service until c. 1970 ... it now houses signal equipment.

Chapter 9

Power

Many historians who study the evolution of man and society in the long view adhere to the theory of Challenge and Response as the principal determinants of the rise and fall of certain peoples and empires in the grand scheme of things. By way of example, they point to the vicissitudes of life in colder climes as being the fundamental pressure that induced more vigorous progress in, say, northern Europe.

We are mildly cautious in accepting this theory without reservation because, if for no other reason, it does not fully explain some exceptions in history.

We must admit, however, that advocates of Challenge and Response could regard B&O as a case in point. The challenge of the Erie Canal produced a response in the form of a wholly new form of transportation; the challenge of the PRR in walling-off Pennsylvania produced the West End; the challenge of the West End produced B&Os virile motive power policy.

In drag service, B&O adopted the eight-coupled locomotive, principally the unique Winans Camel 0-8-0 in the early years. This basic design evolved into the Consolidation 2-8-0 and then into the mallet 2-8-8-0 locomotive. An eight-coupled engine translates into four powered axles ... B&O stayed with four axle power deep into the diesel era. It was not until 1964 that B&O accepted six axle power with the SD35s, with the net result that B&O powered drags over the West End with four powered axles for 116 years. Other configurations were tested and always found wanting ... the severe grades and curvature on the West End were a reality that dictated adherence to a basic design that worked.

In QD and passenger service, the six-coupled locomotive with a four-wheel leading truck was introduced in the form of the Hayes Ten Wheeler in 1853 and, again, the basic design of three powered axles endured through the Pacific 4-6-2 years. Only in the late steam era did eight-coupled, four powered axle Mountains appear on the West End in any numbers.

The 4-4-0 American engine simply could not perform on the West End ... only with the coming of the diesel E unit did two powered axles pull passenger trains (we beg lead to point out that an E unit was really two locomotives in one carbody).

When the West End was being constructed, wood was the primary locomotive fuel on most railroads. With vast soft coal deposits along its line of road, B&O began experimenting with coal and found the results highly favorable ... they even tried coke, but found it too expensive.

That coal became the fuel of choice on all railroads gave the West End a lot of traffic ... in the early years as high as 20% of the coal hauled on the West End was for B&O use. Even with improved efficiency, coal for company use in the later stages of steam operations constituted over 10% of West End volume ... when coal hauled for use of other railroads was included, some estimates ranged as high as 50% of all tonnage moved.

As usual, we shall present the reader with the history of West End power in captions to follow ... successes, failures, warts and wonders. And surprises. "Surprise" is a basic principle of war ... tactical instructors invariably preface their lectures with the admonition that "Gentlemen, by surprise we do *not* mean open-mouthed astonishment." When the reader studies malletization, he will have to decide for himself just how low the jaws of B&O officials did sag.

Electrification came to the West End with the diesel locomotive ... less well known is that B&O considered electrification in the 1920s. Westinghouse Electric prepared an in-depth study of the West End and presented a detailed plan recommending electrification from Cumberland to Fairmont. We have read this report with some amusement ... the Westinghouse engineers were obviously taken aback by the severity of West End operating conditions and one has the feeling that they were not absolutely and completely sure that they could get the job done. Electrification for Norfolk & Western, Virginian, Great Northern and others were success stories, but this West End was something else again. Apparently they also made proposals for electrification east of Washington ... allusions were made in the West End document.

Terra Alta was to be the "power center," with electricity to be purchased from hydroelectric and mouth-of-mine generation. We suspect they planned to use power from Deep Creek Lake and a mine near Albright, but no specifics were provided in the proposal. They did note, perhaps with some misgivings, that West End coal consumption was almost fifty per cent higher than that for the B&O system as a whole.

For a little over eleven million dollars, the West End would be completely electrified with locomotives included. B&O balked and a new proposal from Hardman to Terra Alta was offered for $4,612,916.

The disposition of both plans can be deduced from the dates ... 1 July 1929 for the first and 5 November 1929 for the second.

The West End was electrified, but with diesels. For us to expound upon the virtues of the diesel over the steamer would be akin to telling the reader's grandmother how to suck eggs ... only a few of the more prominent advantages will be recited.

Availability: in 1947 B&O diesel availability was 96% ... *modern* steam around 70%. Multiple-Uniting: units could be tied together to provide exactly the amount of power needed, *with one crew*. Economy of Operation and Maintenance: modern T3 Mountains cost 43.2% more than passenger diesels per million horsepower rated miles ... even the magnificent EM1 cost 25.5% more than FT freight diesels.

In 1947, President R. B. White asked for a report detailing the advantages of steam power over diesel. The list was not impressive:

1. A steam locomotive can be overloaded to the point that it will work at maximum boiler pressure, full throttle and maximum cut off to the point of stalling without serious damage. Such performance for a diesel would seriously damage traction equipment through overheating.

2. The steam locomotive is not as susceptible to damage from mishandling as the diesel.

3. A steam locomotive is capable of accelerating a given train load faster from speeds over about 20 mph because the tractive effort curve of the diesel falls below that of the steamer around that speed.

4. First cost of a steam locomotive is about one-half that of a diesel.

Other advantages were so minor that they are not worth mentioning.

The diesel had another huge advantage that has occurred to the writer, but which we have not seen mentioned in literature of the period. The steam locomotive was at its technological height in the 1940s ... the diesel just at the dawn of development.

Four-unit FT lashups produced 5400 h.p. *Three*-unit SD50s produce 10500 h.p., a 385% improvement in forty years. Moreover, the SD50 has a marvelous "creeper" wheel slip control system, activated by radar measuring speed over the ground, that enables the driving wheels to move about 2 mph faster than the locomotive and adding greatly to effective tractive power.

Whatever the efficacy of B&O motive power policy on the West End, the grades and curves remain. Perhaps ten years ago, a group of European operating officials visited the West End and were taken by auto by their B&O hosts to start their tour at M&K Junction. One of them looked around and introduced a new Age of Innocence by asking, "Why all the power?"

WEST END

THE EIGHT-COUPLED ERA on the West End probably began with this Baldwin-designed 0-8-0. Of the eight locomotives in this series, No. 57 *Memnon* was the second of two built by New Castle (Delaware) ... another was built by B&O and five more by Baldwin. Apparently Baldwin was very busy in 1848 and allowed others to build to their plans. Delivery of all eight was completed 1848-49 and it is likely that a number of them were involved in the construction of the West End. As the 57 still exists in the B&O Museum, we know something about it. With 41" drivers and 150# steam pressure (originally), she produced 8580 lbs. tractive power. This series had 12.65 sf grate area, large enough to produce at least adequate steam volume.

C. S. Roberts Collection

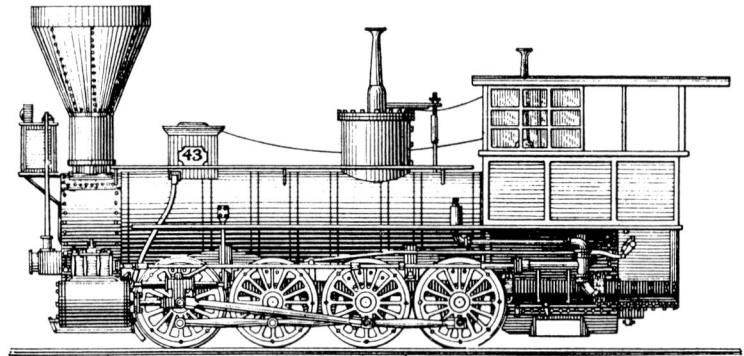

B&O BUILT eleven of these 0-8-0s in their own shops 1850-53. With 43" drivers, horizontal cylinders, 18 sf grate area and all weight on the drivers, these locomotives must have been good tonnage engines in their era. As with the 57 and sisters, we cannot be sure these engines were used on the West End, but it does appear likely.

C. S. Roberts Collection

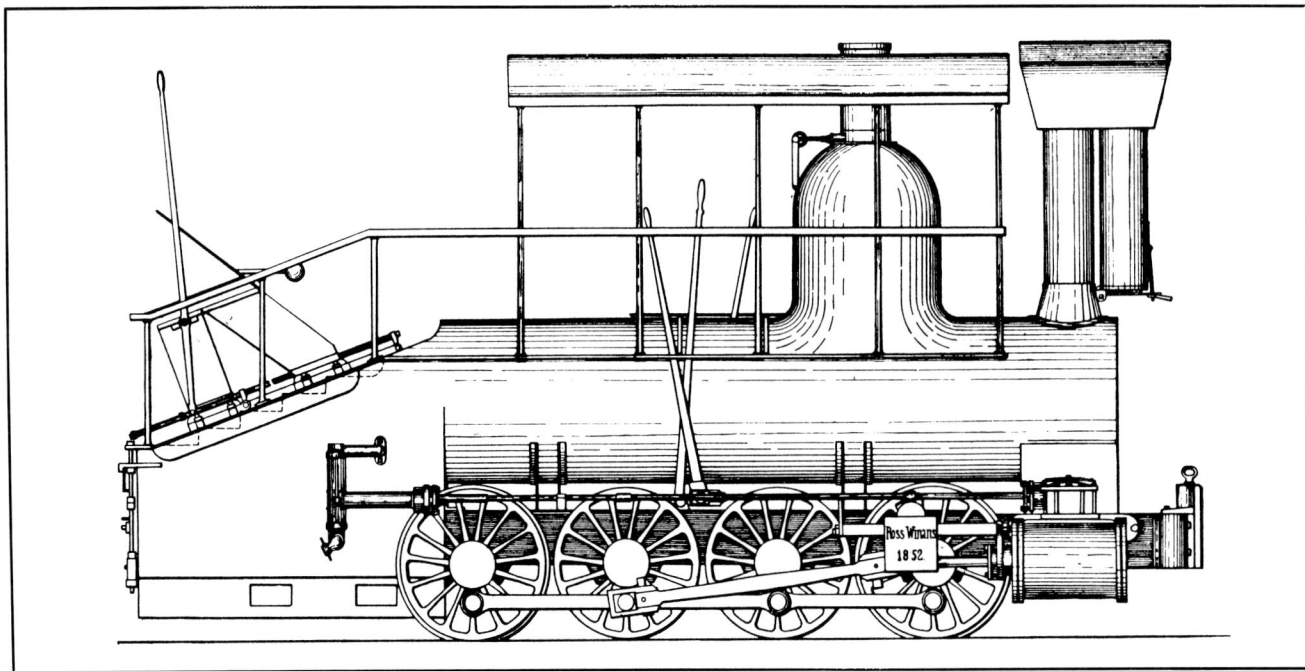

THE ROSS WINANS CAMEL 0-8-0s were, without question, the backbone of tonnage power on the West End from opening and well into its history in the last century. This drawing, as the previous one and most others to follow, was taken from Snowden Bell's seminal 1912 work entitled "The Early Motive Power of the Baltimore and Ohio Railroad." From 1848 to 1857, one hundred and nineteen examples were built in three

POWER

basic versions ... short, medium and long furnace. This is a medium furnace version ... there were thirteen long furnace engines and the balance was split between a few short and many medium in uncertain numbers. All had 43" drivers and ample grate areas ... this version's measured 24.5 sf. The firebox was fed from behind and above ... note the two chutes. Some even had two-platform tenders to facilitate firing and grate shaking. Note that the two center drivers are flangeless. The twin-tube stack and cinder catcher was soon replaced by the standard B&O freight stack as will be apparent in illustrations to follow, but this change did little to alleviate what can only be called a weird appearance. An 1860 locomotive critic described the Camel as "the most peculiar engine in use in the United States ... in every detail of construction this engine is ... in the strongest possible contrast with the proportions, arrangement and workmanship of the standard American engine." The Camel, Ross Winans and the B&O were of a piece ... brilliant, determined and eccentric.

"THE DETAILS of these locomotives had many interesting features, and the whole machine was designed with wonderful skill and ingenuity, and the chief aim of their construction seemed to be to produce locomotives with a maximum capacity at a minimum cost. The safety of the men who had to run them seemed to have received less consideration. The object aimed at was apparently accomplished, as these locomotives certainly did a greater amount of work than any of their contemporaries, and Mr. Winans made a princely fortune by building them." So wrote a former Winans apprentice in an article some years after the event. The Henry Tyson-Winans debate and controversy of 1856, essentially over pilot trucks, drew a lot of critical attention to the Camels as well as the participants and resulted in an airing of the advantages and disadvantages of the locomotive. This debate alone deserves a book ... indeed, Mr. Bell devoted many pages to the subject and seems to have come away with the conclusion that Mr. Winans was both a genius and a nut (if so, not the first or last in B&O history) who was years ahead of his time in every matter except the need for pilot trucks to ease engines into curvature. Whatever the merits of the case, the Camels were luggers with ample steaming capacity, great tractive force and what must have been a very high factor of adhesion ... exactly what B&O needed on the West End. The 55, pictured here, was a short-furnace version with a standard B&O freight stack.

THIS PLAN of a long-furnace Camel presents some detail about the design. Notice the strong, rigid frame and, again, the flangeless middle drivers. The firebox was not waterlegged and was of light construction, so the locomotive was well balanced in spite of its appearance. Mr. Winans wanted *all* the weight on the drivers and practice proved him correct. On the West End, the Camels were used on drags at slow speed (around 10 mph) so the lack of a pilot truck was not serious. The Tyson-Winans debate was really over Ten Wheelers, not 0-8-0s ... Mr. Tyson was correct in demanding pilot trucks for faster-moving locomotives yet his own "Tyson Ten Wheeler" apparently had insufficient weight on its leading truck. Mr. Tyson was B&Os Master of Machinery 1856-59 and made many contributions, but as we shall see B&O ordered more 0-8-0s in 1865.

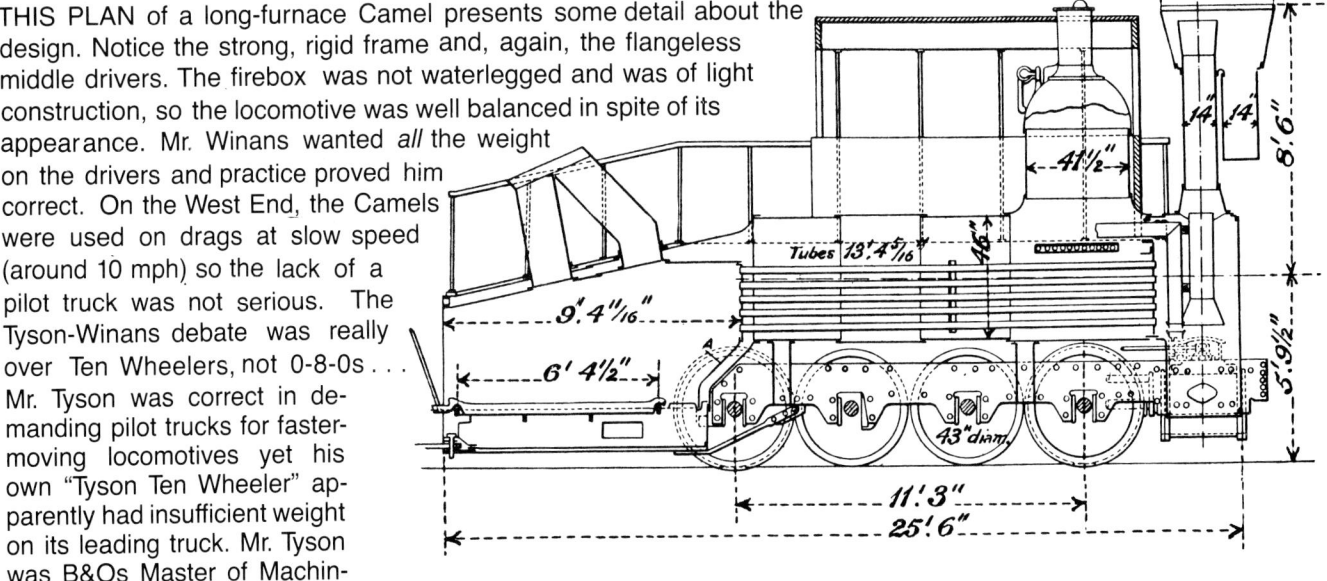

C. S. Roberts Collection

WEST END

MEDIUM-FURNACE Camel 154 is at work at Piedmont c. 1863. Sadly, not one Camel was saved ... we found a photo in the B&O Museum archives captioned, "Last Camel being dismantled Mt. Clare 1898." Mr. Winans named the first locomotive in this class "Camel" and unknowingly gave the name to U.S. railroading ... any engine with the cab on top was known as a Camelback. Except on B&O ... they called them "Mother Hubbards" or "Snappers."

C. S. Roberts Collection

THATCHER PERKINS was B&O's Master of Machinery 1847-51 and 1859-65 ... he designed this 0-8-0 locomotive to replace Winans Camels on the West End and Bell reports 24 examples were built in 1865 by various builders (Sagle in *B&O Power* says 27). The plan shown here is of the first in the series, originally numbered 83 and changed to 32 shortly after construction. This class became known as the "Greenbacks," presumably because of the color of their boiler jackets, and probably worked the West End in some numbers. With 43″ drivers, 100-110 pounds steam pressure, 19.25 sf grate area and all weight on the drivers, they certainly must have been good tonnage engines. There is no record of tractive power of most early locomotives ... only in the case of engines preserved by the B&O Museum is such information known. B&O began to "class" locomotives in this era; Winans 0-8-0 Camels were L and these were L1. Later L would be used only for 0-8-0 switchers. Apparently these L1s were well designed and sturdily built ... it is safe to assume they gave good service until finally B&O decided a leading truck was needed even on drag engines and began producing 2-8-0 Consolidations in 1873 as Class E.

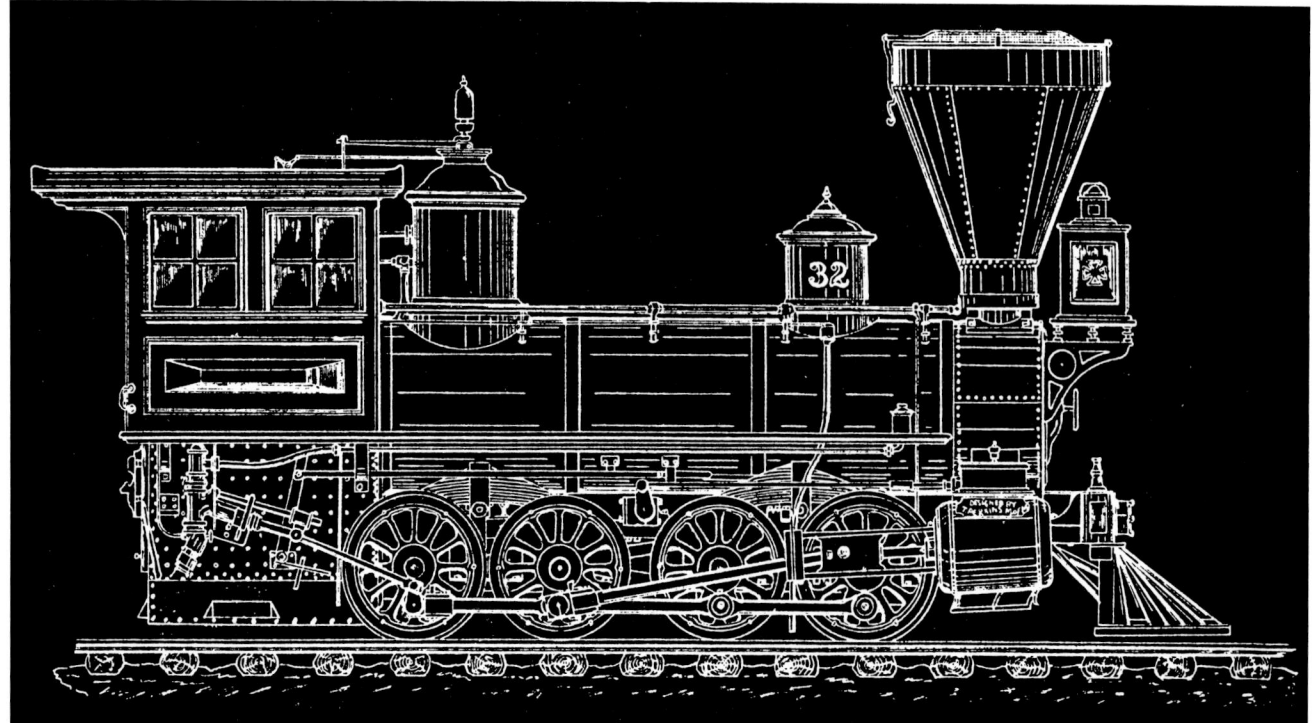

C. S. Roberts Collection

POWER

IT HAS BEEN SAID that the Consolidation locomotive, in league with the 4-4-0 American, built America and there is merit to the proposition. For half a century, these two types dominated all U.S. railroading and the B&O was not an exception. B&O's class E with 50" drivers, 125# sp, 20,400# tractive power was the first in 1873 and the last was class E27 with 62" drivers, 205# sp, 40,800# tp in 1905-10. In between E and E27 literally hundreds of Consolidations were built for B&O and many served on the West End until the Mikado came into service in 1911. The engine pictured here was E17, one of five built by Baldwin in 1898 with 54" drivers, 190# sp, 40,531# tp. Cylinder changes resulted in them being reclassed E17a ... we do not know that the E17s served on the West End but a lot of their sisters did so. From the first to the last, tractive power doubled and this steady improvement certainly helped B&O with their West End problem. *B&OHS*

OF ALL THE CONSOLIDATIONS built and acquired by B&O, which ones served on the West End? We can only report about those *known* to have battled The Hill. Class E2 definitely did so ... the 458 is pictured at Newburg in 1873 in *B&O Magazine* September 1938 along with family recollections that they replaced Camels in drag service on the West End. The E2s, of which 90 examples were built 1873-81, had 50" drivers, 130# sp and 21,216# tp. And we have seen a photo of an E8 at Amblersburg obviously in helper service ... this class was built in 1888 with 50" drivers, 150# sp and 29,200# tp. There is one survivor of this class ... the *A.J. Cromwell* in the B&O Museum is an E8. With classes E13 and E19, B&O reverted to Camel configuration with the cab on the boiler to make room for huge Wootten fireboxes. With typical B&O perversity, they were Mother Hubbards and Snappers rather than Camels. Actually the E13s were built in 1896 with the cab in the rear and with compound cylinders ... in 1904 they were simpled and the cab moved. They had 54" drivers, 180# sp, 35,000# tp and an incredible 4.99 factor of adhesion. Pictured here we see E19a 1844 at Salt Lick Curve, probably in 1906. Construction of this class began in 1900 with compound cylinders ... they were soon simpled. They had 55" drivers, 200# sp and 40,900# tp. *C. S. Roberts Collection*

WEST END

TOMMY'S FAMILY vacationed in Terra Alta and his love affair with the West End began at an early age. His father wanted him to become a stockbroker ... the sight of his first drag creeping up Cranberry launched him into a railroad career that combined vocation and avocation and made him one of B&Os greatest historians. This photo of a Snapper with two Bobbers drifting down Cranberry just west of Terra Alta is undated but has to be one of his very first shots ... he couldn't have been more than nine or ten years of age. Standard operational procedure until the early 1920s was to fill-out drags off Cranberry at Rinard and this Snapper was obviously in such service ... the two cabooses being returned clinch the argument. Tommy was born in 1911. In 1927 Tommy was sent to summer camp in New England and his grandmother mailed him a postcard from Terra Alta with an LL1 featured on the front. For many years Gary Schlerf, now president of B&OHS, was a devoted collector of B&O postcards and was kind enough to let us acquire duplicates for our collection. One evening in the mid-1980s he brought this postcard to us and we noticed the message. Of course, we presented it to Tommy ... sadly, it has not been found in his files. We still consider it an incredible coincidence that this postcard floated around the country for almost sixty years to end up in the hands of the only student who would recognize its provenance.

E. L. Thompson/B&OHS

POWER

B&O WAS AN EARLY PIONEER in the development of the Mikado 2-8-2 locomotive and began ordering large numbers in 1911 as class Q. The use of a trailing truck to support a larger firebox resulted in another increase in tractive power (the Q1s were rated at 50,184# tp) and naturally examples were immediately sent to the West End. The year 1911, however, was also the introductory year for mallet engines on the West End, so the Mike did not become a drag engine to any extent. The Qs were used as road engines on QD trains until the early 1920s and some were used in helper service, although not widely. The glorious role of the Qs on the West End were as passenger engines and helpers, of all things. The Q4s starred in this performance ... their 64" drivers were no impediment on the West End as speeds were low enough to avoid excessive dynamic augment. For a third of a century, almost all passenger trains had Q4 helpers and many were pulled by Q4s alone ... all were built with steam lines. Many West End Q4s received longer Vanderbilt tanks from S and T3 engines ... here we see the 4613 with a T3 tank on Train 29 with P1d 5070 against 10 cars at Altamont on 28 May 1950.

E. L. Thompson/B&OHS

WEST END

Largest Locomotive in the World. Built at Schenectady, N. Y.

THIS UGLY LOCOMOTIVE, so balky it was immediately nicknamed "Old Maude" for a comic-strip mule of the period, was built by Alco for B&O in 1904 and was the largest in the world when built. To have two engines under one boiler was not a new idea ... Frenchman Anatole Mallet built and patented the first articulated compound engine in 1885. This 0-6-6-0, built as the 2400 class O, was a flop. With 56" drivers and 235# sp, it developed as a compound engine 71,500# tp. The 2400 was tried as a helper on Sand Patch Grade and then banished to Willard as a hump engine. It was renumbered 7000 and reclassed DD1 in 1915 and was simpled in 1926 as DD1a with 91,650# tp. There is no evidence that it ever ran on the West End and it was not an eight-coupled engine. Why do we even mention this turkey in a history of the West End? Because this monster was a conceptual success that fathered the mallet revolution and transformed the West End. It all had to do with one number ... 71,500 pounds of tractive power ... almost *double* the output of the most modern Consolidation. That the 2400 ran at all was a stunning development and B&O management quite correctly saw this design concept as a "big solution," to use the military term, in their war with The Hill. Overall, B&O had a good record in preserving its historical heritage ... that they scrapped *this* engine in 1938 has to be regarded as a cultural war crime.

C. S. Roberts Collection

B&O BACKED THEIR BET on the mallet locomotive by spending vast sums to rebuild the West End as we have reported and placed an order with Alco for thirty O1 0-8-8-0 behemoths for delivery 1911-13. They were originally numbered 2401-20 and 2422-31; number 2421 was given to a failed experimental. With 100 sf Wootten fireboxes, 56" drivers, 4.6 factor of adhesion and 210# sp, they developed an amazing 105,000 pounds of tractive effort. They were actually built without stokers ... the designers were kind enough to supply two firedoors, however, no doubt a great solace to the firemen who had to feed these mammoths. Ultimately Duplex stokers were installed ... B&O probably lost too many firemen to exhaustion and hernia. We wish we could say that B&O went on to broad, sunlit uplands with delivery of these powerhouses ... unfortunately, B&O management had ignored the warning that those who do not study history are doomed to repeat it. These engines did not have pilot trucks and naturally developed a distressing tendency to straighten out the rails when they managed to stay on them. Didn't anyone keep notes? Did *one* official recall the Tyson-Winans debate? The 01s were absolute failures as road locomotives and were relegated to helper service ... nine had leading trucks installed and became EL4 2-8-8-0s, but even then the small drivers doomed them for headend use. They were reclassed LL1 in 1915 and renumbered 7020-49 in 1915 ... here we see the 7047 at M&K Junction 28 September 1948 with a lengthened rectangular tender.

E. L. Thompson/B&OHS

POWER

THE O1s WERE all compound locomotives and it is significant that none were simpled when B&O walked away from compounding in the 1920s ... they didn't want to put another penny into these bombs. This builder's photo of the 2427 shows that a sandbox was originally mounted on the pilot deck ... it was later moved to boiler-top position. This engine is what is known as a "second group" O1/LL1 with rounded-top tender.

W. A. Barringer Collection

HAVING SPENT millions upon millions of dollars rebuilding the West End and touting "malletization" from the housetops, B&O management must have been on the edge of panic as they gazed upon their impotent O1s. We cannot say that they lied to their stockholders, but they certainly didn't go out of their way to tell the truth ... at least the first rule of public relations was observed, i.e., they clammed up as they thrashed around for a solution. Other operating statistics on the railroad were improving and B&O employed the time-honored device of cooking the books by burying the bad news under the good. "When in danger or in doubt, run in circles and scream and shout" is the soldier's credo, another pearl of wisdom ignored by B&O management. Hand-in-hand with Murphy, they dashed to Baldwin and ordered thirty Class S ten-coupled 2-10-2s (more about them later) in 1914, managing to produce a debacle on top of a disaster ... these harridan locomotives should have been throttled at birth. Snowden Bell's book was published in 1912 ... perhaps, by 1915, someone in B&O management got around to reading it. At least one unknown, unsung hero did appear with some brains, steel nerves and courage. Perhaps there were several good men ... we simply do not know. We *do* know that a bold decision was made and it was a correct one. The 7212 pictured above was part of the solution.

C. S. Roberts Collection

WEST END

W. A. Barringer Collection

ALMOST HALF of all the 2-8-8-0 locomotives ever built were bought by B&O and they saved B&O from itself on the West End. Thirty were delivered in 1916 ... thirty more in 1917, another twenty-six in 1919-20 and sixteen were purchased from Seaboard Air Line in 1920. They were all classed as ELs. Aside from the SAL engines which we will explore later, they were all basically alike: 58" drivers, stokers, 88 sf grates, 210# sp (initially), compound (some with slide, others with piston valves on the low pressure engine) and producing 101,300 pounds of tractive power. Steam pressure was soon raised to 225# on all and that change pushed tractive power to 108,500 pounds. As road engines on drags and QD trains, or as helpers, these locomotives were splendid performers. The various classes were divided as follows: 15 EL1, BLW, 7100-14; 15 EL2, Alco, 7200-14; 30 EL3, BLW, 7115-44; 26 EL5, BLW, 7145-70. Almost all of these 86 engines were assigned to or ran through the West End. B&O made another audacious decision in 1925 by starting the process of simpling most of them ... this change, with 220# sp, gave each affected locomotive an incredible tractive power of 118,800 pounds. Sixty-four were simpled, as follows: 12 EL1a 1927-32; 8 EL2a 1930-42; 20 EL3a 1927-32; 24 EL5a 1925-30. EL1a 7106 pictured here was a typical example with a 12,000 gallon tank ... most ELs had their tanks lengthened to hold 18,000 gallons, another wise move which improved West End operations. Note the exhaust steam injector ... most ELs were fitted with these "poor man's feedwater heaters."

E. L. Thompson/B&OHS

THE 7125, EL3a, takes water into its long tank at M&K Junction on 13 October 1946. Tommy regarded this photo as one of his best and luckiest. M&K was a smoky bowl ... the wind suddenly blew away the smoke and the sun broke through just before he snapped this shot.

POWER

C. S. Roberts Collection

THE 7163 and mate 7148 were the only two EL5s not simpled ... here we see her taking water at M&K Junction on 28 May 1948, in helper service.

B&O GOT LUCKY in 1920 ... Seaboard Air Line had purchased sixteen compound 2-8-8-2s from Alco in 1917-18 and sold them to B&O in 1920. They had 63" drivers, 88 sf grates and produced 98,000# tp as compounds. Originally classed EE6, in 1923 B&O amputated the trailing truck and reclassed them EL6. In 1927 B&O simpled all of them, which gave them 108,000# tractive power and class identity EL6a ... in the same era they were given extended S1 tanks as reported earlier. They retained Southern valve throughout history. All were assigned to the West End.

W. A. Barringer Collection

WEST END

E. L. Thompson/B&OHS

IT IS HARD TO SAY too much good about the EL6a engines ... they were magnificent and perfectly suited to West End operations. Their 63" drivers were large enough to make them the engine of choice for QD trains, yet small enough to handle drags with ease. Numbered 7300-15, they were replaced by the thirty EM1 7600s delivered 1944-45 and sent west to work Lake trains, which they did with great efficiency. They lasted well into the 1950s, outliving most of their EL peers. Tommy caught the 7301 with a 51 car drag just east of M&K on 13 April 1947 ... 7207-7200 were shoving. The object above the tender's coal bin is a firebox rake. One cannot help but wonder if the EM1s would have been ordered if there had been thirty more of these noble locomotives.

OF ALL THE STEAM LOCOMOTIVES to serve on B&O lines, it is a given that the thirty EM1 7600s were the best. Yet, given a choice, B&O would not have ordered them. B&O had wisely concluded that the diesel was the way to go, but the War Production Board gave priority to other railroads and B&O was desperate for additional power on the West End. Baldwin built thirty of them, 7600-19 in 1944 and 7620-29 in 1945, specifically for West End service. They were 2-8-8-4 engines ... the four-wheel trailing truck was needed to support a huge 117.5 sf firebox. With 64" drivers and 235# sp, they produced 115,000# tractive force ... slightly less than their EL simpled cousins, but with far more steam-producing capacity. They had every modern steam locomotive appliance known and trailed a 22,000 gallon, 25 ton welded tender. Their tenure on the West End was short ... as F7 road diesels began to flood onto the West End in the early 1950s, they were based at Keyser for service eastbound to Brunswick. A few served as helpers out of M&K and Keyser in the early 1950s and they worked the Pittsburgh and Cumberland East End Subdivisions until final transfer to Benwood and Painesville for service on Lake trains. They were certainly the most handsome, and most photographed, engines in B&O history. The 2400 was the first and the 7629 was the last articulated built for B&O ... neither one was saved.

Pontin/C. S. Roberts Collection

POWER

B&O DECIDED to use 7600s on West End express trains and Train No. 29, usually the longest and heaviest, was a natural choice ... one 7600 replaced two or three less powerful engines with substantial crew savings. That practice ended on 21 January 1947 just west of Bridge 88 near Oakland. The 7625 derailed, rolled over and killed her engineer ... Tommy took this photo from Train No. 75 *Cincinnatian* the next day. We have interviewed two engineers who ran 7600s ... the first was running C&O's famous 614 on a tour train in the 1970s and he replied as follows when we asked him how he liked the 614, "A very fine engine, but it's not a 7600." The other engineer was equally complimentary, but pointed out that he thought they were topheavy ... he went into a curve between Cumberland and Keyser and the engine went down on its springs to the point he was sure he was going to leave the railroad. In response to this, a B&O motive power official snarled that "if you run them too goddam fast, you'll roll them over." He also admitted that they did look a little topheavy. They also are reported to have had problems with staybolt leakage, perhaps caused by vertical curves on the West End. When that gigantic boiler started downhill, the water would rush forward and expose the crownsheet until it sloshed back. One can see that the sight of water suddenly disappearing from the glass would unnerve the most steadfast crewman.

E. L. Thompson/B&OHS

C. S. Roberts Collection

WE MUST DIGRESS from our eight-coupled dissertation to briefly review this ten-coupled botch in the motive power history of the West End. The 6007 is, of course, a Class S engine of lately reported infamy. The first S was the 6000 ... with 190# sp, it produced 75,970# tp. The additional twenty-nine (6001-30) engines had 205# sp and 86,500# tp. All were built by Baldwin in 1914 with 58" drivers to "save" the West End ... they were barely able to save themselves and were lucky to survive as helpers in other locales. We have always been curious about the S engines ... as we related in another book, they were the "Genesis" class for the fabulous Bix Sixes. Why did they fail on the West End? We suspect there were two reasons ... first, a ten-coupled wheelbase was simply too long for West End curvature and, second, they only had a factor of adhesion of 3.84. A third reason might be their relative lack of tractive power ... they weren't weaklings, but they didn't have quite enough "dig" to substitute for two Consolidations or one properly designed mallet. Whatever the validity of the foregoing, they came and they went. The 6007 seen here is at Cumberland in 1947.

WEST END

C. S. Roberts Collection

THE "BIG SIX" locomotive was one of the finest and best known steam engines to trod B&O rails. There were 125 of them and they were classed S1/S1a ... the cognomen "Big Six" evolved simply because they were BIG, as this photo of the 6193 at Cumberland 18 August 1946 attests, and their numbers always began with a 6. They were built by Baldwin and Lima as follows: S1 BLW 6100-49 1923-24; S1 Lima 6150-74 1923-24; S1a Lima 6175-99 1926; S1a BLW 6200-24 1926. They all had 64″ drivers, 220# sp and produced 84,300# tractive power. There were only two significant differences between the Big Sixes and the abortive S engines ... driver size and factor of adhesion; the latter on the Big Six was a comfortable 4.12. And the Big Sixes were West End engines, but not on the "central sixty miles." Keyser was awash with them and almost all eastbound drags from Keyser had one on the headend. West of Piedmont, they would be seen only as Piedmont helpers or on passenger trains as helpers.

ONLY ONCE did Tommy see a Big Six on a drag west of Piedmont ... here is the 6171 at Salt Lick Water Tub Curve with just 47 cars and 7128-7040 shoving on 18 October 1947. Almost certainly the 6171 had gone west as a passenger helper and was being returned to Keyser on a drag. Note that this drag had five cars less than usual as compensation for the 6171s lower tractive power in comparison to the typical mallet.

E. L. Thompson/B&OHS

POWER

TRAIN NO. 4 *Diplomat* was just east of Newburg at 5:42 a.m. 18 November 1946 in fog at 31 mph with Diesels 56-56a against twelve cars, the 4416 against the diesels and the 6204 in the lead when a rail broke and things started to go awry. An engineer was killed, one passenger and four employees injured. The 7600 in the foreground is handling the relief train ... the 4416 is in the middle with a crushed cab and the 6204 is buried in the mess on the right. West Enders operating from Piedmont to Grafton did not like or trust ten-coupled engines and this wreck confirmed their suspicions. We have interviewed scores of employees over the years on the West End and this derailment usually comes up in the conversation ... as recently as 1984 an operator alluded to it. All were convinced that the 6204 broke the rail. True or not, B&O management continued to use Big Sixes as helpers on the West End until the end of steam.

THE SIX-COUPLED engine rapidly became the standard design for West End passenger and QD service. The 4-4-0 American type may well have built America and, for that matter, been widely used on the rest of the B&O system, but the West End was a special case. Samuel J. Hayes, Master of Machinery 1851-56, realized early on that the practice of teaming a 4-4-0 with a 0-8-0 Camel on fast trains was bad news and he designed this Ten Wheeler engine to get the job done. Seventeen examples with 50" drivers were constructed 1853-54 by various builders and went straight to the West End where they served for many years and in fact became the model for the better known Davis Ten Wheelers built later. The fundamental approach of combining a four-wheel leading truck and six-coupled drivers was so sound for West End service that it held sway until the end of steam ... a Pacific 4-6-2 is, after all, nothing more than a Ten Wheeler with a trailing truck to support a larger firebox.

C. S. Roberts Collection

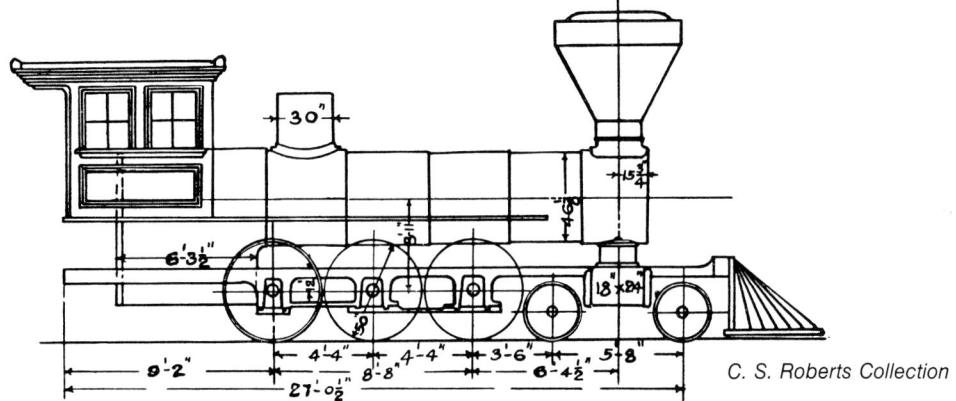

C. S. Roberts Collection

THIS TEN WHEELER design was the cause of the Tyson-Winans dispute over leading trucks which, of course, was won by Mr. Tyson. Nine locomotives with 50" drivers were built in 1857 and sent to the West End. Snowden Bell praised these engines even while noting that they lacked sufficient weight on the leading truck. They were not duplicated per se, but one of them earned approbation in the 1858 Annual Report. The 229 pulled 150 tons from Piedmont to Altamont, "the most favorable performance yet." With the cab in the rear, we can be sure the crews liked the Tyson Ten Wheelers.

WEST END

C. S. Roberts Collection

WE HAVE MET Thatcher Perkins and his 0-8-0 design ... here we see his famous Ten Wheeler. Eleven engines were built 1863-64, one with 64½" and ten with 60" drivers. With the possible exception of the first one, all were sent to the West End where they gave splendid service until c. 1890. The 117 shown here is in the B&O Museum with 58" drivers and rated at 10,350# tractive power with 75# steam pressure. They had 120# sp when built, so the original tractive power must have been much higher and quite welcome on the West End.

THE NEXT SIGNIFICANT Ten Wheeler design to see extensive use on the West End was the Davis ... ninety-eight engines were built 1869-75. Oddly, Mr. Bell had nothing to say about them ... what little we know has been derived from the pleasant circumstance that two have survived. Pictured is the 173 (ex-373) at the National Museum of transport at St. Louis with extended smokebox and altered stack ... the 217 (ex-377) is at the B&O Museum in earlier configuration. The 217 has 50" drivers, 17.24 sf grate area and produces 8,775# tp at 65# sp. Original steam pressure *may* have been as high as 150# ... whatever the real figure, the tractive power was high enough to keep Davis Ten Wheelers in active service on the West End until the late 1890s. The need for six-coupled engines on the West End was a major but not the only reason B&O became a Ten Wheeler railroad. An important factor was rail loading ... B&O was almost always strapped for cash and had difficulty increasing rail weight to support higher loadings.

C. S. Roberts Collection

B&O DID NOT build any Ten Wheelers from 1873 to the late 1880s ... they then began another building spree. Larry Sagle in *B&O Power* reports that eight B7 engines (shown here) were built by Baldwin in 1890 specifically for West End deployment. Numbered 1300-07 and with 25,900# tp riding on 62" drivers, they were certainly suitable for West End use ... it's just that the quantity seems rather low. In any event, the Pacific type appeared on the railroad beginning in 1906 and one can be sure the West End got their share of these more powerful engines.

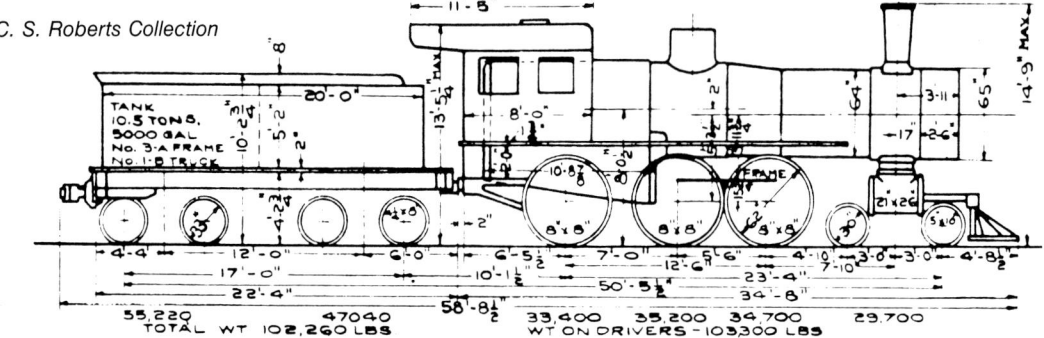

C. S. Roberts Collection

POWER

THE PACIFIC LOCOMOTIVE most widely associated with the West End was the P1d, a heavy 4-6-2 with just 74" drivers and 51,000# tractive power. Thirty-one of them were rebuilt from divers other Pacifics and Mikados from 1928 to 1937 (one blew up and then there were thirty). Their numbers were scattered from 5003 to 5094 ... they were used in mountain territory and were not exclusive to the West End, but if you saw a Pacific west of Keyser it was almost certainly a P1d. Here we see the 5086 drifting through Amblersburg with Train No. 11 on 30 March 1948.

C. A. Brown

THE MOST FAMOUS B&O Pacific was the P7 "President" class ... they were not, however, common on the West End except for the P7d subclass used on *Cincinnatian* trains. Designed for Washington-New York service, they were displaced westward as dieselization progressed and would show up on the West End ... here, on 28 May 1950, is the 5307 trailing the seven cars of Train No. 11 at Salt Lick Curve.

E. L. Thompson/B&OHS

William Hoffman II

PASSENGER DIESELS were not assigned to the West End, but many ran through on first class trains. We have already seen photos of many early E units in action ... here is E9 1464 on 4 September 1968 with Train No. 11 at Rowlesburg. B&O locomotive historians have yet to divine the reasoning behind B&Os decision not to put dynamic brakes on E units, particularly since so many of them passed through mountainous territory. When dieselization was complete on the West End, F units were put on passenger trains as helpers at Keyser and Grafton ... one can be sure their dynamics were welcome.

175

WEST END

EMD's FT DESIGN doomed the steam locomotive. None were West End engines, but, as we have reported, in the mid-1940s they were run through on some QD trains. Here we see a set of four at Cumberland 8 June 1945.

AT A MINIMUM, Baldwin lacked tact when they numbered their Centipede demonstrator the 6000 ... only thirty-four years had passed since the lamented 1914 delivery of Class S 6000s and some motive power people with long memories might still be on the property in 1948. B&Os decision to dieselize helper operations on the West End was a big one and *this* time they tested everything in sight ... EMD, Alco and Baldwin. West Enders called this locomotive "The Spider" ... B&O did not buy this monster and must have smiled when PRR suckered on it. The 6000 was on the West End twice ... in March 1948 she helped east out of M&K and it was promptly learned that coupler limiting blocks were essential on West End curves. The 6000 came back in May ... here she has just cut-off a drag at Terra Alta 31 May 1948. For several weeks she headed QD trains through the West End and was returned to Baldwin with a "thanks but no thanks" note. A sidenote ... one veteran West End operator told us that he distinctly remembered seeing a *steam turbine* engine being tested on the West End. N&W and C&O historians take note.

E. L. Thompson/B&OHS

POWER

MALLETIZATION of the West End got off to a rocky start ... dieselization was a quick and complete success. Seven four-unit EMD F7 sets were delivered to M&K in the Fall of 1949, each set with 6,000 hp, 209,600# continuous tractive power and 245,100# starting tractive power. With *one* crew. The DH1s, as B&O classed them, were specifically geared for helper service and shoved away with sturdy dependability (they were later regeared for road service). Business fell off in 1949 and early 1950 ... several sets were put into QD road service and performed admirably. We will spare the reader an explanation of B&Os numbering scheme ... let us just call this set the 186. A veteran engineer told us, "They were a big thing when they arrived," and he was right. EMD F7s flooded onto B&O property during the early 1950s and, on the West End, a pattern of powering evolved that held for over a decade ... three F7 units on the front of drags and four on the rear. On QD trains, four on the rear and two or three on the front was the standard practice. B&O laughed and The Hill frowned.

B&OHS

BY THE LATE 1950s, B&O was broke. In the early 1960s C&O took control of the railroad ... by the late 1960s a process of operational melding began that has progressed to this day, involving a medley of railroads and equipment. Motive power distribution became centrally controlled with the net result that on the West End you could see anything on anything at any time. B&O was a GP railroad, not seeing the sense in buying and operating extra axles when GP multiples could be deployed at will. B&O did acquire five SD7s and ten SD9s ... 1500 hp and 1750 hp units used for special situations, e.g. an SD9 was stationed at M&K for subdivision and turn work c. 1960. This photo at Rowlesburg 6 September 1970 says it all ... an eastbound QD train with five units ... GP40, GP35, GP38, GP35, GP30, numbers 3703, 3517, 3805, 3542 and 6939.

William Hoffman II

WEST END

A GOOD EXAMPLE of the eclectic nature of power assignment in the last third of this century is this photo of two GP9s (6456 and 6529) on 7 September 1965 working the M&K subdivision near Rowlesburg.

William Hoffman II

IN THE MID-1960s, B&O motive power people relented and acknowledged that SDs weren't *all* bad. As usual throughout history, the West End was a special case. In 1964 B&O bought twenty SD35s (7400-19) and in 1965 four more (7437-40) ... C&O bought twelve in the same years. The SD35s were 2500 hp units and in sets of four produced 308,800# tractive power. By all accounts these locomotives were among the finest in B&O history ... they remain in service with 4500 numbers to this day, although long in the tooth after a quarter of a century of assaulting The Hill. If a train watcher on the West End were to find motive power consistency 1965-85, it would be the SD35s in helper and drag service. On 6 September 1970, 7404-39-40-06 move west over Bridge 92 in a move to Hardman to shove an eastbounder.

William Hoffman II

APPARENTLY HAPPY WITH SD35s, B&O purchased seventeen SD40s 1967-69 ... nine of them (7482-90) were leased to Central Railroad of New Jersey; eight entered B&O service as 7491-94 and 7497-7500. C&O purchased another thirty-three units 1966-69. Each SD40 unit produced 3000 hp and 82,100# tractive power ... they would be seen in West End service. Other CSX railroads contributed SD40s to the pool ... various renumberings 4600-21 and 8301-8488 have occurred. As we shall see, SD40s of varied ancestry still appear in West End lashups.

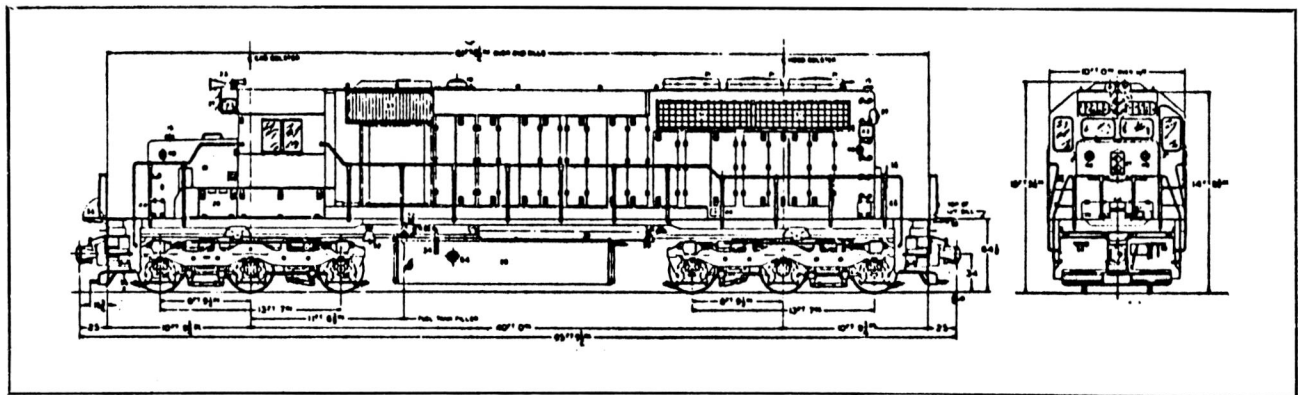

C. S. Roberts Collection

POWER

C. S. Roberts

AN SD50 against the train and two SD40-2s behind are shoving a drag east by Newburg on 4 May 1991, introducing the two latest classes of SDs ordered by B&O for primary service on the West End. Twenty SD40-2s were delivered early in 1977 numbered 7600-19, borrowing their numbers from long-gone EM1s. These are 3000 hp units with tractive power in the 81,000 to 83,160# range ... they can be seen in road or helper service. For example, in the Fall of 1978 we rode a single SD40-2 shoving out of Piedmont. These engines are good, but not perfect power ... they have a tendency to overload on grades. They are now numbered 8000-8261. The splendid SD50s appeared on the West End in the Spring of 1984 in the form of C&O units ... in August twenty B&O units numbered 8576-95 were on duty (the last locomotives, incidentally, to be delivered to B&O before corporate extinction in 1987). The SD50s are 3500 hp units, each producing 96,300# of tractive power. The era of four-unit helpers ended with the arrival of the SD50s ... three of them could do the job. Combined CSX SD50s are now numbered 8500-8643 ... the engine shown here is not a B&O unit. Against the chance that the casual reader might be puzzled by constant renumbering of locomotives, let us point out that a railroad cannot have two engines with the same number. Extra trains (and most of them are extras) take their identification from the number of the leading road locomotive. To have two trains on the railroad with the same number is inviting disaster.

Chapter 10

Trains and Cars

With one exception, all forms of transportation share a basic similarity. They involve self-propelled units carrying cargo. Man, animals, watercraft, wagons, trucks and iron birds are all integral structures with propulsion power inherent in the design. A tug towing some barges or a tractor with a couple of trailers are minor variants that merely illustrate the basic premise.

The unique form is the railroad. Power units, alone or in combination, haul large numbers of cars in trains. Other than watercraft where the water supports the load, the railroad is by far and away the most efficient mode of transportation in existence.

Adhesion is the secret. The coefficient of friction between like metals is very high ... thus the iron wheel on the iron rail or the steel wheel on the steel rail tend to adhere to one another. With enough power in the propulsion unit and enough weight on the driving wheels to maintain adhesion, you can pull enormous tonnages at speed with an extremely high payload-to-power ratio.

We have discussed power and the constant drive to create ever more powerful locomotives. The point of this exercise is to pull more and more weight in a train and further improve overall efficiency.

The cars are the point of the power ... indeed, the whole point of the railroad itself. After all, the cars carry the payload. In the case of railroad cars, a few problems arise. Whereas, say, a wagon merely has to carry a load, a railroad car has to carry a load and be capable of doing so in trains consisting of scores of other cars.

To design a railroad car to carry a load is rather simple. A car is in effect a bridge ... the trucks are the piers and the carbody the bridge itself. Man has been building bridges for thousands of years. Various forms or combinations of girders and trusses and cantilevers and cables can be employed to support the load. One can spring and reinforce the trucks to absorb road shocks with no particular problem.

Bridges, however, stay in one place. Railroad cars do not. They are coupled together in trains of ever increasing length and hauled away. That "hauling away" introduces a few very nasty problems.

First is slack. Couplers are mounted and spring-loaded in draft gear on the carbody to dampen shock and the couplers themselves (whether links and pins in the early years or knuckle automatic couplers in later years) must have a little space between pulling faces in order to function. Thus there is sprung (controlled) slack and free (uncontrolled) slack in every car. Multiply that slack by a hundred cars and there is a lot of slosh in the train.

That slosh is either stretched out or bunched up or a mixture of the two. The place where stretched and bunched slack meet is called the node. The node, unfortunately, is very contrary and refuses to stay in one place. As the node rushes back and forth, it creates some additional problems called buff and draft forces ... innocuous sounding, brutal in action.

Buff forces are compressive ... one car slams into another and compresses the frames. Draft forces are the opposite ... pulling creates tension on car frames and couplers.

Slack, buff, draft and load-bearing forces combine to create problems in car design. And the West End, with its grades and curves, as always made it a "special case", i.e., the problems were magnified. Curves create resistance and add to draft forces. As trains got longer, more and more cars were wrapped around more and more curves and multiplied draft strain. And, of course, the grades are an insult to gravity ... the steeper the grade the more weight hanging on couplers and frames.

When slack runs in, curve resistance helps a little but not enough to compensate for the impact of momentum and gravity.

Slack isn't all bad ... a locomotive unable to start a stretched train can bunch slack and break inertia by starting bits of the train at a time.

TRAINS AND CARS

Good and bad together, early car designers had to reconcile all these demands and come up with cars able to take the beating and carry loads at a profit. Car design progress has been steady and impressive, none more so than on B&O in the early years.

We will take the reader on a succinct tour of B&O car design in the usual pattern later in this chapter, concentrating on cars likely to have been in service on the West End ... open-top hoppers, box, stock, grain, passenger, express and caboose cars. As railroading evolved, cars were interchanged between roads and common approaches to car design were mandated ... when the West End first opened, cars did not usually leave home rails and consequently B&O could concentrate on car development to meet the requirements of its own severe environment ... it was no accident that iron hoppers and box cars appeared on B&O quite early. Happily, B&O selected 4'-8½" for its gauge and avoided the trauma suffered by some other roads when that distance between the rails became standard.

Cars plus power equal trains and the most prevalent train on the West End would be, of course, the drag.

As we begin, let us introduce the reader to some abbreviations which will be used: ETT/Employee Timetable ... DRMT/Dispatchers Record of the Movement of Trains ... STUDY/company analysis of 1919 West End operations ... A/actual tons ... AT/adjusted tons.

Here is a precis of one hundred years of eastbound drag operation with helpers on the West End:

GRAFTON TO PIEDMONT

Year	Power	Avg. Run Hours	Avg. MPH	Avg. MPH up Cranberry	Cars Per Train	Tons
1855 ETT*	Stm 080	10½	7	9	9	144A
1919 STUDY	Compound Mallet	9	8½	8	50	3600A
1945 DRMT	Simple Mallet	8	10	8	53	4500AT
1956 DRMT	F7 Diesel	5½	14	13	61	5500AT

*Scheduled time with five meets. Other times actual.

This analysis demonstrates some simple facts. First, steam power improvement increased train length and load, but not running times. Second, simpling mallets was very productive. Third, the diesel improved everything.

Diesel productivity has, of course, leapt forward since 1956 ... for example, a typical 1991 drag contains 75 cars of 9000AT.

There is another way of looking at it, however, and it is more sobering.

Year	Cars Pulled Per Powered Axle	Tons Pulled Per Powered Axle
1855 ETT (est.)	2.3	36
1919 STUDY	2.1	150
1945 DRMT	2.2	188
1956 DRMT	2.2	196
1984 Author's Notes	2.4	214
1991 Author's Notes	2.2	265

After almost a century and a half of constant improvement in power and car capacity, *the number of cars pulled per powered axle has not changed.* Many other things have changed and everything is relative, but the bald fact remains that the West End is still a cyst on B&Os posterior and The Hill hasn't given up an inch. The Hill is unconquered and perhaps unconquerable.

The story of westbound coal car movements is substantially the same ... doubled train length and roughly halved running times do not change the dismal fact that returning empties is a very high cost operation on the West End.

The arrival of the F7 DH1s for helper service in 1949 was accompanied by a lot of fanfare (after B&O was sure the change was a success ... there was no advance publicity ala the mallets ... once burned, twice shy). On Cranberry, helper time per drag was reduced by a third and B&O promoted this accomplishment with a blizzard of press releases. Crew costs were also reduced by a third on the grades and this was no minor gain. As we have shown, average MPH up Cranberry increased by more than fifty percent. Still, it is necessary to keep all these dramatic improvements in perspective ... almost all of the time and turnaround gains were the result of diesel availability. Diesels did not have to stop at, say, 42 for water and they were immediately available for another shove when they arrived at M&K or Hardman without any time being lost for servicing.

Thus dieselization on the West End provided a large one-time gain. Additional gains would be incremental and achieved a little bit at a time over years. It took thirty-five years to increase tons pulled per powered axle by 35%.

WEST END

With QD trains, the pattern of tonnage east and empties west was the norm throughout history except that the split was not as severe as with drags ... while the relationship varied over the years, a typical split would be three loads east for every one west.

Usually QD trains were numbered, although QD extras and additional sections appeared frequently when business was good. By the turn of the century, storied train numbers 88, 94, 96, 97 and 196 began to appear on schedules. After World War II as B&O fought for non-commodity business, QD trains began to sport names, e.g. Timesaver, Trailer Jet, Gateway, TOFC, St. Louisan and others.

A typical day would see six or more QDs east and three west. And on the West End, B&O would pile on helper power to move them over The Hill ... until 1985. In a decision that stunned West End watchers, B&O announced in July of that year that *all* QD trains and grain extras would be rerouted via the Chicago line and the West End would see only open-top hopper trains. We will discuss the reasoning behind this move in the Operations Chapter ... in effect, B&O surrendered to The Hill after 132 years of war. In November of 1985, The Hill took out Bridge 92 in response.

In December 1987 B&O reinstated two QD trains (Nos. 316 and 317) on the West End because of other developments west of Grafton, but in reality these trains should more correctly be called "junk trains" ... they are slow and do switching en route.

The following table gives the reader an insight into QD operations on the West End:

Year	Train	Avg. MPH	Between
1855 ETT (1)	Stock East	9	Grafton-Piedmont
1884 ETT (2)	85 (East)	10	Grafton-Piedmont
1886 ETT (3)	145 (West)	10	Piedmont-Grafton
1911 ETT	94	21	Grafton-Piedmont
1919 STUDY (4)	94	15	Grafton-West Keyser
1919 STUDY (4)	97	16	West Keyser-East Grafton
1928 ETT (5)	94	19	East Grafton-Viaduct Jct.
1928 ETT (5)	97 (Cin.)	12	West Keyser-East Grafton
1948 ETT (6)	94 (St. L)	20	East Grafton-Viaduct Jct.
1948 ETT (6)	97 (Cin.)	19	Viaduct Jct.-East Grafton
1956 DRMT (7)	88	20	East Grafton-Viaduct Jct.
1956 DRMT (7)	97	34	Viaduct Jct.-East Grafton
1990 Sch (8)	316	16	East Grafton-Viaduct Jct.

(1) Scheduled time with 3 meets; **(2)** Passenger Car attached-Train Number is correct; **(3)** Passenger Car attached; **(4)** Q1c on point; **(5)** Simple mallet on point; **(6)** EM1 on point; **(7)** F7 diesels on point; **(8)** Running time scheduled.

For the reader with the image of fast-stepping QDs streaking through the countryside, the average speeds in this table must be startling. Well, that's the West End ... to attain even these average speeds, B&O throughout history had to employ *one powered axle for each 1.6 cars*.

We cannot let Train 85 in 1884 pass without comment. Railroads run in only two directions, usually East and West. Timetable trains are numbered "even east" ... *all* eastbound trains carry even numbers and *all* westbound trains carry uneven numbers (extras, of course, carry the road locomotive number as in Extra *East* 7691).

Not on B&O in 1884 ... they did it the other way around. By 1886 and later, "even east" numbering was practiced. But not in 1884 and earlier. This typical B&O eccentricity may not seem like much to the reader, but it drove your writer up the wall as he labored for hours trying to make sense out of running times. When the light finally dawned, we swore for twenty minutes in outrage at having been *again* snared by B&Os gleeful habit of deploying traps for historians. Students be warned.

B&O sold passenger tickets for West End travel for 118 years, from 1853 to 1971. From opening of the line until late in the last century, the West End was part of the Main Stem from Baltimore to Wheeling and Parkersburg ... *all* through traffic funneled over The Hill to and from Chicago, St. Louis and points between. The line to Chicago from Cumberland via Pittsburgh was not fully functional until the 1890s and the Main Stem cognomen was not dropped until early in this century.

Passenger, or more accurately First Class, trains as a category included more than the well-known "feature" trains. Mail, express, tour, troop, special and even Presidential trains were regularly scheduled through the West End. History's first large troop movement went through the West End during the Civil War and MAIN trains (as troop trains were called in this century) were frequent movements until after the Korean War when aircraft were used to get cannon fodder to the front more speedily.

Express and Mail business was always a major source of West End revenue. In 1855 there were three First Class trains scheduled in each direction, named *Mail*, *Express* and *Accommodation* ... while the first two probably carried passenger cars, it is obvious that self-loading cargo was only a part of this picture.

TRAINS AND CARS

In 1948, by way of example, Through-Train Passenger Consists called for 39% of the assigned cars to be express or mail. By 1958, when passenger business was melting away on all railroads, express/mail cars were 46% of the total. The last first class trains to be run on the West End were venerable Nos. 11 and 12 *Metropolitan Special*, throughout history an express with a few passenger cars attached.

In the Spring of 1971 Amtrak took over all inter-city passenger trains and, unfortunately for the West End, West Virginia Representative Harley O. Staggers was a powerful presence in Congress in that era ... B&O was stuck with running the "Staggers Special" over The Hill. Operating under various names and numbers, this train ran from September 1971 to May 1973 and again from October 1976 to September 1981, losing money by the barrel and complicating West End operations by requiring high superelevation.

Amtrak did manage a great comedy act during the first half of 1972 when they introduced the Turbo Train on the West End. B&O took one look at this abortion and refused to accept any responsibility if it ran over 25 mph on the West End. Their fears were ill-founded ... it rarely got above 15 mph when it was running at all. The gnarled Hill must have looked at this experiment with astonishment ... is that a train or a moped?

The premier passenger train numbers on any railroad are the lowest and the West End had the most prestigious by 1884 ... Numbers 1, 2, 3 and 4. By 1965 the West End still had Nos. 1 and 2, but lowly *Metropolitan Special* outlasted them all.

Following is an overview of first class operations on the West End.

PASSENGER/EXPRESS TRAINS

Year	Train	Avg. MPH	Total Trains Both Directions	Between
1855 ETT	Exp West	20	6	Piedmont-Grafton
1855 ETT	Mail East	20	6	Grafton-Piedmont
1855 ETT	Acc East	17	6	Grafton-Piedmont
1884 ETT (1)	1 East	27	10	Grafton-Piedmont
1886 ETT (2)	1 West	28	10	Piedmont-Grafton
1906 ETT	2	26	13	Grafton-Piedmont
1929 ETT	2	33	15	Grafton-Piedmont
1949 ETT	76	37	12	Grafton-Piedmont
1965 ETT	2	33	4	Grafton-Cumberland
1970 ETT	11	33	2	Cumberland-Grafton
Amtrak	8	34	2	Grafton-Cumberland

(1) See preceding diatribe.
(2) See preceding diatribe. ETT says "No trains to stop at Mountain Lake Park on Sundays." One hopes the bars were open in Loch Lynn.

Average first class speeds over the West End were faster than those for QD trains, as one would expect, but they certainly were not record-breaking. And the historical record for powered axles per car? One.

"Why all the power?"

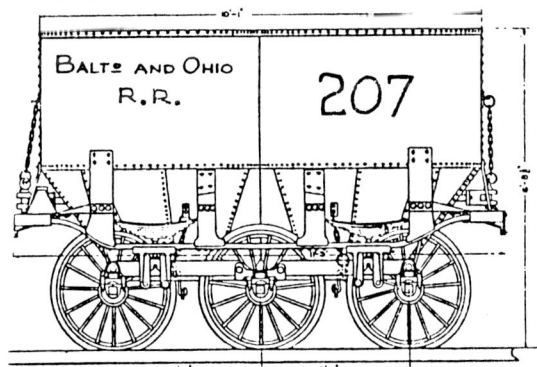
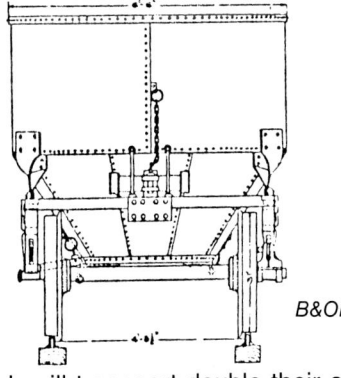

THIS SIX-WHEEL open-top hopper car was not the first car produced by B&O to haul coal, but it was a member of the first class of cars designed by Ross Winans that got the job done with a load capacity that exceeded the tare, i.e., it could carry a load heavier than the car itself. Mr. Winans patented this design in 1847 and it is a reflection of his genius. "The transportation of coal and all other heavy articles in lumps has been attended with great injury to the cars, requiring the bodies to be constructed with great strength to resist the outward pressure on the sides as well as the vertical pressure on the bottom, not only to the weight of the mass, but the mobility of the lumps ... tending to 'pack' ... by my improvement I am enabled to make cars which will transport double their own weight," he stated in his patent application. This car weighed 3 tons and carried 7½ tons, a remarkable breakthrough in design which presaged a fleet of similar cars on B&O and other railroads. The car also featured a "continuous drawbar ... to relieve the body from strain due to draft (forces)," another material improvement. The six-wheel car quickly evolved into the eight-wheel design ... by 1854 B&O had only 254 six-wheelers. In that same year B&O had 770 eight-wheel wooden gondola cars, some of which were used to haul coal even though improvements in this design resulted in a tare/load relationship of only 6½ to 9 tons. Gondola cars, of course, evolved, but not as primary coal haulers.

WEST END

IT IS POSSIBLE that these four-wheel cars, shown at Piedmont c. 1872, hauled coal when built. If so, their tare/load relationship must have been poor. We believe that these are "dump" cars, of which B&O reported 138 in 1854 and 128 in 1860 without specifications. It is also possible that they were MOW cars for ballast or demoted to that service.

B&O Museum

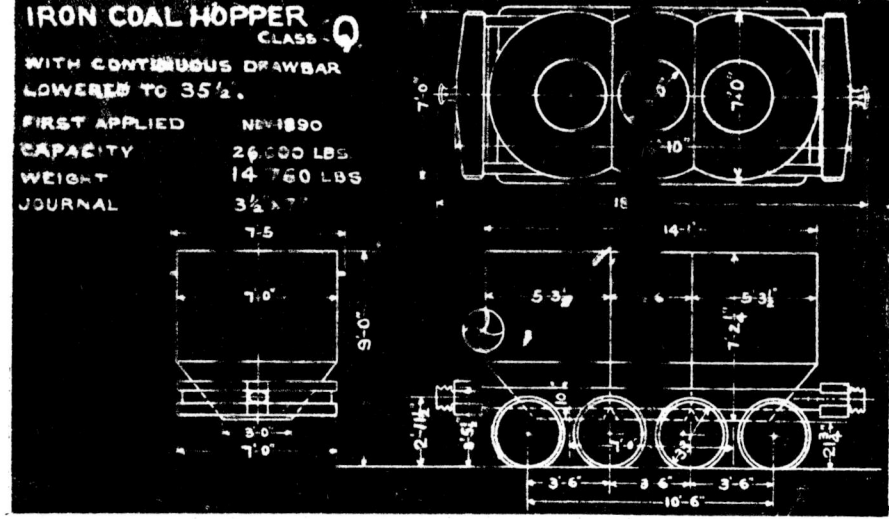

AS COULD BE IMAGINED, the six-wheel rigid base car tended to derail, so Mr. Winans quickly designed this eight-wheel car. It weighed slightly over 7 tons and carried 13 tons, a small retrogression in tare/load which was more than offset by better trackability and increased total load.

C. S. Roberts Collection

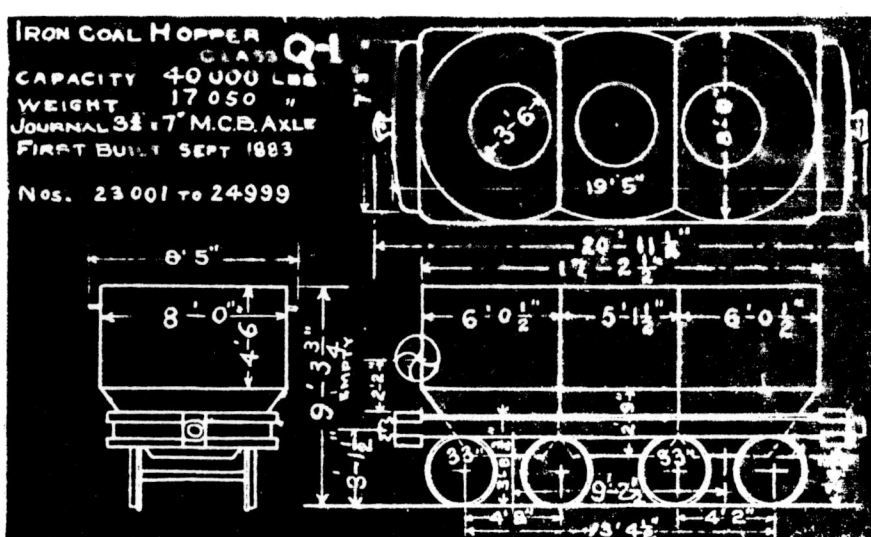

THE POT HOPPER, as it became known, was constantly improved over the years by lengthening of the car and utilization of the pots to form part of the structure of the car. This version was built in 1883 with a tare/load of 8½ to 20 tons ... a relationship that compares to the very earliest eight-wheel pot (not pictured) of 4 to 8½ tons. The pots, of course, were built of iron. Two 1884 examples of this class of car are in the B&O Museum ... they have a rod running the length of the car, tied to the coupler pockets, to add strength to the wooden underframe and pot "cantilever." A lot of these cars were built ... for example, B&O went from 773 in 1854 to 1,756 in 1870 and continued building them until the late 1880s.

C. S. Roberts Collection

TRAINS AND CARS

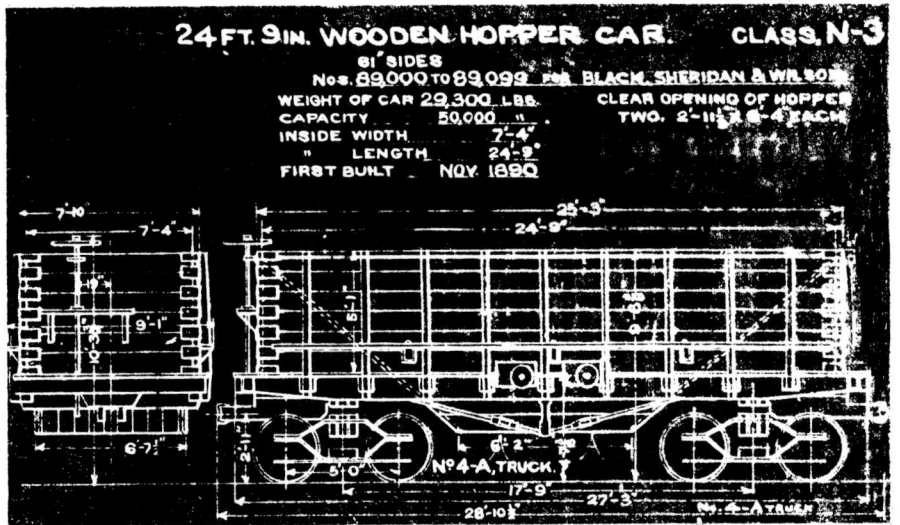

C. S. Roberts Collection

IN THE LATE 1880s, B&O began building truss-rod rectangular wooden hoppers ... this example of an N3 was built in 1890. These hoppers were cheaper to build than the "pots" and improved cubic capacity in relation to the length of the car ... at a price of a more modest tare/load of 14½ to 25 tons. Total capacity, however, was higher than a contemporary "pot." We should note that truck design is an important factor in the equation of car design ... heavier cars require stronger trucks to carry the load and absorb shocks.

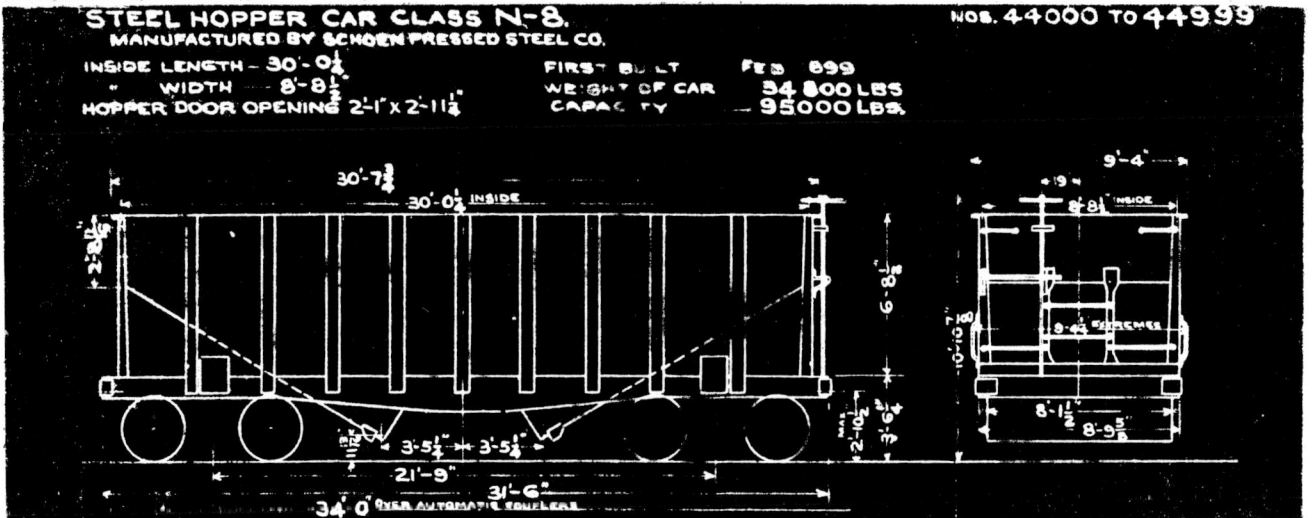

C. S. Roberts Collection

THE STEEL HOPPER CAR era dawned in the late 1890s and with it a dramatic increase in the tare/load ... this N8 car boasted 17 to 47 tons. Early steel hoppers had fishbelly side frames as well as steel main frames to add support to the cantilever car sides.

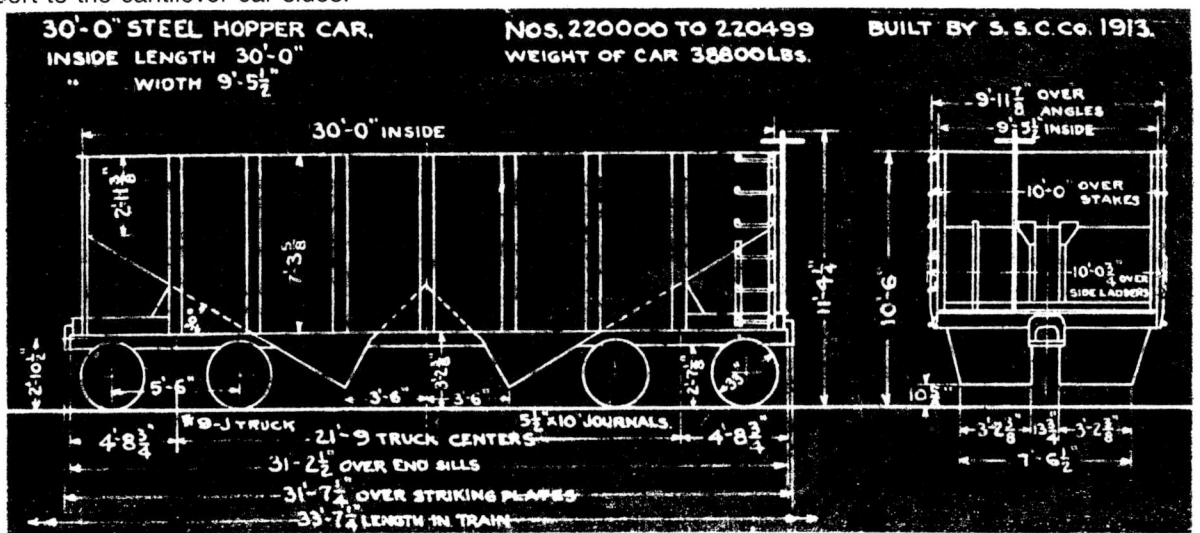

C. S. Roberts Collection

BY 1913, steel hopper design was steadily improving ... this N12 car weighed 19½ tons and carried 55 tons. One should note that hopper car design was restricted by customer usage, e.g. if coal users had trestles and bins built to handle 30 foot cars they could not accommodate longer cars.

WEST END

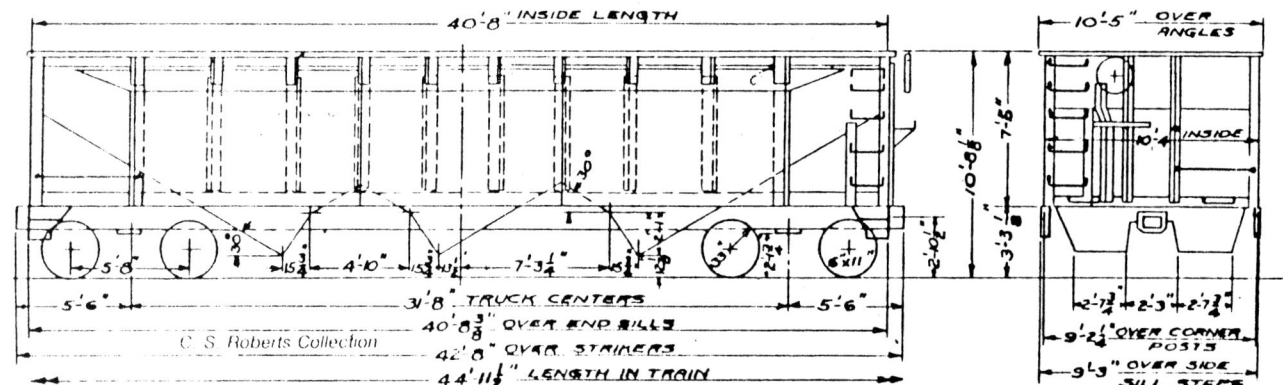

OFFSET-SIDE car design as well as lengthening increased cubic capacity and total load. The side ribs were placed inside the car except at the top ... in this W7 car built in 1947 with three hoppers, tare/load was 24 and 81 tons. B&O had been building 40 foot offset hoppers with four hoppers (quads) for some years before 1947, yet as late as 1/1/1949 seventy-seven percent of B&O hoppers were twins and only twenty-three percent triples and quads.

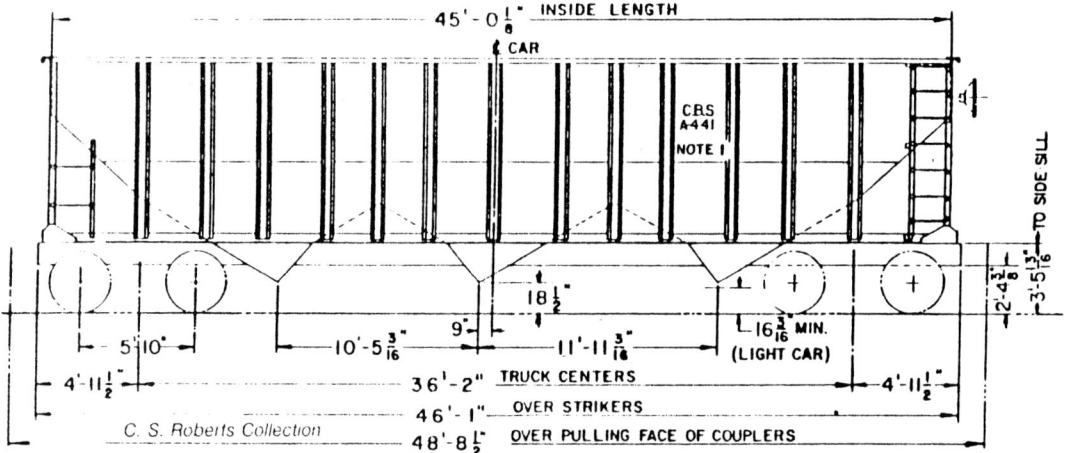

THIS H48 car was built in 1976 for B&O/C&O and fairly represents the modern hopper car. Offset-side cars passed into disfavor for maintenance and first cost reasons ... the side-ribbed car is now virtually universal. This car weighs 30 tons and carries 102 tons ... this 3.4 ratio is about as good as it's going to get unless some magic new metal alloy appears. B&O experimented with aluminum and corten steel hoppers in the 1930s, but no production orders resulted. Roller-bearing trucks are nearing universality, adding to efficiency.

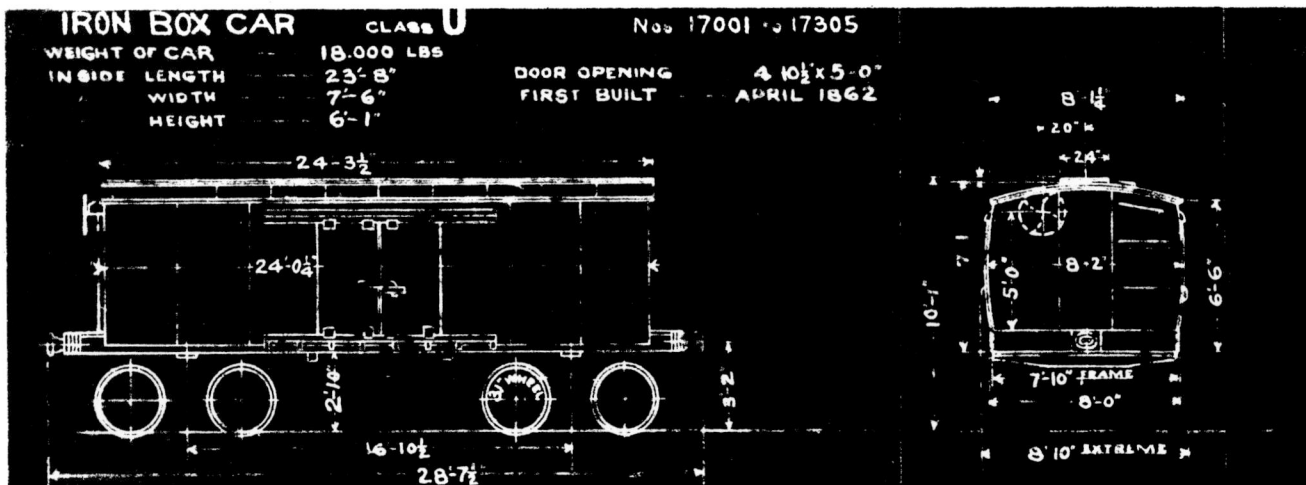

THE "HOUSE" CAR, as it was called in the early days, was as ubiquitous on the railroad as the open-top hopper ... it provided an enclosed, weathertight container for divers ladings. In the 1880s this design would become known as a Box Car, a class name that remains to this day. By 1854 in Main Stem service B&O had 1,056 "House" cars, eight-wheel, tare 6½ tons, capacity 7 tons ... by 1870 there would be 1,779 such cars of various tare/load ratios. This early iron car was produced in large numbers ... one still exists in the B&O Museum. However, not all early cars were made of iron ... while records are non-existent, some photos show house cars obviously made of wood.

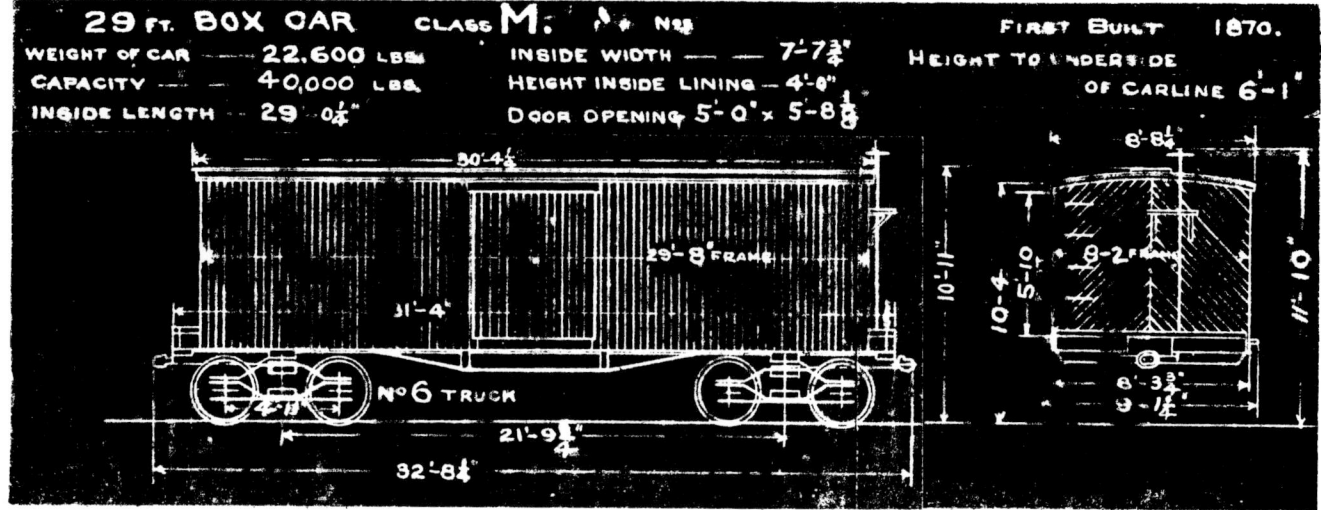

THE WOODEN BOX CAR became predominant on all railroads, including B&O, in the last century. Underframes came to be truss-rod affairs as on this car ... turnbuckles on the rods were used to adjust tension. The sides of box cars were also part of the structure and formed a truss. Shifting cargo brought attention to end designs, which also evolved. The tare/load ratios of box cars have never reached the heights of those on open-top hoppers, in great measure because it wasn't necessary. Ladings in box cars covered the gamut of cargo types ... feathers to booze ... and rarely was a box car loaded to capacity.

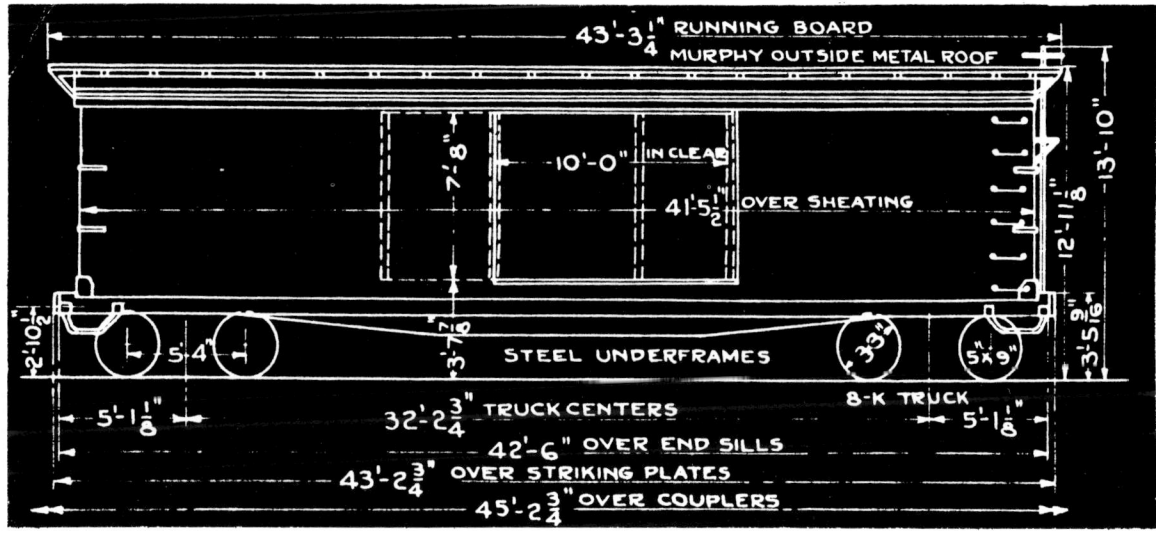

INCREASING TRAIN LENGTH multiplied stresses on cars and box cars, among others, were designed with steel fishbelly underframes as in this M15 car produced in 1910-11. Two thousand of these cars were built with a tare/load of 22 tons and 40 tons. The "box" was still wood, although in this case with a metal roof. Note that car *capacity* and length was increasing ... it was the tare/load *ratio* that stayed about the same as earlier cars.

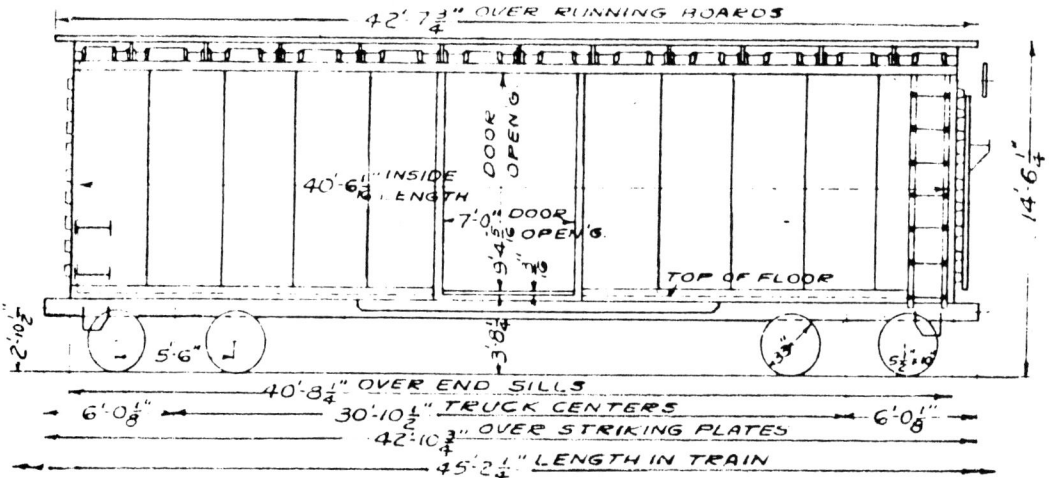

THE ALL-STEEL box car inevitably evolved with corrugated ends and roof ... this M55c car was built in 1945 and boasted a favorable tare/load of 22½ tons to 62 tons. This particular subclass of car became famous when a number of them were painted in silver and blue "Sentinel Service" livery just after World War II.

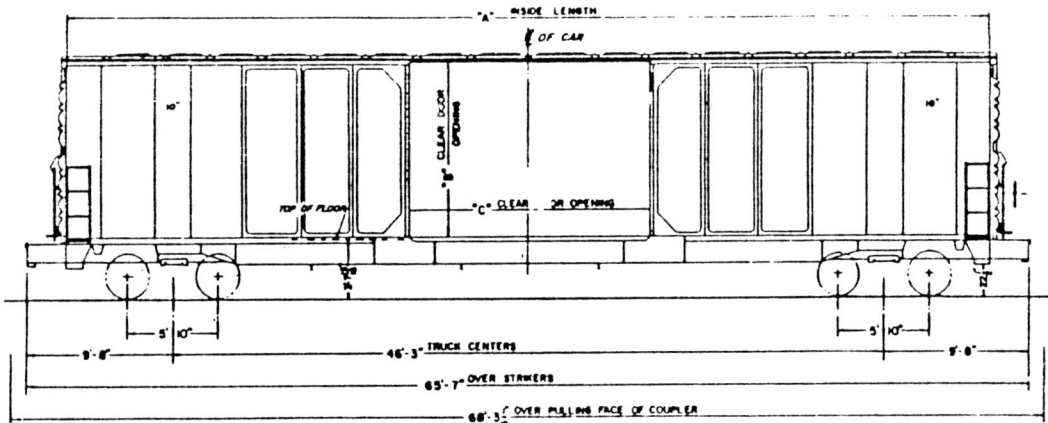

THE HI-CUBE box car began to appear on all railroads in the 1960s and this B102A car is typical ... while only five specific examples of this car were built in 1970, it is a classic modern-day box car of 60 foot length and tare/load of 41½ tons and 90 tons.

C. S. Roberts Collection

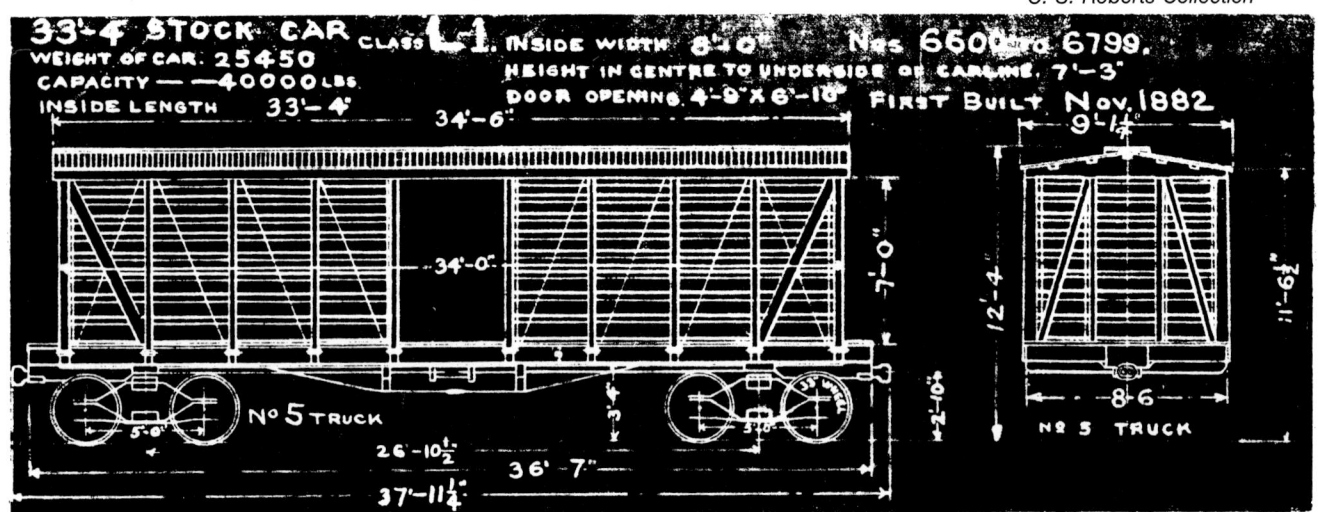

FOUR-LEGGED FOOD was a major source of revenue for B&O and particularly through the West End ... B&O lines ultimately tapped lush Midwestern agricultural areas and much of the meat moved "on hoof" in stock cars. From opening of the line until the mid-1950s, solid stock trains were the norm ... in addition, meat and produce moved in Refrigerator cars over the West End. For example, for many years QD No. 88 was almost solid Reefers when it left St. Louis. This 1882 wooden, truss-rod car was typical. Actually, stock car design changed little over the years and the length hardly at all because stockyard chutes were spaced for short cars. In the early 1850s some B&O stock cars were open-top, a practice that stopped when the viciousness of West End weather was recognized. In this connection, one wonders if perhaps B&O inadvertently pioneered the transport of frozen meat.

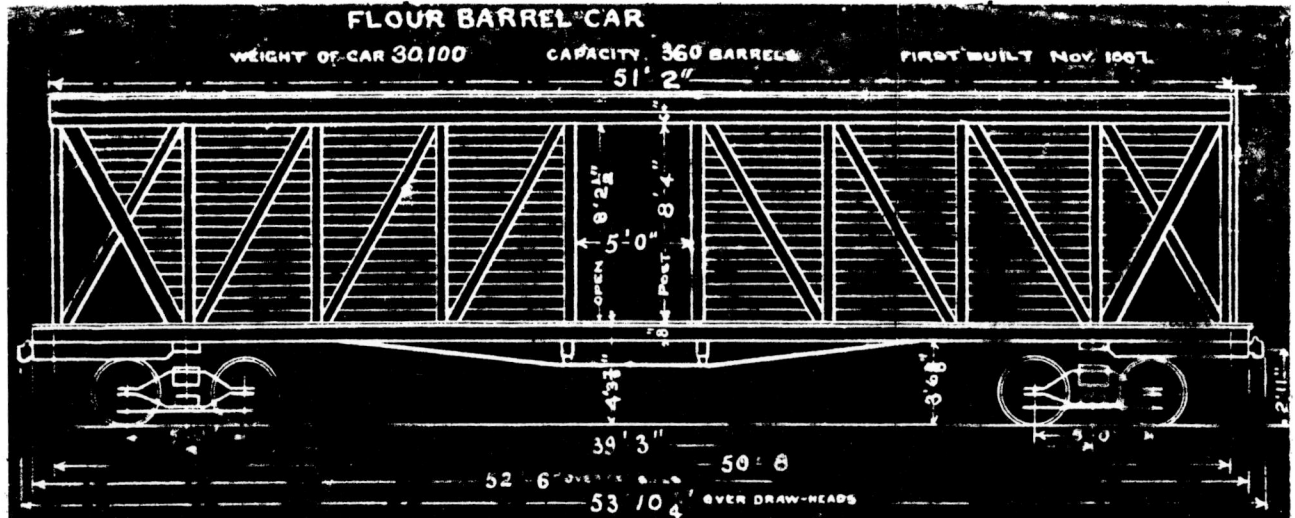

GRAIN MOVEMENTS were another major source of West End tonnage from opening of the road until the mid-1980s, much of it for export from Baltimore. Whether in bags, barrels or loose, the Midwest granaries produce a torrent of this commodity and much of it moved in drags through the West End until B&O diverted such movements to the Chicago line. Until recent times, much grain moved in box cars ... this 1887 flour barrel car is so unusual, however, we couldn't resist presenting it. We doubt if many were built.

TRAINS AND CARS

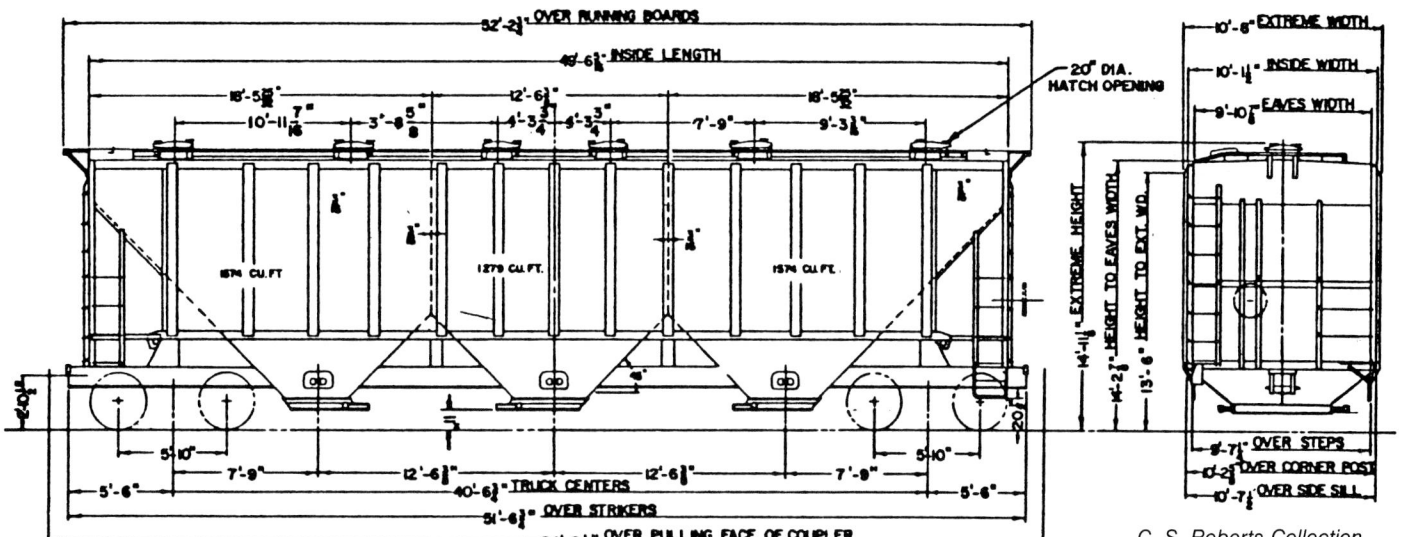

C. S. Roberts Collection

IN MODERN TIMES, grain moves in large covered hoppers ... this HC30 car, built in 1970, is typical with a tare of 30 tons and capacity of 101 tons. While one must grant that this style of car design moves grain economically, it is apparently topheavy and susceptible to overloading. These two faults plus a long wheelbase have resulted is a car liable to rocking on curves to such an extent that it will leave the railroad at speeds between 10-25 mph, an undesired turn of events. For years, crews with this category of car in their consists have been cautioned to keep train speed below 10 mph or above 25 mph and to assiduously watch their train for "excessive" rocking, whatever that is. We assume that rocking is "excessive" when the train is all over the county. Crews are also required, of course, to keep eyes focused ahead of the train for obvious reasons ... how crews are to reconcile these conflicting missions remains unremarked. And on West End curvature, one can rarely see the train let alone go swiftly through the danger speed zone between 10-25 mph on West End grades ... grain extras are, after all, drags. When B&O removed QD trains from the West End, they also stopped grain extras.

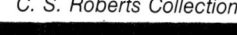

C. S. Roberts Collection

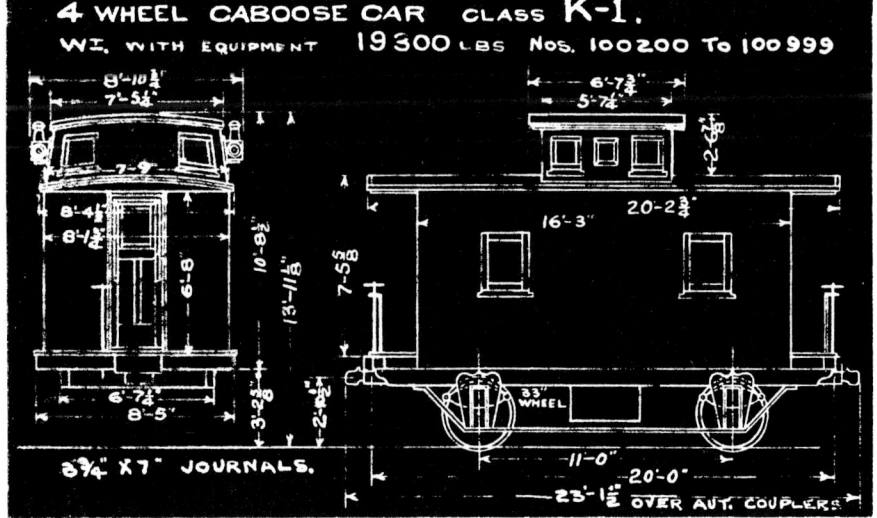

DRAG OR QD, the end of every freight train had a caboose. Well, not quite. It was not until 1866 that B&O even mentioned having any cabooses and the total was only four ... by 1872 there were one hundred and forty-three. Prior to the advent of the caboose, trainmen rode out on their trains without relief in all weather. On the West End, brakemen rode out until the 1950s! In recent years, the end-of-train device has eliminated the caboose on almost all trains and the whole crew rides up front. Pictured is a K1 four-wheel "bobber" caboose, a classic early B&O design. The presence of a caboose was a special problem on the West End when shoving started ... the helper could crush the caboose against the train or pop it out of the train, neither scenario commending itself to management or crews. So, The Hill laughed as B&O had to take the time on the West End to splice-in helpers ahead of the caboose and then return it at the summit.

WEST END

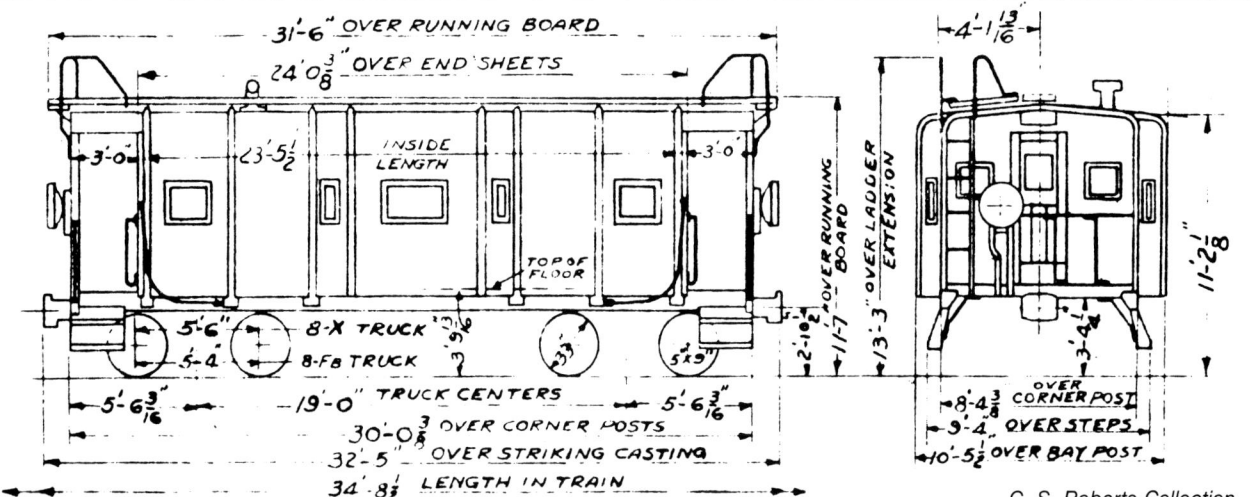

THE ULTIMATE SOLUTION to the West End caboose problem came with the all-steel wagontop design ... at last, B&O had a caboose that could withstand the buff forces from helpers. While a few examples were tested in the 1930s, real relief came with one hundred of these I12 cars ... built appropriately enough, at Keyser in 1941 just in time for the surge in war tonnage.

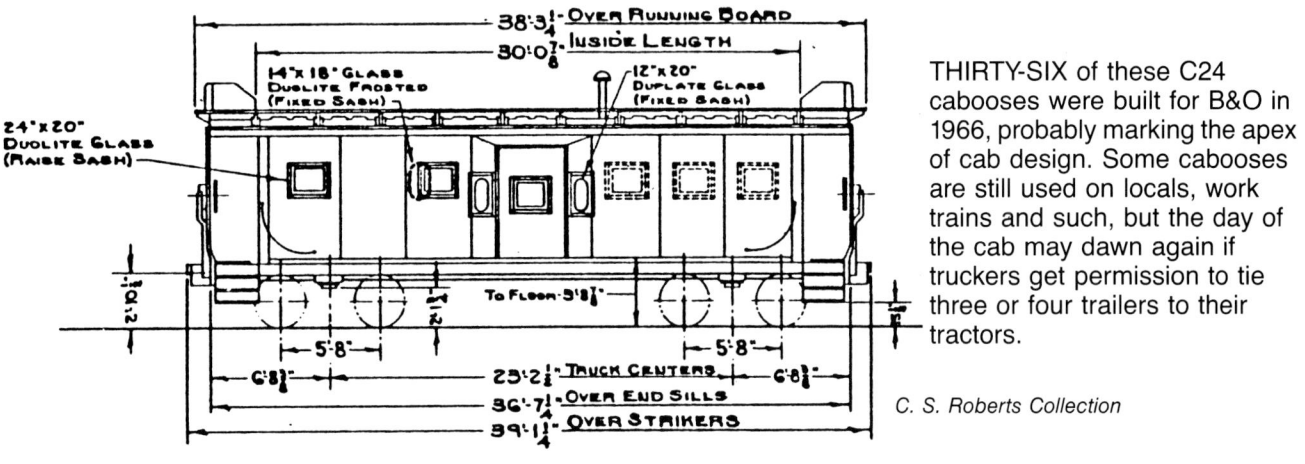

THIRTY-SIX of these C24 cabooses were built for B&O in 1966, probably marking the apex of cab design. Some cabooses are still used on locals, work trains and such, but the day of the cab may dawn again if truckers get permission to tie three or four trailers to their tractors.

C. S. Roberts Collection

B&O SOLD the first passenger ticket and by the time the West End was built, enjoyed a thriving passenger business. Here we see an early 54-seat wooden, truss-rod coach with duckbill clerestory built in 1870 which probably saw service on the West End ... note that it only weighed 22 tons.

C. S. Roberts Collection

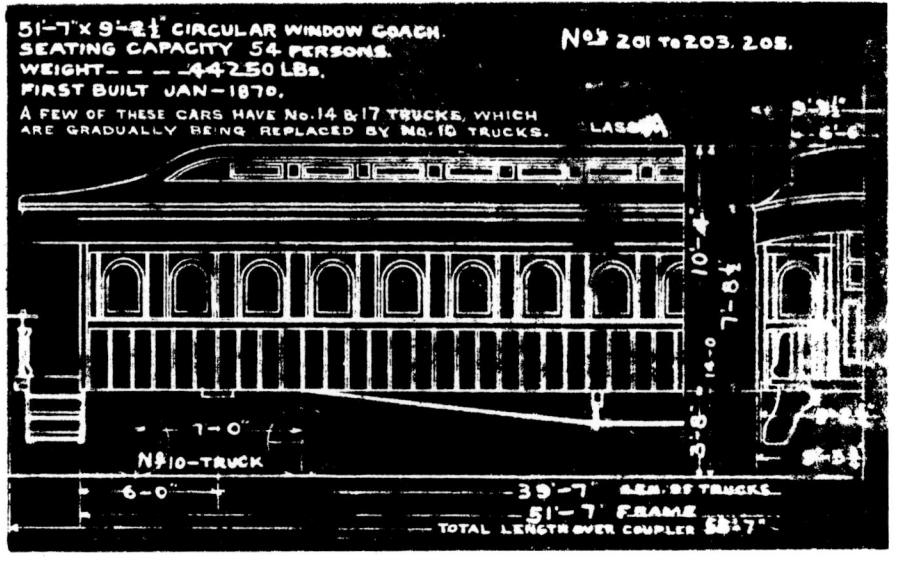

TRAINS AND CARS

B&Os MAIN STEM enjoyed a hearty express business from opening until the end of passenger service and a lot of it funneled through the West End. This C2 express car was built in 1886 and weighed almost twenty-five tons ... since 25 of these cars were built, it is virtually certain that examples rode on West End trains. Note that clerestory end-shape has evolved to the configuration that would endure to the end of the steel standard passenger car era.

MORE THAN ONE mail-user wishes that the Rail Post Office would come back to life and reinstitute the movement rather than storage of written communications. Here we see a 30-ton Postal Car built in 1885 ... note that B&O is beginning to use six-wheel passenger trucks, a practice that would become standard on all B&O passenger-hauling cars in the next century.

B&Os WAGONTOP design is generally recognized as still another major advance in car development ... the C16 express cars, seen on the West End in large numbers, were converted to express use from original 1937 construction as M53 box cars. These cars were built at Keyser and were ultimately changed back to box cars. Of course, B&O carried a lot of express in baggage cars ... a category which included working mail, storage mail, express, newspapers and other high-priority ladings.

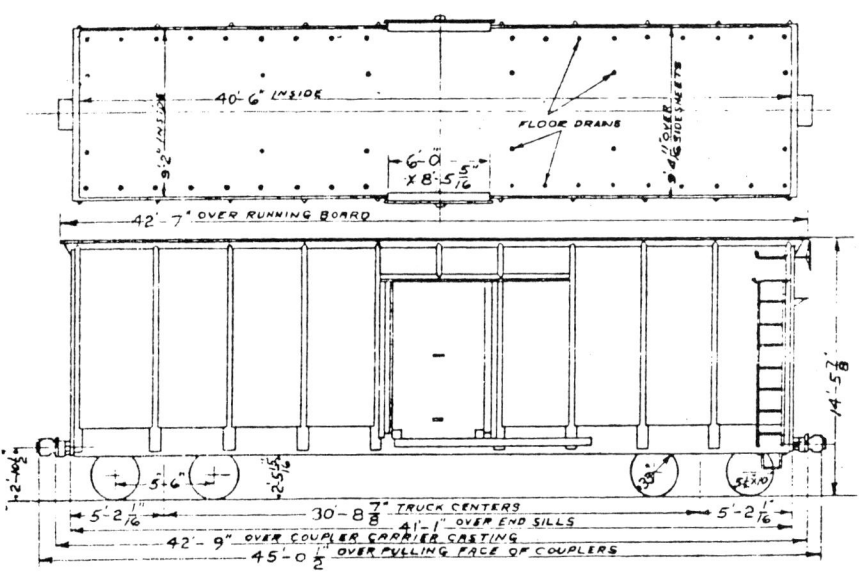

C. S. Roberts Collection

WEST END

THE STEEL PASSENGER CAR began arriving on the B&O early in this century ... whatever the benefits derived in the areas of safety and comfort, the tare/load ratio worsened to the extent that major increases in power were required. We have seen an 1870 coach that weighed 22 tons and carried 54 people ... this updated A19b modernized coach weighed 80 tons (Pullmans weighed even more) and carried 68 people. B&O pioneered air conditioning in passenger cars and certainly it was a welcome advance, but a heavy price was paid in weight what with all the generators and A/C equipment sucking on the power up front. We have shown how West End passenger operations employed rear helpers to relieve coupler strain on first class trains (until an official tired of it) ... a lesser known fact is that B&O was a "hard spring" railroad. Increasing passenger car length combined with B&O curvature introduced the possibility that sway might cause the cars of two trains passing on a curve to "kiss." B&O management was as lusty as the next, but this form of embrace might have unwelcome consequences. B&O hardened the springs, choosing safety over a soft ride. We recognize that the reader can have a lot of fun with the last three sentences and would welcome copies of any word plays that evolve ... we must, however, close the subject by pointing out that West End curves were many but not all of the ones on B&O responsible for this decision.

C. S. Roberts Collection

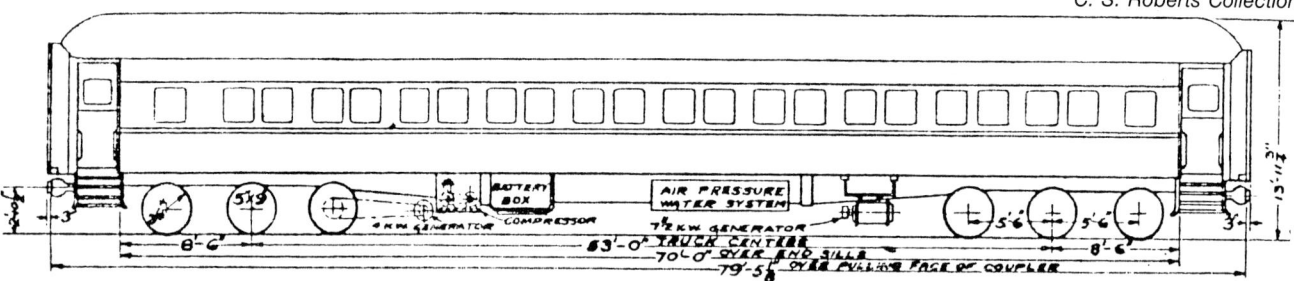

THIS SUBLIME PHOTOGRAPH of Train 76 *Cincinnatian* Engine 5302 besting Cranberry Grade at Salt Lick Curve on 13 March 1949 ... running on time ... says it all for Mr. Barr, the B&O and the West End. On 21 May 1947, Tommy was aboard Train 76 Engine 5301 and recorded the following in one of his incomparable trip logs: "Left Grafton 15 seconds late, Engineer Cregan. Yellow signal approaching Thornton, and then red near MP 6.2, proceeding at one-quarter speed for 1.2 miles, where green signal received. Apparently whole signal bridge out-of-order, as No. 11 stopped on the westbound track. Slipped twice on Newburg Grade, due to sand clogging up, and couldn't seem to get good traction through Kingwood Tunnel. Approaching M&K Junction, engineer climbed down and tried to open the sanders, and failing, he stopped at the engine house. Shop men hit all pipes, and sand began running again, but soon after starting up Cranberry Grade, it clogged again, and engineer had extreme difficulty keeping the high-wheeled engine moving. Rain or wet rail entire run. Road Foreman of Engines (Wild Bill Henry) came running out and got aboard, running engine to Keyser. And run it he did! The times were sensational over this piece of railroad, and notwithstanding instructions in the timetable calling for 32 minutes *minimum* from Altamont to Piedmont, the run was made in 26½ minutes! The intermediate times explain themselves and it is doubtful if they have ever been bettered. Did 58 mph uphill coming to Altamont." Wild Bill was 12½ minutes late at Terra Alta and *on time* at Keyser ... *without* going up either safety spur on Seventeen Mile Grade. This, dear reader, says it all for Wild Bill.

Chapter 11

Glimpses

C. S. Roberts

WE THOUGHT the reader might appreciate viewing the cover photograph free of typesetting. SD40-2 7604 is shoving about 160 coal cars with veteran engineer H. M. "Snuffy" Dunnivan at the throttle passing Bond on 20 October 1978. The coal cars arrived at Piedmont "stepping lively" as the road engineer wanted to get to Grafton ahead of a following train. Mr. Dunnivan preferred steam power and expressed the opinion that steam would have prevailed if sufficient research had been applied.

WEST END

SD40-2 8253 resting at West Keyser 3 May 1991 resplendent in the latest CSX coloring. When working, this engine hauls Georges Creek coal west to the Mt. Storm power plant off the old WM line.

C. S. Roberts

GP38 4816 is the lead locomotive of this coal car train as it approaches Piedmont to pick up a helper ... this is the same train being shoved in the preceding and cover photograph. The flagman is on the ground on the opposite side inspecting the train as it passes the helper spur.

EARLIER IN OCTOBER of 1978, an eastbound QD train rolled over a rail and dumped a lot of cars into the Potomac River at Bloomington ... this photo was taken from the deck of the coal car helper. The flagman on the helper was on the headend of the QD train, which left the railroad about the fiftieth car ... the shock bounced him around a bit. A lot of new automobiles ended in the river and promptly became "used."

GLIMPSES

Gary Schlerf

PASSING BOND in April of 1978, GP38 4818 and a GP40 plus two additional units lead a westbound QD train with the path of the old safety spur seen on the hillside to the right.

WEST END

Homer T. Newlon

PROBABLY ON TRAIN 30, T3b 5567 is topping the summit at Altamont on 12 August 1953 and about to descend Seventeen Mile Grade. This photograph was the subject of a painting reproduced and published in print form in 1973 ... the 5567 was colored blue in that rendering. While there were some blue T3s, it is unlikely that the 5567 was one of them.

GLIMPSES

B&OHS

C&O "SOLD" ten Alco RSD12s to B&O in the summer of 1969 and here is the 2013 leading a QD train east at Altamont on No. 1 track. The date of this photograph is uncertain … we know that B&O renumbered these 1800 hp, 12 cylinder units 2007-16 and that they were off the property in 1972. Known as "Notch Nose" engines, these units were built in 1956 with C&O numbers 6700-09. Several of them were sighted at M&K Junction in October of 1962, which probably makes them the first six-axle diesels on the West End.

CSX HAS AT LEAST some sense of soul … the famous marker at Altamont was being maintained in pristine condition on 11 August 1991. This view looks eastward.

ORIGINAL MILEPOSTS installed when the railroad was built can still be found on the West End … this one is at Altamont just east of the "summit" marker, again on 11 August 1991.

C. S. Roberts   *C. S. Roberts*

WEST END

TWO SD40s in CSX "Stealth" paint scheme lead a third unit on a drag at Mountain Lake Park 4 May 1991 with 76 trailing cars and helpers on the rear with the old "MK/PK" tower in the background.

C. S. Roberts

THE HELPERS ON THIS DRAG, which went through to Altamont, were SD50 8461, SD40-2 8258 and SD50 8560 ... two still in Chessie paint and one in stealth.

C. S. Roberts

GLIMPSES

THE MOST STATELY structure on the West End is the magnificent Oakland Station, seen here in two views on 3 May 1991.
C. S. Roberts

WEST END

C. S. Roberts

THE TERRA ALTA Station in late December of 1977 is not quite a hundred years old and is in fairly good condition. Little if anything has been done in the way of maintenance since then and its appearance today is poor ... one can only hope this interesting structure has a future.

CA TOWER at Terra Alta on 10 August 1991 is without a mission ... the plant it served for years has been completely removed.

C. S. Roberts

GLIMPSES

LIGHT POWER WEST approaching Salt Lick Curve on 4 May 1991 ... six units led by SD50s 8574 and 8589.

A WORK TRAIN east on No. 1 track in December 1978 is about to enter the frigid Glades with two feet of snow on the ground and about to pass a very chilly photographer.

WE GOT as far as the famous cut on Salt Lick Curve that December day and decided to go back to a warm fire and wee dram.

NUMBER TWO TRACK is being rebuilt near Rodemer in October of 1978 with this rather monstrous machine.

C. S. Roberts

WEST END

STILL PRESENTING a dignified appearance on 4 May 1991 even if not in use for its intended purpose, the Shrine dominates M&K Junction. The hoppers contain utility ash returning home and the power works the branch during the week. Away down No. 1 track one can see light engines about to cross Bridge 92 enroute to Grafton.

C. S. Roberts

IT IS DIFFICULT to find Sun at M&K, let alone on the North side. We got lucky on 10 August 1991 and can present an angle on the engine house seldom seen. Many years ago the corner of the house was brutally pranged, probably by an engine … the black paint covers plywood replacement walls. We do not know the details about the incident but can say that it occurred prior to 1976. On the far left, notice the lighter brick … this is the 1947 addition.

GLIMPSES

ANOTHER ANGLE on the engine house 10 August 1991 ... look closely at the right end and one can see how far the lower wall was shoved eastward.

C. S. Roberts

Andrew A. Holzopfel

MODELING is an art form and a preservation technique ... here is the Shrine in the steam era as created in HO by Andy Holzopfel in another of his wondrous works. The detail is incredible and fidelity to the original breathtaking .... the *inside* has also been re-created! And he is building another model, on commission, of the Shrine in the diesel era. If Andy ever deigns to allow an exhibition of his fantastic models, we suggest that the reader make a pilgrimage to attend.

WEST END

"ROWLESBURG" tower *nee* MK at the dawn of middle age on 10 August 1991, one of the few active towers remaining on CSX.

C. S. Roberts

YAWNING after a few months vacation, plow X26 is preparing herself for still another winter in September of 1972 at M&K Junction. During heavy snows, plow turns simply start at one end of the West End and work back and forth to the other end to keep up with the downfall and drifting.

Gary Schlerf

B&O TAKES POWER where it can find it ... here at M&K Junction on 4 May 1991 we find, of all things, a D&H GP in a branch lashup resting for the weekend. As CSXT appears under the engine number, we assume the 7408 is leased.

C. S. Roberts

GLIMPSES

A QD TRAIN moves east as the branch engine shifts coal cars at M&K Junction in December 1978.

C. S. Roberts

SD50 8607 and two SD40s pause at Rowlesburg for a crew change 4 May 1991 ... the lead locomotive is in Seaboard livery and before the year is out will probably wish she was back in warmer climes.

SHABBY but still in existence ... the Rowlesburg Station on 10 August 1991.

205

WEST END

THE EAST PORTALS of the Kingwood Tunnels in December 1977 ... the old bore on the right, of course, has been closed for many years.

C. S. Roberts

WEST END TOWER in April 1984, still active but already on the list to go into retirement.

THE FIRST SD50s from C&O appeared on the West End in the Spring of 1984 ... B&O units arrived later. Here we see a helper set at West End in April of 1984. Actually, some foreign SD50s were tested earlier and B&O was happy with their performance. These locomotives are astonishingly quiet ... we watched this set shove out of Hardman and wondered for a moment if they were being towed.

GLIMPSES

A CLASSIC SD35 set of four awaiting 88 at Hardman on 21 October 1978 ... the young man is Number Five Son Robert, who brought 7402 and mates down Newburg Grade with aplomb after two minutes training. We sat for four hours awaiting 88 and the senior engineer noted, "The pressure on this job will kill you."

C. S. Roberts

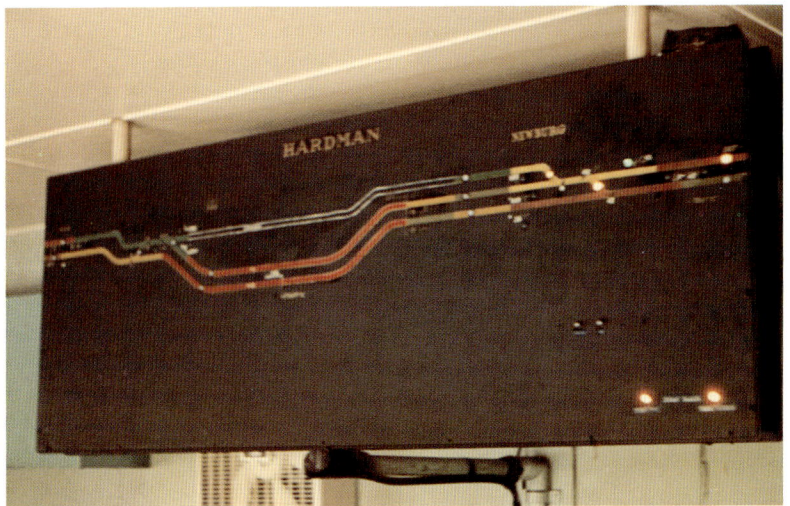

ONE HUNDRED AND SIXTY coal cars at Hardman on 4 May 1991 with a power consist typical of CSX operations today ... front to rear 3 SD50s (8609, 8632, unknown), B36-7 GE 5819, GP39-2 4301 and GP40-2 6085.

THE BOARD at Hardman (Q) in April of 1984 ... note that Newburg is controlled remotely from this tower. Hardman is still active.

207

WEST END

THE WEST PORTAL of the old Kingwood Tunnel, taken 4 May 1991, is the only remaining monument on the West End that dates from the construction of the road aside from a few original mileposts. The parapet is original ... the three insets memorialize Messrs. Latrobe, Bollman and another gentleman who was in charge of arching. The parapet on the east portal disappeared some years ago ... we have recommended removal of this artifact to the B&O Museum. Laurel Mountain continues to assault the bore ... a stream has forced its way out under the closure blocks and we would bet most of the roof has collapsed. Rest in peace, old warriors.

C. S. Roberts

Chapter 12

Operations

We have described the construction and physical evolution of the West End as well as progress in motive power and car development. In military analogy, we have presented the terrain and the weapons available at any given point in time for deployment in the battle. Now we shall discuss the tactics employed as B&O closed with the enemy over almost a century and a half of campaigning.

The Infantry School is the Holy City of wisdom and doctrine for the U.S. Army, and several of its pithy principles of operations are quite transferable to the West End.

If nothing else, the outlook of the School is pragmatic: "*Everything* depends upon the situation and the terrain," intones the most basic dictum. "If it works, it's right; if it doesn't work, it's wrong," states another fundamental rule. And the lowliest troop leader learns to orient his map toward the enemy, not north on top.

On the West End, the B&O "army" is in Grafton and the enemy is to the east . . . if B&O can win the eastbound drag battle through to Piedmont, the westbound battle will have been won by default. Get the drags through and the QD/First Class problem will solve itself.

Placing the map looking from west to east, the terrain must now be studied. This map recon is jarring and verges on the alarming. Two seething boils . . . Newburg and Cranberry . . . are implanted on the axis of advance and cannot be bypassed. Both are followed by sickening plunges . . . Cheat River Grade (short, but mean) and Seventeen Mile (long and terrorizing). Between Terra Alta and Altamont lie the Glades, wracked by violent weather and with two grades . . . 58 Cut (annoying) and Deer Park (short, but nasty).

Even the approaches to Newburg are a problem, curvy and just steep enough to force deployment.

Recon on the ground does nothing to improve the outlook. The terrain is unstable and the enemy untiring . . . "Come to me, Baby," grins The Hill.

Whether in 1853 or 1991, one can easily envision the troops contemplating the mission and asking if they can get a transfer out of this chicken outfit.

There are only two tactical solutions to the West End problem. First, one may apply sufficient power at Grafton to take a given train straight through to Piedmont in one movement. Alternatively, one can adjust the size of the train at various locations en route by adding or subtracting power and cars. There are advantages and disadvantages to each of the "solutions."

The "straight through" approach has the advantages of simplicity and speed. The disadvantages, however, are many and marked. Power is wasted to greater or less degree en route . . . many sections of the route do not require the amount of power necessary to surmount the facing grades. Also, there are a lot of short trains to space, reducing the capacity of the line. Power pileup at Piedmont is maximized and power availability reduced . . . you need more locomotives and they spend a lot of time at the wrong end of the battlefield. In the steam era, servicing stops were still required on the way and time was lost.

The "helper and train adjustment" tactic mitigates all the negative aspects of "straight through," but introduces some new problems, i.e., there is no free lunch. This tactic takes more time, requires yard facilities for tonnage adjustment, servicing facilities for helpers and track space for returning helpers.

At one time or another B&O has tried every variant of the two methods. Let us explore the tactics used in different eras, the parameters of which we must set somewhat arbitrarily.

First 1853 to 1880. The line was basically single-track, although as we have shown double-tracking was progressing a section at a time. Power was the 0-8-0, with the 2-8-0 beginning to appear. The capabilities of the car fleet were steadily improving, as was true throughout history. There were no air brakes and couplers were link-and-pin. There were only two "helper stations," at Newburg and Piedmont, and a minor facility at Terra Alta. There were wyes at Newburg, Terra Alta, Altamont and Piedmont. Water stations were numerous. How did B&O fight the battle in this time frame?

What historical data is available? Very little. We have an 1863 report giving average train lengths by divisions; an 1864 Rebel After Action report; a gaggle of 1850s etchings and 1870s maps and photos; excerpts from an 1850s book describing train handling, spacing and procedures.

Now we must caution the reader that we are about to promulgate a theory and advise him of the admonition that an historian who labors to prove a theory risks distorting the truth. Let the reader beware.

There is a wealth of information in the 1863 report. We can dismiss passenger trains ... average number of cars per train on the main four divisions ranged from six to seven. We have already presented evidence in earlier chapters that double-headed Ten-Wheelers provided the power on the West End and the train length is plausible.

Tonnage trains from Piedmont to Baltimore averaged 25-30 cars ... from Wheeling to Grafton 20 cars and from Parkersburg to Grafton 15 cars. Each car was assumed to weigh 16 tons total, probably actual.

On the Third Division from Grafton to Piedmont, the figures were split into two groups. Trains of 9 cars were reported on grades exceeding two percent and 18-30 cars on grades not exceeding one percent.

The 1864 Rebel After Action report on the raid 5 May 1864 at Piedmont details the capture of two *eastbound* freight trains, each consisting of one engine and nine cars. They also captured the *eastbound* Mail with one engine, one baggage, one mail and four passenger cars. (Incidentally, the Piedmont operator truthfully told the Rebel commander that an eastbound troop train was due ... Johnny Reb thought he was being joshed and a merry firefight resulted.)

We believe the two reports point to the following conclusion ... trains of 18-30 cars were dispatched from Grafton to Newburg and there split into 9 car trains, each with one locomotive, and thence sent *all the way to Piedmont* without further adjustment in power or cars.

Westbound movements were carbon copies ... 9 car trains with one engine all the way to Newburg, thus balancing the flow. In Chapter 8 on Newburg Grade, we pointed out the lack of water service for eastbound trains just east of Newburg engine house and this makes sense in our scenario ... westbound trains would simply water at that location while waiting for yard space as a matter of convenience and eastbounders would water and coal west of that location at the engine house.

To keep power and crews balanced, trains of 18-30 cars from Newburg to Grafton and west were dispatched.

In other words, helpers per se were *not* used on tonnage trains for about a quarter of a century and the problem of returning light helpers on a single track line was avoided.

Train handling and dispatching during this era can only be described as having all the elements of a nightmare, especially on the West End. In sustained combat, the infantryman has only two ways out ... the litter or the grave. The same can be said of trainmen until the 1950s.

Before automatic couplers, the mere act of coupling cars was tantamount to a suicide mission. The trainman had to stand between the cars as they closed, balance the link with a stick to guide it into the receiving pocket and drop the pin by hand when the cars joined. And that was the easy part of his job. He still had to fulfill his job description of *brake*man. There were no air brakes ... he had to run from car to car on a moving train to tie down one car at a time ... in *all* weather.

On the West End, a train consisted of an engine and nine cars ... in the early years, there were no cabooses. A "bell cord" was run from the end of the last car to a bell in the engine cab. The conductor was enjoined to perch on the sill of the last car with the bell cord in one hand and a red flag or lantern in the other *at all times* ... the question of

OPERATIONS

how to hang on was unaddressed. The brakeman must travel on the top of his chosen car at all times ... in the case of an empty coal car, he could ride on the sill.

The engineer would blow one short to signal "brakes off" and the brakemen would scamper from car to car to release them. When he wanted "brakes on," he would blow two shorts in quick succession ... when he *really* wanted them, he would blow another two shorts.

If the conductor (who, after all, was the boss) wanted to signal the engineer, he rang the bell with the bell cord. We assume that a ringing bell meant *stop* ... just what other signals could be sent were unspecified.

The rules of the day called for a brakeman for every five or six cars ... we doubt if a brakeman could handle that many on West End descents. We do know that the fireman was required to become a brakeman when descending "heavy" grades ... the West End certainly qualified for that definition. The conductor must protect the rear of his train and assist with braking ... just how he could move in two directions at the same time was not explained in the rules.

Today, if a train breaks in two, the brakes go on automatically and both parts stop. In those days, a "separation" on West End grades was a calamity ... the hind end would take off downhill like the proverbial bluebird toward the following train and "concentrate the minds" of trainmen beautifully, to borrow a phrase.

Trains ran in "convoys" in olden times ... thus a "Stock Train" might run in a number of "sections" as they would be called in more modern days. The lead train of, say, a five-train convoy would display a large placard displaying the number "5" and the countdown would continue until the last train would display "1," thus signaling all concerned that the last train in the convoy was arriving.

Trains were spaced a half mile apart ... in theory very conservative, in practice meaningless. The front train might maintain a steady 10 mph, but anyone with convoy experience will tell you that the last one will be going 2 mph or 20 mph accordian-style.

At least speeds were low, mostly because the rigid wheelbases of 0-8-0 engines precluded anything in excess of 10 mph. And enginemen were warned to reduce to half speed over wood and iron bridges and by cuts.

As one can imagine, "bumping" was a problem ... a polite way of saying that rear-end collisions were frequent.

B&O rules were adamant on one issue: "In all cases of doubt, take the side of safety!" The only "safe course" for trainmen was not to show up for work.

In all candor, with personal weather experience in West End territory, we must say that we do not understand how these men did it. That they did so is a matter of historical fact ... how they did it is beyond our comprehension. You are a better man that I, Gunga Din.

The year 1880 marked the beginning of another phase in West End operating history that lasted until 1985. The opening of a helper station at Rowlesburg, completion of most double-tracking, conversion to automatic couplers, the advent of air brakes and steadily improving cars and locomotives heralded a change in tactics in favor of the "helper and train adjustment" approach.

During this one hundred plus year period, sweeping improvements were instituted on the West End as we have shown. The pattern of operations was consistent. Maximize tonnage to Thornton, Hardman or Newburg ... add the helper power necessary to get the train to West End or Tunnelton and then drop it ... drift down Cheat River Grade to Rowlesburg/M&K Junction ... add power to crest Cranberry ... fill-out trains at Rinard ... help up Deer Park Grade.

During the 1880's, air brakes and automatic couplers began to appear and were mandated by law by the Railroad Safety Appliance Act of 1893. There was, of course, a transition period as with all car improvement projects. Most railroads tended to apply both improvements when cars were shopped, so the practice was to put modern cars on the front and old cars on the rear.

We believe shoving began during this era. The reader must understand that one can shove or pull cars with no difference in operational effect other than the slack aspect. When you are shoving uphill, the slack is bunched ... pulling, the slack is stretched.

At any point in history, including today, the capabilities of the car fleet control how much power can be safely applied to the train. Any consist at any time has a mixture of old and new cars with different draft/buff characteristics. On all railroads at all times management is trying to maximize efficiency by increasing train length and that is especially true in West End drag service where savage grades and curves magnify the problem.

If you have two engines on the rear of a drag and one on the front, on average two thirds of the train has bunched slack and one third stretched. The draft strain is relieved on most of the train which in turn tends to compensate for older, weaker cars. While it is true that you can buckle or pop a weak car while shoving, the more likely source of mishap is in draft ... a broken knuckle or pulled draft gear.

During the Consolidation era and even deep into the mallet period, helpers were cut into the middle of trains at Newburg/Hardman and Rowlesburg/M&K to relieve draft strain ... in addition, of course, to the rear helper. A Consolidation could handle about eight cars and a mallet about sixteen ... thus one could see a variety of power locations in the train. As the average consist improved, the time came when mid-train helpers were dropped ... probably in the late 1920s.

We will be quoting the experience of Mr. Harry C. Eck, Superintendent of Locomotive Operations (retired), Chessie System, in many of the following paragraphs. For many years, his duties included constant attempts to improve tonnage per train on the West End and he spent much of his time in that activity.

Mr. Eck has noted that constant car fleet improvement enabled him to add tonnage in one year that would not have been possible just a few years earlier. Much to our astonishment, he also pointed out that knuckles don't always break ... sometimes they just simply open up! That says a lot about progress in metallurgy as well as power.

By the 1960s, drag tonnage had increased to about 9100AT ... five F7s were put on the headend at Grafton and four F7 helpers on the grades. One operational change in the diesel era was the tendency to leave helpers on the train down Cheat River Grade. If a helper crew change was imminent at M&K, the helper would follow its train down ... if another train was due soon at Hardman, the helper would cut-off at West End.

The arrival of the outstanding SD35s was greeted with some caution ... could B&O cabooses take the buff strain of twenty-four powered axles on the rear? They could and did. The GP35s were EMDs worst engines, yet the SD35s were splendid ... curious that the same generation would produce such opposites. SD35s had a tendency to automatically cut back on power at low speeds, not a joyful situation in drag service ... brilliant B&O electrical men adjusted relays so effectively that EMD copied the system on later models and B&O scored another "first." The long wheelbase and design of the SD35 truck produced excessive wheel and rail wear, a problem EMD ultimately solved through redesign ... B&O made do, however, and compensated by periodically turning engine sets at the Terra Alta wye to equalize wheel wear.

A seemingly small and yet important advantage to the SD35 over the F7 was minimum speed in heavy drag service ... the F7 had to be kept to 11 mph, yet the SD35 could drop to 9.4 mph. On Cranberry, that was a big plus.

The SD40s did their bit ... prior to their arrival, B&O would put five F7s on at Grafton and shove with four SD35s. B&O found that two SD40s could be substituted for four F7s and yet train weight of 9100AT be maintained.

And the SD50s boast some electrical wizardry ... in the 8-11 mph range an intricate control system takes applied power to the thin edge of endurance without damaging traction motors.

With all these major advances in power, Newburg and Cranberry still demanded special attention ... even after firemen could be legally removed from diesel freight cabs, B&O kept a fireman on M&K helpers. If a unit went down while shoving, it was essential to have a fireman to rush back and get it back on line if possible before the whole train stalled.

Not surprisingly, the West End has always been a test ground for B&O on the sound reasoning that if it worked there, it would work anywhere.

For example, B&O Chief Electrical Engineer (ret.) C.M. Machin invented the "rate of change wheel slip system" which was tested on the West End and ultimately "borrowed" by EMD as their IDAC system. This was a slip *control* system, not a "creeper" device, and it was a big improvement over earlier methodology.

B&O also experimented with *very* heavy trains on the West End in 1969, utilizing mid-train "Locotrol" equipped locomotives, i.e., Remote Controlled Multiple Units. Several 15000AT and

OPERATIONS

18000AT drags were run ... in addition, a 240 coal car train was dispatched. The heavier train gave some problems, but by and large the tests were a success on the West End and elsewhere on the system. Yard capacity was the limiting factor in these tests and it remains unlikely that such trains will appear on eastern railroads to any significant extent unless some form of unit-train system can be evolved.

In 1964, B&O continued its long tradition of "firsts" by producing three thousand W10 hoppers with composite brake linings. These were the first mineral cars ever built with such linings and they attracted a lot of attention from other railroads. Observers from many roads rode drags down Seventeen Mile Grade with full consists of these cars and went away suitably impressed.

One day a PRR man was aboard such a drag and his presence irritated The Hill ... after all, the PRR was the cause of the West End being built in the first place and The Hill has a long memory. The Hill caused a leak in the flat maintaining equalizing reservoir which in turn caused the brakes to go on harder. Since the train was on the lower part of the grade, the engineer decided to simply pull against the brakes for awhile. When the train and visitor arrived in Piedmont, the train was inspected and it was found that the brake linings were burned to the extent that most had to be replaced. We have to admit that the thought of poetic justice has occurred to us and we would like to have seen the PRR man's face as he contemplated the near-run thing he had just experienced. Since that time, B&O operating rules for the West End emphasize that thou shalt not pull against brakes for more than two miles.

As we further explore operations on the West End, we feel we should give a simplified explanation of brakes and brake systems for the benefit of those readers who are mystified by the subject.

On each *car*, the air brake system consists of two reservoirs (one for normal service and one for emergencies). These reservoirs are interconnected to a "triple valve" and a piston ... each *car* is then connected to a "train line" that runs to the locomotive and its air compressors.

At the start of the cycle, the air compressors on the locomotive pump air into the train line which fills the reservoirs with a predetermined amount of air pressure. When this pressure poundage is reached, the triple valve flips and equalizes the pressure between the reservoirs and the train line.

When the engineer wishes to make a brake application, he *reduces* pressure in the train line and that causes the triple valve to flip to a new position which feeds air from the service reservoir on each car to the piston which in turn applies the brakes through linkage rods.

When the engineer wishes to release brakes, he adds pressure to the train line which tickles the valve to put the additional air into the reservoirs and release the brakes.

If the train line should be broken or if the engineer wants to make an emergency application, the air rushes out of the train line and the triple valve dumps the air from the emergency reservoirs into the pistons which in turn slam on the brakes so hard that the wheels stop turning.

Each car also has a "retainer" valve, a *hand-activated* valve near the hand brake wheel that can be set to four positions ... off, two different poundage settings and slow release. If this valve is set to one of the two middle positions, the air brakes on that car cannot be released after they have been applied even if the engineer wishes to do so. In the slow release position, the brakes will go off over a period of several minutes. In the modern diesel age, cars still have retainers but they are rarely used. In the steam era, it was essential when descending severe grades to "set retainers" at the top of the grade to one of the three possible positions on a certain percentage of cars in the consist to be sure the train would always have brakes applied on those cars regardless of what happened to the rest of the train. Once the engineer made a brake application, the cars with retainers "up" would apply brakes and *keep them on*. At the bottom of the hill, the retainers would have to be turned "down" by hand so that the brakes would function normally. On QD trains, this was done *while moving* near the bottom of the grade to save time.

The diesel "dynamic" brake is really just a reversal of the power flow. The diesel engine turns a generator that feeds electric power to the traction motors between the wheels. In braking mode, the traction motors become generators and the electricity generated is dissipated as heat ... the drag slows the locomotive.

Also, each locomotive ... steam or diesel ... has an *engine* brake that works only on the locomotive, independently of the train.

On most *passenger* cars, the system is more

213

elaborate and allows for graduated *release* as well as graduated *application*.

On freight cars, however, the brakes are "dumb." The engineer can make graduated *application* of brakes, but the system only recognizes "on" or "off" ... in other words, they "release" all at once.

Think about the last paragraph, dear reader. You are taking a 9000 *ton* train down a steep grade and you have to stop on the grade. Now you want to go. The brakes will go off *all at once* and the train will *instantly* plummet down the hill. Whiplash will be the least of your problems.

Now in the chapter on M&K Junction we stated that *engine* brakes would hold but not stop a drag. We must qualify that statement ... we meant to get over that engine brakes would hold a train on a West End grade when *helpers* were on the rear assisting with their brakes.

The suggestion that engine brakes alone would hold a 9000 ton train on, say, Seventeen Mile Grade without helpers on the rear is laughable.

One last commentary in regard to brakes. There is always leakage of air in the train line and the cars ... as one would expect, in cold weather it usually worsens. When the brakes are *off*, the compressor on the locomotive simply pumps more air through the train line to replace the lost air.

Before the advent of flat maintaining brake systems (pressure maintaining is synonymous), there was a problem when the brakes were *on*. The engineer would make a reduction in the train line to put brakes on and then put the handle in "lap" to hold that reduction. On the old systems, the "lap" position *precluded* the addition of air to the train line and leakage was not replaced. The marvelous flat maintaining system has a bypass valve that eliminates this problem by feeding air to the train line while in lap.

The combination of diesel dynamic and flat maintaining brakes appeared in the 1950s and enabled railroads to dispense with the use of retainers and allow trainmen to come in out of the cold. Nowhere was this development more welcome than on the West End.

Having pitied the poor trainmen, the reader might think that enginemen had a soft touch on the West End. Their lot was somewhat safer and perhaps a little warmer, but they had to carry the twin burdens of frustration and stark terror.

Some years ago, with typical B&O progressivism, a school for engineers was created in Cumberland for the training of new and retraining of older enginemen. New men would go to school for several months and then be sent out on the railroad. Engineers to be posted to the West End, however, were treated differently.

B&O would assign them as firemen on the West End for a full Winter and *then* send them to school. Management wanted these trainees to have experienced at first hand train-handling up and down the grades, winter air leakage, frozen brakes, frozen sand, draining of disabled locomotives and all the other myriad things that would go wrong on this bitter battlefield.

At this point in our saga, we can see that the reader would have the impression that once an eastbound drag reaches Terra Alta the battle is all over except for the shouting. Steam or diesel era, the worst is yet to come.

Quite aside from the weather in the Glades, the Deer Park Grade lies ahead. In steam days, this grade was named "Wonder Hill" and the name has stuck. The reference has nothing to do with the splendid scenery in the area ... very simply, the engineer "wonders" whether he is going to get up.

The approach to Wonder Hill begins at Weber, about a mile east of Oakland where Route 219 crosses the railroad. From there to the Deer Park Hotel road crossing the gradient ranges between .15% to .59% for about four miles. Of course, this is not a serious rise and there is a lot of tangent. The next four miles to Altamont, however, leaps from .65% all the way up to 1.33% at the summit and there are a lot of curves.

As we have seen, in steam days Wonder Hill required a helper. Even with a helper it was touch and go ... the road engine's fire was in shambles after hammering up Newburg and Cranberry and the grade had to be surmounted from a dead stop made for the helper.

Until very recent years, the diesels also had a hard time of it. Helper service disappeared with the steam engine and that small rise from Weber was just stiff enough to preclude gaining any meaningful momentum ... you cannot accelerate a drag like a sports car.

Mr. Eck has taken many a diesel-powered drag up Wonder Hill and he describes the experience as akin to "hitting a stone wall." The deceleration is so sharp that the engineer slides forward in his seat and the speed falls off to the point that he "wonders" if he will stall.

Assuming the engineer does get his drag up Wonder Hill, the frightening part of the trip begins... he has to get down Seventeen Mile Grade.

As the engine tops the grade, the dropoff is so severe that "you can feel your feet get light." As the descent starts, more and more of the train is coming over the top and the train is accelerating at a very rapid pace... "the train comes against you and pushes you back in the seat." And it is a long, long way to the bottom.

Unfortunately, the grade has a bear-trap at Swanton called the "Flat." There is a very short section of track that is almost level. On the surface one would think this is good. It is not, as we shall see.

As the drag is coming over the summit, the engineer must slowly reduce his power until about half the train is on the downgrade. Then he will make about an eight pound reduction and engage the dynamic brakes. The train is still accelerating and the temptation to make another heavy reduction is quite strong... in all candor, the engineer is apprehensive. The temptation must be resisted because of the Flat... another reduction of about three pounds should be made.

About this time the train enters the Flat and starts to slow. If the second reduction was a little too much, the train will stop... if not quite enough, the train will grind through the Flat and take off down the other side.

The reader should now recall his lesson on "dumb" brakes. One cannot *gradually* release brakes... they go off all the way all at once and to completely release the brakes in this situation is tantamount to suicide.

Each train is a little different and no hard and fast procedure is possible for this descent... the reductions prior to the Flat are a guessing game.

If the train is obviously going to come to a stop, the engineer has two unpleasant choices. He can apply power and pull against the brakes. This is hard on wheels and brake linings... in no case may it be done for more than two miles ala composite linings. Or, he can let it stop... it's an engineer's judgment call.

If the train stops, a whole new set of problems arise. The engine brakes will not hold the train. A release is out of the question. The only thing to do is walk back and tie-down hand brakes on a number of cars.

The engineer then braces himself in his seat and releases the brakes. A nine-thousand ton train will now go from zero to ten miles per hour in a fraction of a second. The dynamics begin to bite and the engineer makes a heavy reduction to keep the train under control.

It is still *twelve miles* to Piedmont.

One way or another, the engineer is through the Flat and now must make one or two small reductions to "balance the grade." If all goes well, the train will grind its way down without incident. Of course, he may have to make another stop... restricting signal, penalty application, obstruction, whatever. If so, the drill is repeated.

There is one constant in all descents of Seventeen Mile Grade, for all engineers of whatever skill or experience: "It is always awfully good to see Piedmont!"

For all that happened between 1880 and 1985, the basic operational tactic of "helper and train adjustment" remained. In 1985 an epoch ended.

B&O pulled all QD and grain drags off the West End, leaving only open-top drags. Shortly thereafter, helpers were based in Grafton and the tactics reverted to the original "straight through" method. Helpers would be added at Grafton or Hardman and kept on at least to Terra Alta and usually all the way to Altamont. The interlockers at West End and Terra Alta were completely removed.

We have alluded to this change as "surrendering" to The Hill and have presented a host of hints as to factors which may have contributed to the decision... grain car instability, QD rail rollover, high helper costs and so on. We have yet to talk to a West End employee or devotee who is not convinced that B&O finally tired of heavy helper costs and made the determination accordingly.

In fact, the West End situation had no bearing whatsoever on the decision.

We have spoken to senior operating and traffic people privy to the study which preceded the decision and all agree that the West End wasn't even mentioned.

The only remaining shippers of consequence on the railroad from Cincinnati to Grafton could be served by other lines and it made no sense to maintain miles and miles of mainline for traffic

WEST END

that could be routed to Deshler, Willard and east over the "Chicago" line. In a sense, The Hill has won a victory but not through its own doing. B&O is still on the West End and, for the moment at least, intends to stay. An average of three 9000AT drags traverse the West End every day and B&O is still giving the finger to The Hill. We hope the show continues.

In the early 1980s, Mr. Eck met with Mr. Arch W. McElvany, General Manager Operations Chessie System (ret.), to discuss matters pertaining to the West End.

Mr. McElvany, a man whose career with the railroad hovers on the legendary, made a statement to Mr. Eck that will stand for all time as an epithet for that "central sixty miles."

"There is no such thing as an easy eastbound trip on the West End."

THE BALTIMORE AND OHIO RAILROAD COMPANY
CUMBERLAND DIVISION - WEST END
ADJUSTED TONNAGE RATINGS FOR STEAM AND CLASS DH-1 DIESEL LOCOMOTIVES

WESTBOUND						EASTBOUND				
Remarks	S-1	EL-5A	EM-1	Service	Run	Service	EM-1	EL-5A	S-1	Remarks
Single	950	1200	1400	97-Q.D.Extra	Grafton-Keyser-Cumberland	All Q.D.	1300	1200	875	Single
Helper"D"	1650	1900	2100	"	" " "	"	2350	2250	2000	Helper "A"
Helper"E"	1900	2150	2350	"	" " "	88	2800	2700	2400	Helper "B"
Helper"F"	2550	2800	3000	"	" " "	94	3000	2900	2600	Helper "B"
Single	1050	1300	1500	Ton.& RT-89	" " "	96-Stock	3300	3200	2900	Helper "B"
Helper"D"	1825	2075	2275	" "	" " "	196	3650	3500	3200	Helper "B"
Helper"E"	2100	2350	2550	" "	" " "	Q.D.Extra	4000	3900	3575	Helper "B"
Helper"F"	2875	3125	3325	" "	" " "	Tonnage	3100	3000	2675	Helper "A"
					" " "	"	4600	4500	4175	Helper "C"
Single	1050	1300	1500	Tonnage	(Fairmont)Grafton-Keyser	Tonnage	4600	4500	4175	Helper "C"
Helper"D"	1825	2075	2275	"	" " "					
Helper"E"	2100	2350	2550	"	" " "					

Note: Doubleheaders will be rated at 100% of combined ratings of engines used.

FULL SLOW FREIGHT RATINGS FOR SINGLE LOCOMOTIVES OVER RULING GRADES

RATING DISTRICTS	Grade	STEAM						DIESEL	
		EM-1	EL-5A	S-1	KB-1	Q-4	Q-1C	6000 HP DH-1	3000 HP DH-1
Grafton - Thornton	0.60	6700	6000	4700	4300	3500	3000	8500	4250
Thornton - Terra Alta	2.40	1600	1500	1175	1075	875	750	3000	1500
Terra Alta - Altamont	1.20	4100	3500	2900	2650	2100	1850	7000	3500
Altamont-Keyser (Desc)	2.50	5500	5000	5000	4600	4000	3500	6500	5500
Keyser - Cumberland	0.50	8500	7200	6000	5500	4300	3700	11000	5500
Cumberland - Keyser	0.50	8500	7200	6000	5500	4300	3700	11000	5500
Keyser - Altamont	2.50	1500	1300	1050	1000	775	675	2600	1300
Altamont - Grafton	2.30	2050	1750	1400	1300	1050	900	3500	1750
Sabraton-M&K Jct. E&W	2.25	2150	1850	1500	1375	1100	950	-	-

Note: When Class EL-6A Locomotive (Numbered 7300 to 7315) is used, the rating will be 100 Adjusted Tons Less than the rating shown for Class EL-5A.

DESCRIPTION OF HELPER SERVICE

"A"	1-3000 HP DH-1 or 1 Mallet on Newburg and Cranberry Grades
"B"	1-6000 HP DH-1 or 2 Mallets " " " "
"C"	1- " " " " " " " " " "& 1-Q4 on Deer Park Grade
"D"	1-Q4 on 17 Mile Grade and 1-3000 HP DH-1 or 1-Q4 on Cheat River Grade
"E"	1-S1 on 17 Mile Grade and 1-3000 HP DH-1 or 1-S1 or 1-Q4 on Cheat River Grade
"F"	1-S1 and 1-Q4 on 17 Mile Grade and 1-3000 HP DH-1 or 1 Mallet or 1-S1 and 1-Q4 on Cheat River Grade

ADJUSTMENT IN TONS PER CAR

Districts	A Above 35°	B 20° to 35°	C 0° to 20°	D Below 0°
West End, including M&K, East & Westbound	4	6	8	10

R. A. J. Morrison
Superintendent

Office of Assistant to Vice President, Operation & Maintenance (J.H.H.),
Baltimore, Maryland - August 15, 1949.

Miscellany

Perhaps *potpourri* would be a more appropriate heading for this section of the book as it will prove to be an odd assortment of parenthetical thoughts, elucidations, comments, elaborations and statements of questionable context. The reader is, by this time, well aware of his writer's weakness for tangential wanderings and will find he has written these last pages with gleeful abandonment of any attempt at literary discipline.

CHAPTER ONE: It was apparent to all even in the 1840s that the northerly reaches of the Midwest were developing more rapidly than the southern areas simply because of easy access to water transport ... the Great Lakes and numerous water courses laced the entire region and provided the only truly efficient means of transportation before the coming of the railroad.

Mr. Swann was well acquainted with this simple fact of life and discussed it in many reports ... he acknowledged that B&O was being forced by the Pennsylvania Railroad to reach the Midwest to the south of the main prize and would have to make do with what turned out to be third place.

It was true, as we quoted Mr. Latrobe on page 16, that none of the other railroads could "compare with the B&O in directness of connection with the commercial centers of the Mississippi Valley" and B&O did wrest a significant portion of this business from the New Orleans/Ohio River gateway ... to this day, B&O enjoys heavy, long-haul traffic from these sources.

And B&O attempted to grasp business from the northerly regions by reaching west from Wheeling toward Chicago ... again, as Mr. Swann reported at the time, being forced by Virginia to reach the Ohio at Wheeling was not all bad. This route, however, was long and expensive to operate ... particularly on the West End. Over history, B&O did capture some of this business but not enough to become a major player.

Virginia's obstructionism in regard to the Parkersburg Branch hurt B&O, but not fatally ... when the Civil War began, nobody gave a damn what Richmond thought and B&O acquired a very direct route to Cincinnati and St. Louis. The Supreme Court ultimately ruled that PRRs "Berlin Wall" along the Pennsylvania border was not in the public interest and B&O did reach Pittsburgh and Chicago over Sand Patch, but the pickings were slim as the other railroads had seized the "high ground" simply because they had gotten there first.

To be sure, the PRR had to cross the mountains and they did so west of Altoona through the well-known "Horseshoe Curve" and topped at Gallitzin. Historians make much of this "brilliant" engineering achievement, but it is all nonsense ... the PRR crossed over a solitary pimple.

At the time of construction, questions were raised whether steam power could traverse such incredible grades. B&O was already operating over worse branch line grades near Cumberland and knew it was possible albeit expensive ... Mr. Swann's famous "first trip up Seventeen Mile Grade" was merely a public relations drama.

The great celebration at Wheeling upon the opening of the line in the McLure House (which, incidentally, still operates under that name in a different location ... B&OHS held a convention there a few years ago) was awash with wine and whiskey to the extent that one wonders if Mr. Latrobe seized the entire supply from his Irish and Moonshiner foes. The toasts were beyond count and we will admit that we are not sure the toast quoted was in deference to The Hill ... in fact, we are not sure just what most of them were toasting. Any excuse for a party is a good one, however, and B&O certainly had just that.

The reader might wonder why the mountains west of Cumberland were unwashed, so we will treat that subject with thanks to Gary Schlerf's knowledge of geology.

The mountains did not pop up overnight and water was draining toward the seas even when the mountains were still plains. As the mountains slowly rose through the pressures of continental drift, the streams and rivers continued to flow along their original courses and simply scoured the sides of the rising mountains ... the paths of these rivers did not change significantly because the process was so prolonged.

The erosive power of water is directly related to velocity, however, and the waters draining toward the Atlantic Ocean from the Continental Divide had only a short distance to go to reach sea level. As the mountains rose, the "eastward" water picked up velocity and swept the slate clean, so to speak.

Drainage west of the Divide, however, had a very long and tortuous way to go before reaching sea level at New Orleans. Longer and gentler decline, less erosive power, less "washing."

The reader who has stayed the course to this paragraph certainly suspects that we regard the West End as Sacred Ground and we wish to confirm that view. Any ground on Earth soaked in blood and treasure is Sacred in our philosophic opinion and the West End qualifies.

When did this railroad become the West End Subdivision? We are confident that the name evolved c. 1903 when this division became part of the Cumberland Division ... it is just that we have yet to find a specific written reference to that effect.

CHAPTER TWO: In recent decades, the West End boundary on the east actually begins about a half-mile east of Viaduct Junction and, of course, since 1985 the West End is in reality not a true part of the St. Louis line. It remains, however, a mainline subdivision.

A single-track span over the Potomac River on the Patterson Creek Cutoff remains in place, rusting and rotting away. And the reader will be happy to know that the "sag" at McKenzie which ruined the operator's day in 1951 (see page 29) still exists.

The Great Coal Boom of ten or so years ago was triggered by the Solidarity Strike in Poland and other strikes in the South African and Australian coalfields. Residents of the Chesapeake Bay region will recall fifty or more colliers anchored in the Bay as far south as Annapolis awaiting dock space, sometimes for weeks on end. Martial Law was declared in Poland and the other strikes were settled ... the Boom went into history.

Throughout the book we have presented photos of relief maps to give the reader a visual appreciation of the terrain on the West End. Reproduction is poor because the originals are small and fuzzily printed, yet we feel the only thing worse than a poor photo is none at all. In fact, all photography on the West End is difficult. Weather is usually overcast and the Sun seldom reaches points of interest in the valleys.

217

WEST END

We should point out that the descent from the east portal of Knobly Tunnel to Patterson Creek was also a retainer grade in that era.

Both spans at 21st Bridge were washed out in 1896 and we believe the through-truss bridges pictured on page 26 were built at that time.

CHAPTER THREE: Cold air is heavy and in all seasons the air in the Glades is colder than in the valleys. Almost every day of the year, this colder air flows down Seventeen Mile Grade in an invisible torrent that reaches all the way to Keyser before it is deflected. In May of 1991 we were on the road bridge by Keyser Station and the blast of air almost blew us into the traffic lane. Yet off the bridge it was perfectly calm.

The control panel at Bond has survived and is now in the collection of B&OHS. When the tower was closed, it was learned that operators had stuffed old Station Sheet records into the walls to reduce drafts from this wind flow and many of them were recovered to end up in the author's files. They provide an invaluable insight into Seventeen Mile Grade operations in scattered time frames.

Operators would write pithy comments on these sheets not expecting them to be read. One pathetic comment reads, "No coal, no wood, no heat, no food ... Shit!" No duty on the West End was easy.

The 1985 flood that took out Bridge 92 also weakened the roadbed east of Hitchcock ... a coal car train with four units, moving slowly, triggered a landslide. The first unit passed, but the middle two tumbled down several hundred feet to a stream bed and killed the fireman riding on one of the units. No duty on the West End was safe.

There were two jugs at 37 Water Station ... we have just learned that the older of the two was demolished for parts between 22-28 February 1952.

There was a telegraph office at Wilson for many years and water at least in the years 1913-17.

CHAPTER FOUR: Mountain Lake Park lost its call letters MK to M&K Junction in the mid-1950s and was known as PK until closure in 1961.

The 1868 depot at Terra Alta was torn down about a week before our arrival in early May 1991 ... almost, but not quite.

CHAPTER FIVE: Some years ago we were taking a shortcut through some woods to get to a photo location when we heard some voices. A little bird suggested that we be cautious, so we moved silently to a vantage point and saw two armed men carrying on a vigorous conversation. It did not strike us as being wise to exit the woods with a camera on our chest, so we faded away. Some years later we related this incident to a resident with local knowledge and learned that the two were Shiners with mean dispositions.

CHAPTER SIX: We have just learned that the Rowlesburg Southern was out-of-service 30 June 1950.

With temperature at 17 degrees below zero, Harry Eck walked from Mrs. Howard's to the engine house without noticing that one of his ears was exposed. The poor ear was frostbitten and blew up like a balloon. Since M&K Junction is one of the warmer spots on the West End, the reader can imagine what it was like in the Glades that day.

There is a narrow gravel road from M&K Junction to the top of Lantz Ridge and we drove up it one cold December day. Traction was fine until we went around a bend and found a spot where the Sun never shines. We had to throw the vehicle into the ditch to avoid rolling down the side of the mountain ... when we got out, the ice was so bad we almost slid off the edge. It was a long drop.

CHAPTER SEVEN: The photograph at the top of page 124 was taken from the top of Lantz Ridge. We will spare the reader tales of our struggle to get to this location. As we approached a fence enclosing the open field where we planned to take our pictures, we saw a very large sign that stated simply, "Anyone who crosses this fence will be shot." With more than a little trepidation, we decided to proceed. As we were taking photos in the field, four armed men came out of the woods and strode determinedly to our site. We decided to be friendly and said, "Hi there!" Much to our relief, the conversation was very pleasant and non-threatening. We finally felt emboldened to inquire about the sign. It seems the owner was sick and tired of having city hunters shoot his cows!

As to the wreck of the *Gateway*, the one trackworker who had experienced a derailment told us his story. The gang was correcting a Sun-kink on the middle track on Newburg Grade when "pop" went another one on No. 1 track as a coal car train was approaching. The gang scattered save for this one brave soul who tore off his shirt and raced toward the train waving violently.

The rules say, "Thou shalt stop at once if any earnest signal is seen." The fireman waved back and the train went straight into the soup. The fireman said later he thought the trackworker was just being friendly.

CHAPTER EIGHT: The decision was made to demolish the Hardman helper facilities on 11 January 1951 and the operation was reported as 95% complete by October 1951.

The station at Independence was torn down in late 1946 and replaced by a waiting shed ... the materials gained were used to reconstruct a freight house at Newburg, completed by January 1947. The Newburg Station was apparently closed in that month and the platforms razed.

CHAPTER NINE: If one could select a scene from the past to visit as a fly on the wall with big ears, we would choose the day Daniel Willard was informed of the malletization failure. We doubt that Mr. Willard employed the Greek practice of killing messengers delivering bad news ... he must have been tempted, however, when he was informed about the S engines a few years later.

B&O's many "firsts" are established features in railroad history ... two additional ones met the Greek requirements for Comedy and Tragedy. While neither occurred on the West End, the reader should know that B&O had the first female engineer to put an engine into a turntable pit and the first to be killed in the line of duty. The latter lady was where she was supposed to be, doing what she was supposed to be doing ... the collision was caused by gross negligence on the part of the crew of a facing train that ran past a meet point in the face of functioning restricting signals.

CHAPTER TEN: The late Wild Bill Henry left the West End in the summer of 1948 and rose to Supervisor of Locomotive Operations for two divisions. The 1958 recession savaged the B&O and in company with all others,

MISCELLANY

Mr. Henry bounced back to engineer... Mr. Eck fired for him twice and on each occasion found him to be stern, meticulous and competent. Mr. Henry's descendants believe that he ran, at one time or another, every class of engine on the B&O during his career.

As to slack, the operating assumption on B&O is that each car has one foot of it.

CHAPTER ELEVEN: We have visited the *east* portal of the old Kingwood Tunnel, which is buried in overgrowth, and wish to report that it is *possible* that the original parapet is still in place.

CHAPTER TWELVE: The reader might feel that we have employed dramatic hyperbole in describing descents of Cheat River and Seventeen Mile Grades with tonnage trains, pointing out that engineers have safely arrived at M&K and Piedmont for almost a century and a half.

"A good Sea Captain is afraid of the Sea." A good engineer is afraid of these two grades.

Almost all of the eastbound coal on the West End today is destined for utility use at Dickerson near Washington D.C. and to Curtis Bay for off-loading to barges and colliers.

The author has modeled in HO the West End from the Flower Garden east to the road bridge at M&K and from the Salt Lick water tub east to the wye at Terra Alta. Grades and train length are prototypical for the Fall of 1948. Our experience in operating this layout parallels that of the real railroad in every particular.

CONCLUSIONS: Historians, we are told, are required to come to conclusions so we shall.

Should the line to Wheeling and Parkersburg through the "central sixty miles" have been built in the first place? We must say that the answer to this question is an unequivocal "yes." In the context of the times, B&O had to build to Wheeling or give up... the latter was out of the question.

Would the line have been built if B&O had been allowed to meet the Ohio at Pittsburg[h]? While history does not provide answers to the results of alternative courses of action, we find it hard to believe any sane organization would attempt to build a mainline railroad through such terrain if any other choice was available. Certainly some branch lines to tap resources would have been constructed, but it is almost inconceivable that the West End itself would have been built.

The Pennsylvania Railroad, for the most part through political chicanery and not railroading skill as some would have us believe, administered many defeats to B&O... in our view, none was more devastating than the closure of the Mason-Dixon line in the 1840s. B&O became a "hard property to make money out of," to use an accurate if grammatically poor expression, and remains so to this day. There is some wry solace in noting that B&O was the last as well as the first eastern trunkline railroad in history... the PRR and NYC merged and then collapsed in 1970 while B&O dates its corporate existence to 1987.

Rumors are about that CSX is having certain "discussions" with Conrail. We suggest that CSX people read some history, take long spoons to all meetings and remember that Conrail is merely the old Pennsylvania Railroad disguised as gentlemen.

All in all, we feel that B&O was dealt a very bad hand and played its cards quite well throughout history, particularly on the West End.

PAEANS: Whatever degree of approbation may devolve upon this work, all the credit should be given to the people presented in the following paragraphs. They are the lions of the saga... the author merely supplied the roar.

The reader should study the bibliography for the names of the people, from William Prescott Smith to the most recent authors, who compiled and presented so much information for the use of historians to follow.

The book is dedicated to Tommy Thompson, the West End's single most praiseworthy student. Through credit lines, the photographers are honored ... special thanks must be extended to Howard N. Barr, Sr., in our opinion the most skillful of them all. The full and vast resources of the Baltimore and Ohio Railroad Historical Society were placed at the author's feet through the person of President Gary Schlerf... his efforts were truly untiring. He also educated the author in geology and edited some chapters, ignoring the caution that an editor has but two duties... to applaud and change nothing.

John Hankey, Chief Curator, and Anne Calhoun, assistant Archivist, of the B&O Museum deserve special praise and thanks. Harry Eck must be thanked still again and the late Carl B. Welch, Jr., Trainmaster Cumberland Division, was always helpful and outgoing.

The book is graceful in appearance and all credit in this regard goes to artist Warren Somerville, typographers Frances Weber and Diana Ennis of The Type House in Baltimore and the craftsmen of Baltimore's Art Litho Company, represented so ably by Bob Greenlee.

And the following names are in random order: Engineers Clarence Jennings, Tom Dawson, the late G. T. Jackson, a Mr. Boling, Junior Jennings, H. M. Dunnivan and F. B. Hooten; Operators Monroe Maier, Pete Johnson, Clint Shrout, Paul Chidster, the late Eugene Hoffman, Paul Felton and Jeremy Browning; Trainmen Tom Arnold, Keith A. Young and P. D. Lambert; Track Supervisor the late Mr. Snyder; Bill Henry, grandson of Wild Bill; Ray Stern; Don Everly (WVN); Herbert H. Harwood, Jr.; Harry Stegmaier; Andy Holzopfel; those scores of other B&O employees whose names we did not get; finally, those individuals who are victims of our poor memory, but have earned our heartfelt gratitude.

Responsibility for all the flaws in this work rest solely upon the shoulders of the author.

PASSING AND FINAL THOUGHTS: We have chosen to write this book in the third person as a mark of deference... those who assume such usage was meant royally should take it just that way.

We deplore the modern tendency to make political statements in historical works, but have not resisted the temptation. They are in there... you find them. And this will probably be our Swan Song as an author... if the reader misses that pun, he has not been paying attention.

Those thousands of men and women of all stations in life who fought on the West End throughout history and fight today are entitled to one reward. When they die, their souls proceed to a depot where they show their service records, and they then board a non-stop special train that speeds directly to Heaven. They have already served their time in Hell.

WESTWARD.

Distance from Cumberland.	Train Order Stations.	West End Cumberland Division. TIME-TABLE No. 16. April 28, 1929.	Passing Sidings. Capacity in Cars.	FIRST CLASS.									SECOND CLASS.		
				3	**55**	**29**	**21**	**35**	**11**	**1**			**97**	**97**	**97**
				DAILY	DAILY	DAILY Ex. Monday	DAILY	DAILY Ex. Sunday	DAILY	DAILY			Cin. DAILY	Cols. DAILY	St. L. DAILY
				A. M.	A. M.	A. M.	P. M.	P. M.	P. M.	P. M.			A. M.	A. M.	A. M.
	DN	**CUMBERLAND.**		S 4.05	S 6.50	......	S 1.35	S 2.40	S 8.11	......					
0.5	DN	VIADUCT JCT.		4.07	6.52	......	1.37	2.42	8.13	......					
6.7		BRADY.		......	F 7.04	......	......	F 2.54	......	......					
9.0	DN	McKENZIE.		4.21	F 7.08	8.00	1.50	2.58	8.25	9.50					
13.0	DN	RAWLINGS.	124	4.27	F 7.17	8.05	1.56	S 3.08	8.31	9.55					
18.6		DAWSON.		......	F 7.27	......	......	F 3.18	......	......					
23.1	DN	KEYSER.		S 4.45	S 7.38	S 8.25	S 2.11	S 3.26	S 8.51	S10.13			1.40	2.20	11.00
24.5		WEST KEYSER TOWER.		4.48	7.41	8.28	2.14	3.29	8.53	10.15					
28.1	DN	PIEDMONT.	90	S 5.00	S 7.51	8.34	S 2.21	S 3.38	S 9.02	10.21					
29.3		W. VA. C. JCT.		......	F 7.57	......	......	F 3.42	......	......					
30.1		BLOOMINGTON.		......	F 8.02	......	......	F 3.47	......	......					
33.0		BIG CURVE.		5.17	8.10	8.49	2.36	3.55	9.17	10.34					
34.0	DN	BOND.		5.20	F 8.14	8.52	2.39	F 4.00	9.20	10.37					
35.8		FRANKVILLE.		......	F 8.20	......	......	F 4.07	......	......					
38.7	DN	STRECKER.		5.36	F 8.28	9.10	2.52	F 4.15	9.33	10.50					
41.0		SWANTON.		......	S 8.36	......	......	S 4.25	......	......					
44.8	DN	ALTAMONT.		5.55	F 8.47	9.31	3.09	F 4.37	9.50	11.06					
47.6		DEER PARK.		......	S 8.53	......	......	S 4.42	......	......					
48.0		DEER PARK HOTEL.		6.01	F 8.56	9.37	3.15	S 4.45	9.55	11.11					
51.1	DN	M'T'N LAKE PARK.	134	6.07	S 9.02	9.42	3.21	S 4.52	10.00	11.15					
53.7	D	OAKLAND.		S 6.18	S 9.09	9.47	S 3.29	S 5.00	S10.07	11.19					
58.3		EDGEWOOD.		......	F 9.17	......	......	F 5.06	......	......					
59.2	DN	HUTTON.		6.29	S 9.23	9.57	3.39	S 5.13	10.17	11.28					
59.9		CORINTH.		......	F 9.25	......	......	F 5.14	......	......					
62.7		RINARD TOWER.	99	6.35	F 9.31	10.02	3.45	F 5.22	10.23	11.33					
63.7	DN	TERRA ALTA.		S 6.39	S 9.36	10.05	S 3.47	S 5.27	F10.25	11.35					
68.9	DN	RODEMER.		6.51	F 9.46	10.16	3.58	F 5.39	10.35	11.45					
72.2		AMBLERSBURG.		......	F 9.52	......	......	F 5.46	......	......					
74.1		McMILLAN.	131	7.02	F 9.56	10.27	4.06	F 5.51	10.43	11.54					
75.3	DN	M. & K. JCT.		S 7.05	S 9.59	10.30	S 4.09	S 5.54	10.46	11.56					
75.8		ROWLESBURG.		......	S10.03	......	......	S 5.57	......	......					
80.4	DN	BLASER.	204	7.27	F10.18	10.47	4.27	F 6.11	11.02	12.12					
82.1		TUNNELTON.		S 7.31	S10.22	10.50	S 4.32	S 6.16	11.05	12.14					
85.6	DN	WEST END.		7.34	F10.27	10.53	4.35	F 6.20	11.08	12.17					
85.5		AUSTEN.		......	F10.32	......	......	F 6.26	......	......					
89.1		NEWBURG.	105	S 7.46	S10.41	11.03	R 4.45	S 6.34	11.19	12.27					
90.3		INDEPENDENCE.		......	S10.45	......	......	F 6.38	......	......					
91.8	DN	HARDMAN.		7.51	F10.49	11.09	4.51	F 6.43	11.25	12.33					
96.4		THORNTON.		7.58	S10.58	11.16	4.58	S 6.55	11.33	12.39					
100.1	DN	EAST GRAFTON.		8.05	11.05	11.24	5.05	7.05	11.40	12.45			7.30	8.20	4.00
102.2	DN	**GRAFTON.**		A 8.10	A11.10	A11.30	A 5.10	A 7.10	A11.45	A12.50					
				A. M.	A. M.	A. M.	P. M.	P. M.	P. M.	A. M.			A. M.	A. M.	P. M.
		Time over Division........ Average speed per hour......		4.05 25.0	4.20 23.6	3.30 26.6	3.35 28.5	4.30 22.5	3.34 28.6	3.00 31.1			5.50 13.4	6.00 13.2	5.00 15.4

Passenger trains will not exceed a speed of 45 miles per hour.

Speed as shown in Special Instruction 5, and such other restrictions as may be in effect, will not be exceeded.

BIBLIOGRAPHY

BOOKS

Howard N. Barr, Sr./William A. Barringer, *(B&O) Q*, Barnard, Roberts & Co., Baltimore MD 1978.

J. Snowden Bell, *The Early Motive Power of the B&ORR*, Angus Sinclair Co., New York 1912.

Ele Bowen, *Rambles in the Path of the Steam Horse*, Bromwell and Smith, Baltimore MD 1854.

B. F. G. Kline, Jr., *Tall Pines and Winding Rivers*, by author, Lancaster PA 1976.

Robert A. LeMassena, *Articulated Steam Locomotives of North America*, Silverton CO 1979.

Deane Mellander, *The C&P Railroad*, Carstens, Newton NJ 1981.

J. G. Pangborn, *Picturesque B&O*, Knight and Leonard, Chicago 1883.

Lawrence W. Sagle, *B&O Power*, Staufer, Medina OH 1964.

William Prescott Smith, *History and Description of the B&O RR*, John Murphy and Co., Baltimore MD 1853.

William Prescott Smith, *Great Railway Celebrations of 1857*, D. Appleton and Co., New York 1858.

John F. Stover, *History of the B&O RR*, Purdue University Press, West Lafayette IN 1987.

Charles S. Roberts, *B&O Great Photos*, Book 1 (H. N. Barr, Sr.) 1977; Book 2 (H. H. Harwood, Jr.) 1977; Book 3 (J. C. Kelly) 1977; Book 4 (E. L. Thompson) 1977; Book 5 (Bob Lorenz) 1979; Barnard, Roberts & Co., Baltimore MD.

Charles S. Roberts, *B&O Salute*, (M. Davis), Barnard, Roberts & Co., Baltimore MD 1987.

Betty Whittaker White, *The Past is a Key to the Future*, Melody Mountain, Terra Alta WV 1990.

Stephen Schlosnagle, *Garrett County*, Garrett County Bicentennial Commission, Oakland MD 1978.

(unknown), *Photographic Views of the B&O RR and its Branches from the Lakes to the Sea*, first series, Cushings and Bailey/Hagadorn Brothers, Baltimore MD 1872.

PERIODICALS

Baltimore and Ohio (Employees) Magazine, various issues, October 1912 to February 1962, B&ORR, Baltimore MD.

B&O Railroader, various issues, January/February 1972 to March 1978, Neilson Wood, Jr., Levittown PA.

Engine 5304, Run Extra, various issues, January 1979 to September 1982, B&ORR Historical Society, Baltimore MD.

Glades Star, issues June and December 1984, June and September 1985, Garrett County Historical Society, Oakland MD.

Railway Age Gazette, issue 9/15/1911.

Sentinel, various issues, December 1983 to May/June 1991, B&ORR Historical Society, Baltimore MD.

Light Iron, Short Ties, issue March 1987, Three Rivers Narrow Gauge Historical Society, article *Twin Mountain and Potomac* by William L. Reddy.

Trains, November 1945 E. L. Thompson; May 1991 Jay Potter; June 1991 Kevin McKinney; Kalmbach Publishing Co., Milwaukee WI.

B&ORR PUBLICATIONS AND RECORDS

Annual Reports: 1848 to 1977.

B&O Coals: mid-1940s.

Bond (BD) Station Sheets: various days in 1931, 1932, 1933, 1942, 1946, 1947, 1948, 1949, 1950, 1951.

C&O/B&O Freight Equipment: 1 Jan 1970.

C&O/B&O Motive Power: 1 May 1969.

Chessie System Freight Cars: 1 Jan 1977.

Clearance Diagrams: Steam, diesel, revenue and non-revenue cars, from c. 1907 to c. 1964.

Dispatchers Record of the Movement of Trains: West End Cumberland Division 16 Nov 1945, 10-14-15-16 Dec 1951, 30 Jan 1952, 9 Feb 1956; East End 30 Jan 1952, 9 Feb. 1956.

Electrification, Report on, B&ORR from Cumberland to Fairmont, Westinghouse Electric Co., 1 Jul 1929; Internal B&O Memo Hardman to Terra Alta 5 Nov 1929.

Employee Timetables Cumberland Division: 23 Apr 1855, 21 Dec 1884, 30 May 1886, 25 Nov 1906, 27 Nov 1910, 26 Nov 1911, 24 Nov 1918, 13 Jun 1920, 30 Apr 1922, various dates in years 1926, 1928, 1929, 1931, 1933, 1935, 1942, 1944, 1945, 1947, 1948, 1949, 1950, 1951, 1955, 1956, 1957, 1960, 1962, 1963, 1964, 1965, 1967, 1970, 1974, 1975, 1987.

Form 6 (Official List): 1 Sep 1889, various issues 1904, 1905, 1906, 1907, 1911, 1912, 1913, 1914, 1916, 1917, 1929, 1935, 1941, 1948, 1954.

General Orders Cumberland Division: various dates from 12 Aug 1933 to 1 Dec 1961.

Grafton Improvements Report: 16 Sep 1912.

Improvements: Folders A, Nos. 9 to 13, 12 May 1915, detailing improvements from Grafton to Keyser.

Maps: c. mid-1870s Altamont to Grafton: c. 1946 to c. 1969 Terra Alta to West End.

Plans: M&K/Hardman engine, oil and rest houses.

Special Instructions Helper Service: 1 Apr 1990 CSXT.

Summary of Equipment: all issues from 1 Jul 1912 to 1 Jan 1960.

Track Charts Cumberland Division West End: c. 1916, 1930, 1948, 1964; Signal Chart c. 1950.

Through Passenger Train Consists: various issues 1 Apr 1921 to 26 Oct 1958.

Various Correspondence files, reports and memos.

West End Cumberland Division Slow Freight Operation: study 20 Jul 1919.

MISCELLANEOUS

U.S. Army Topographic Command Map 1969.

U.S. Geological Survey Maps 1959.

Author's interview and analytical notes 1976-1991.

INDEX

Albright 100, 159
Alco 166-68-69, 197
Alleghenies 16
Allegheny Front 11
Alpha Portland Cement 111-112
Altamont et al 11, 13-15, 35, 36, 38, 49, 51-57, 59, 68, 106, 196-197, 210, 215
Amblersburg 77, 82, 89-92
Amcelle 17
Amtrak 131, 182
Anderson 115, 117, 134
Atlantic Ocean 36, 217
Austen 140, 145-146

Backbone Mountain 11, 35, 36, 39
Baldwin, E. Francis 67
Baldwin Locomotive Works 160-163, 167-168, 170-172, 174, 176
Baltimore 10, 210
B&O Museum 160, 162-163, 174, 184-186
Bell, Snowden 160-161, 173
Big Curve 35, 38-41
Big Savage Mountain 36
Black Oak 17
Blaser et al 13, 98, 113, 120, 133-135, 140
Bloomington et al 35-38, 194
Blue China 122
Bollman, Wendel 25, 107-108
Bond et al 38, 41, 42, 48, 193-195, 218
Bottling House Curve 59
Brady 17
Brains Curve 141
Brakes 210-211, 213
Bridges 11, 15, 25, 59, 92-94, 107-110, 114, 171
Briery Mountain 11, 77
Browning, George D. 59
Brunswick 19, 29
Buckeye et al 114, 122-125
Buckhorn et al 114, 124, 127, 129, 131-133
Buckingham, Irene 118

Carrico Crossing 121
Cars 180-192
  Box 19, 186-188
  Caboose 19, 56, 101, 189-190, 212
  Gondolas 183-184
  Hoppers, Covered 19, 189
  Hoppers, Open Top 33, 183-186, 213
  Passenger/Express 190-192
  Plow 204
  Stock 188
Cassidy Summit Ridge 115
Cheat River 11, 77, 93, 107-108, 114, 128

Cheat River Grade 11, 15, 105-106, 113-139
C&O Canal 10, 36
Chicago 17, 21, 182, 188, 216-217
Cincinnati 10, 215, 217
Civil War 15, 122, 147, 182, 210
Clements Fountain 127-128
Commercial House 118
Consolidation Coal Company 23
Continental Divide 36, 51
Corinth 58, 70
Crabtree et al 11, 35, 36, 38
Cranberry Glade 77-92, 106
Cranberry Summit 11, 58, 60, 76, 82
Crane Bridge 78
Cranesville Swamp 13
Cresap, Col. 36
CSX 18, 219
Cumberland 9-13, 17, 18, 27, 29, 142
Cumberland Viaduct 17, 19
Cumberland & Clarksburg Road 51
C&P RR 23, 31, 34
Curtis Bay 219

Dan's Mountain 11
Davis, Henry G. 61
Davis, J. C. 174
Dawson 17
Deep Creek Lake 13, 36, 59, 159
Deer Park et al 53, 54, 58-63
Dickerson MD 219
DuBois & Bond Bros. 41

83 Fill 141
Electrification 158, 159
Empire 35
Erie Canal 10, 158
Erie RR 10
Everett Tunnel 35, 38, 39

Fairmont 141, 147
58 Cut 70
Fink, Albert 33, 107, 125
Flower Garden 127-128
42 Water Station 90
Frankville 38
Frostburg 18
Fuel 158-159

Galloway, A. K. 54
Garrett County 13, 14, 51, 66
Garrett, John W. 13, 59, 60
Garrett, Robert 59, 60
Georges Creek et al 18, 20, 23, 30, 31, 194
Glades 11, 13, 14, 25, 58-76
Grafton 10, 11, 97, 99, 142, 157, 208, 210, 215
Graveyard Curve 77, 82, 88
Great Coal Boom 17, 20, 65, 217

Great Pine Swamp 13
Great Raid 15
Greenbrier, Cheat & Elk RR 144
Gulf of Mexico 36

Hardman 13, 95, 97, 98, 106, 135-136, 140-141, 152, 153-156, 159, 207, 211, 215, 218
Haystack Mountain 17
Hayes, Samuel 173
Henry, William 85, 192, 218
Hepburn Railway Act 61
Hitchcock Tunnel 45-48
Hooten Tavern 115, 118
Hopemont 58, 71
Howard, Annette 116, 118
Hudson River 10
Hutton 58-60, 70

Ice Age 13
Imboden, John D. 15
Independence 140, 147, 153, 218
Irontown 140, 156

Jackson, G. T. 119
Jacksonville 106
Jones, William 15

Kelly Springfield 17
Keyser et al 17-20, 23, 26-29, 172
Kingwood 100, 121
Kingwood Tunnels 113, 135-137, 139-143, 206, 208, 219
Knobly Mountain/Tunnel 17, 18, 24
Kyers Run 105, 114

Lantz Ridge 100, 110, 123, 218
Latrobe, B. H. 10-12, 14, 16, 20, 25, 39, 45, 117, 122, 125, 141, 217
Laurel Mountain 11, 113-115, 117, 142-143
Lee, Robert E. 15
Lesmalinston 140, 157
Lima 172
Limestone Run 18
Loch Lynn 58, 59, 63, 64
Locotrol 212-213
Lowndes 17
Luke 30, 35

Main Stem 13, 182
Manheim 95, 100, 111-113, 122
McCabe, Virginia 118
McCarty Family 66
McGuire Tunnel 77, 86, 87, 89
McKenzie 17, 18, 24, 25, 217
McLure House 217
McMillan 77, 82, 90, 94
Monogah Division 141

222

M&K Junction 65, 77, 80, 82, 93-112, 134, 202-205, 211
M&K RR/Subdivision 94, 95, 99, 100, 102, 106, 111, 113
Morgantown Turnpike 153
Mt. Storm 30, 194
Mountain Lake Park 53, 58-65, 106, 198, 218
Murray Tunnel 141, 145-146

Negro Mountain 36
New Creek 15, 18, 20
New York 10
New York Central System 10, 82, 219
New Howard Hotel 115, 118
New Orleans 217
Newburg et al 15, 93, 95, 106, 115, 133, 136, 140-157, 210-211, 218
Northwestern Turnpike 20, 114, 156

Oakland et al 15, 58, 59, 66-69, 199
Ohio River 9-11, 13, 217
Operations 209-216

Parkersburg 10, 182, 210, 217, 219
Patterson Creek et al 17-19, 22-24, 27, 29, 218
Pennsylvania 16
Pennsylvania RR 10, 82, 158, 213, 217, 219
Perkins, Thatcher 162, 174
Philadelphia 10
Piedmont 12, 14, 15, 17-20, 23, 30-34, 36, 41, 162, 210
Pittsburg[h] 10, 17, 182, 217, 219
Potomac 17, 24
Potomac River 11, 17, 18, 20, 24, 35, 36
Power 160-179
 0-8-0 158-162
 2-8-0 158, 159, 162-164
 2-8-2 163-165
 4-8-2 158-159, 165, 196
 2-10-2 165-167, 171-173
 4-4-0 158-159, 163
 4-6-0 158-159, 161, 173-174
 4-6-2 158-159, 175
 Mallet 41, 158-159, 166-171
 Diesel 30, 55, 102, 104, 175-179 181-212
Preston County 100, 136
Preston RR 59, 70, 121
Raccoon Crk/Br 11, 147, 150-151, 153, 156
Rail 11
Rawlings 17
Rinard 59, 60, 71, 211
Roberts 17
Roberts, C.S. back cover
Rodemer 77, 80, 82, 88, 89, 201
Rowles, Thomas 115
Rowlesburg 15, 80, 89, 93, 95, 98, 99 105, 108, 113-119, 123, 143, 205
Rowlesburg Sou RR 94, 103, 106, 108, 218

St. Louis 10, 21, 182, 217
Salt Lick et al 77, 79-85, 163, 201
Savage, John 36
Savage River 11, 36, 37, 41
Seventeeh Mile Grade 11, 12, 32, 35-57, 215, 217
76 Fill 11, 105, 119-121
Simpsons 147
Skipnish 59
Smith, Wm P. 11, 13, 59, 79
Snowy Crk & Cranesville RR 71
Spruce Run 77, 90
Staggers, H. O. 183
Strecker 38, 48-50
Summitville 51
Swan Family 51
Swann, Thomas 10-12, 51, 217
Swanton 14, 35, 38, 48-51, 215

Terra Alta 13, 58, 60, 71-76, 80, 93, 159, 206, 210, 215, 218
37 Wtr Sta 38, 41, 218
Thomas, Francis 38
Thornton 20, 140, 156, 211
Three Forks Crk 11, 141, 156
Tonnage Ratings 13, 216
Tray Run et al 15, 114, 122, 124-127
21st Bridge 11, 15, 17, 18, 25, 26, 218
Tunnelton 113, 115, 120, 121, 134-138, 211
TK&P RR 121
Turbo Trn 183
Twin Mtn & Potomac RR 20
Tygart River 11
Tyson, Henry 161, 173

Viaduct Jct 17-21, 106, 217
Virginia 10, 217

West End 11, 13-16, 18, 20, 134-135, 143-144, 206, 211, 215
West Grafton 140-141, 157
West Keyser 29, 30, 32, 106
Westvaco 30, 35
West Virginia 18, 124
West Virginia Central RR 18, 35, 61
West Virginia Northern RR 121, 139
Western Maryland RR 18, 26, 30, 35
Westernport 18, 20
Wheeling 10-12, 14-16, 182, 210, 217, 219
Willard, Daniel back cover
Wills Crk 17-19
Wilson 35, 38, 52, 218
Winans, Ross 158, 160-162, 173, 183
Wonder Hill 214

Youghiogheny River 58, 59

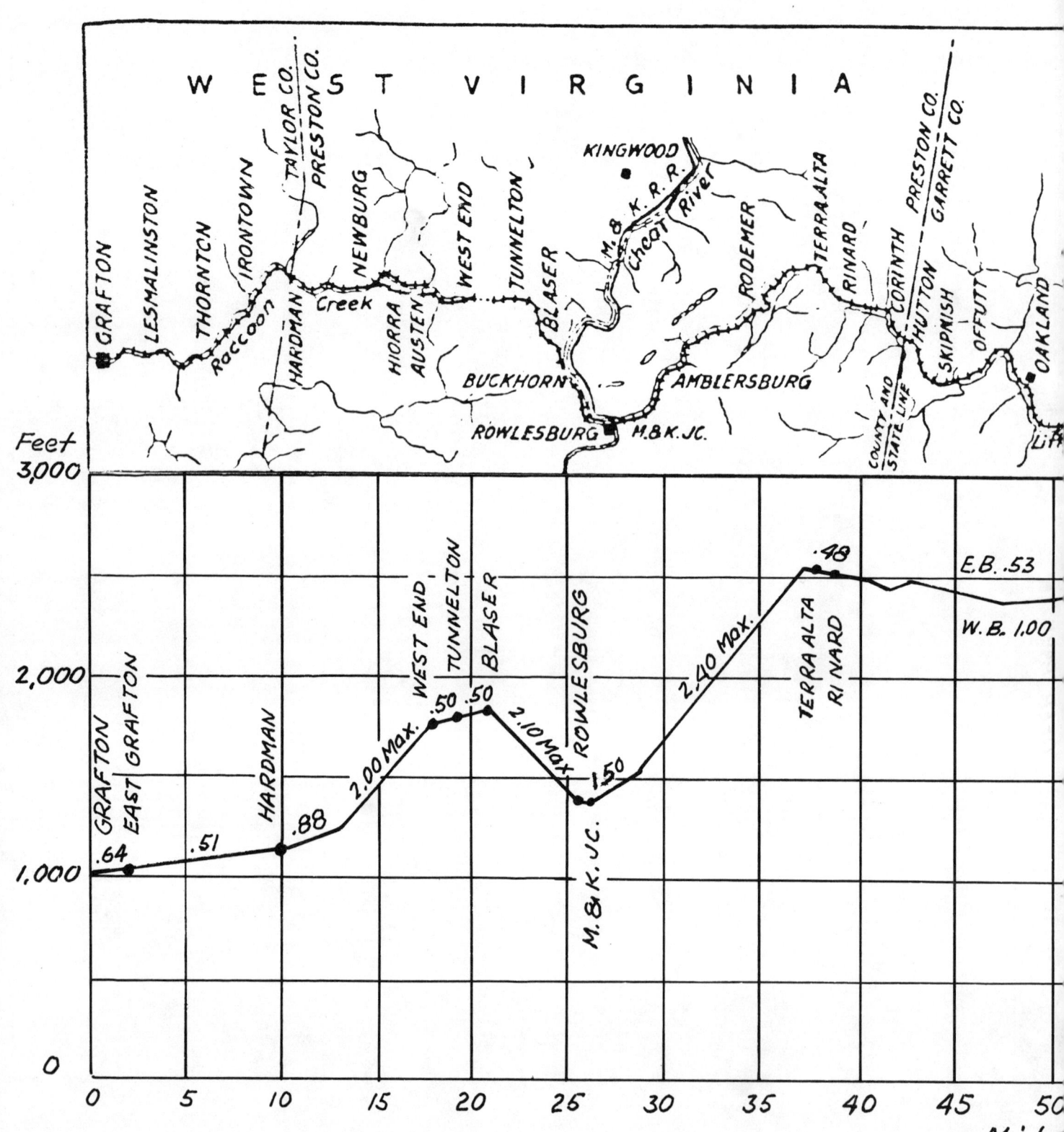